Victorian Classical Burlesques

Bloomsbury Studies in Classical Reception

Bloomsbury Studies in Classical Reception presents scholarly monographs offering new and innovative research and debate to students and scholars in the reception of Classical Studies. Each volume will explore the appropriation, reconceptualization and recontextualization of various aspects of the Graeco-Roman world and its culture, looking at the impact of the ancient world on modernity. Research will also cover reception within antiquity, the theory and practice of translation, and reception theory.

Also available in the Series:
Ancient Magic and the Supernatural in the Modern Visual and Performing Arts, edited by Filippo Carlà and Irene Berti
Greek and Roman Classics in the British Struggle for Social Change, edited by Henry Stead and Edith Hall
Imagining Xerxes, Emma Bridges
Ovid's Myth of Pygmalion on Screen, Paula James

Victorian Classical Burlesques

A Critical Anthology

Laura Monrós-Gaspar

Bloomsbury Academic
An imprint of Bloomsbury Publishing Plc

B L O O M S B U R Y
LONDON • NEW DELHI • NEW YORK • SYDNEY

Bloomsbury Academic
An imprint of Bloomsbury Publishing Plc

50 Bedford Square	1385 Broadway
London	New York
WC1B 3DP	NY 10018
UK	USA

www.bloomsbury.com

BLOOMSBURY and the Diana logo are trademarks of Bloomsbury Publishing Plc

First published 2015

© Laura Monrós-Gaspar, 2015

Laura Monrós-Gaspar has asserted her right under the Copyright, Designs and Patents Act, 1988, to be identified as Author of this work.

All rights reserved. No part of this publication may be reproduced or transmitted in any form or by any means, electronic or mechanical, including photocopying, recording, or any information storage or retrieval system, without prior permission in writing from the publishers.

No responsibility for loss caused to any individual or organization acting on or refraining from action as a result of the material in this publication can be accepted by Bloomsbury or the author.

British Library Cataloguing-in-Publication Data
A catalogue record for this book is available from the British Library.

ISBN: HB: 978-1-47253-785-0
PB: 978-1-47253-786-7
ePDF: 978-1-47253-787-4
ePub: 978-1-47253-788-1

Library of Congress Cataloging-in-Publication Data
Victorian classical burlesques : a critical anthology / Laura Monrós-Gaspar.
pages cm
Includes bibliographical references and index.
ISBN 978-1-4725-3785-0 (hardback)—ISBN 978-1-4725-3786-7 (pbk.)   1. Burlesque (Literature)—History and criticism.   2. English drama (Comedy)—Classical influences.   3. English drama (Comedy)–19th century—History and criticism.   4. Women in literature.   5. Blanchard, E. L. (Edward L.), 1820–1889. Antigone.   6. Talfourd, Francis, 1828–1862. Alcestis, the original strong-minded woman.   7. Brough, Robert B. (Robert Barnabas), 1828–1860. Medea, or, The best of mothers with a brute of a husband.   8. Talfourd, Francis, 1828–1862. Electra in a new light.   I. Monrós Gaspar, Laura.   II. Blanchard, E. L. (Edward L.), 1820–1889. Antigone. 2015.   III. Talfourd, Francis, 1828–1862. Alcestis, the original strong-minded woman. 2015.   IV. Brough, Robert B. (Robert Barnabas), 1828–1860. Medea, or, The best of mothers with a brute of a husband. 2015.   V. Talfourd, Francis, 1828–1862. Electra in a new light. 2015.
PR731.V53 2015
822'.809—dc23
2015014063

Series: Bloomsbury Studies in Classical Reception

Typeset by RefineCatch Limited, Bungay, Suffolk

To him who inspired my love for English literature.

Contents

List of Illustrations	viii
Acknowledgements	ix

1 Why Classical Burlesque? 1
   Enacting the past and the present 1
   The histories of Victorian classical burlesque 8
   Texts and contexts 17
   Note on the texts and this edition 39
   List of representative nineteenth-century classical burlesques ... 46
   Notes 49

2 *Antigone Travestie*, Edward L. Blanchard (1845) ... 61

3 *Alcestis, the Original Strong-Minded Woman*,
   Francis Talfourd (1850) 87

4 *Medea; or, the Best of Mothers, with a Brute of a Husband*,
   Robert Brough (1856) 135

5 *Electra in a New Electric Light*, Francis Talfourd (1859) ... 207

References 281
Index 295

List of Illustrations

1.1. Playbill of Mendelssohn's *Antigone* at the Theatre Royal Birmingham (1845) © Laura Monrós-Gaspar — 20
1.2. Playbill of J. R. Planché's *The Golden Fleece* at the Theatre Royal Haymarket in London (1865) © Laura Monrós-Gaspar — 25
1.3. 'Madame Ristori as Medea' (*Illustrated Times* 14 June 1856, p.433) © Laura Monrós-Gaspar — 27
1.4. 'Frederick Robson as Medea (from a Photograph by Herbert Watkins)' (1856) © Laura Monrós-Gaspar — 27
1.5. 'Scene the Last from the New Ballet of "*Electra, or the Lost Pleiad*" at Her Majesty's Theatre in London' (*Illustrated London News* 5 May 1849, p.293) © Laura Monrós-Gaspar — 37
1.6. Folio 170 of the Manuscript of E. L. Blanchard's *Antigone Travestie* © The British Library Board, BL MS 42982 ff.165–173 — 44
1.7. Folio 645 of Francis Talfourd's *Alcestis, the Original Strong-Minded Woman* © The British Library Board, BL MS 43028 ff.633–653 — 44
1.8. Folio 22 of Robert Brough's *Medea; or, the Best of Mothers, with a Brute of a Husband* © The British Library Board, BL MS 52960, K — 45
1.9. Folio 7 of Francis Talfourd's *Electra in a New Electric Light* © The British Library Board, BL MS 52982 — 45

Acknowledgements

This book would not have been possible without the support and encouragement of various people. First and foremost, for intellectual inspiration I must thank Fiona Macintosh, who also deserves profound and sincere gratitude for her encouragement and support for the project from the beginning. I should also like to thank Carmen Morenilla and Miguel Teruel, who always respond to my work generously and constructively, and all the members at the GRATUV (Universitat de València) and the APGRD (University of Oxford), from whom I have learnt much about the reception of the classics.

Among the many individuals who have helped me in various ways, I am particularly indebted to Jesús Tronch, for his expert advice and infallible eye. For discussions related to divorce laws in England I should like to thank Ann Heilmann. I also wish to thank the members of the International Federation of Theatre Research (IFTR) Historiography working group who provided valuable feedback on early versions of the book. Particular thanks are due to Hayley Bradley, Jim Davis, Kate Newey, Janice Norwood and Yael Zahry-Levo, for their insightful comments and suggestions to various sections of the volume. Flavio Ferri and Nuria Llagüerri also deserve my gratitude for the helpful references provided. Mike and Gina Hardinge should be thanked for a 'precious present', and Sergio Urzainqui for his help in digitalizing images. Finally, it has been a pleasure to work first with Charlotte Loveridge and Dhara Patel, and then with Anna MacDiarmid and Alice Wright at Bloomsbury.

For financial support of this project I am grateful to the Spanish Ministry of Education and the Universitat de València, for awarding me substantial research grants towards the writing of this book (FFI20012-32071 and UV-INV-PRECOMP14-206579). I am also indebted to the Departament de Filologia Anglesa i Alemanya at the Universitat de València for its support during the carrying out of this project.

Among the staff of the libraries visited for this project, all of whom were extremely helpful, I should like to thank librarians and staff at the British

Library at St Pancras and Colindale, the Senate House Library of the University of London, The Bodleian, Sackler and Taylorian libraries in the University of Oxford, the *Archive of Performances of Greek and Roman Drama* (APGRD) at the University of Oxford, and the Theatre Museum (London). Finally, I would also like to thank the readers of this manuscript for their insightful comments and suggestions.

1

Why Classical Burlesque?

Enacting the past and the present

The plays collected in this book span the decades of the 1840s and 1850s, a period when Londoners witnessed the expansion of an all-engulfing city, which eventually became the multilayered London that we know today. The growing numbers of new city dwellers led to the influx of a differentiated audience that demanded a new assortment of places of entertainment to frequent for their leisure. As Bratton points out, this was the making of the West End.[1] Yet the variety of entertainment that the experience of London offered did not spring into existence as the showcase of commercial Englishness that it is at present. Before being taken up by the forces of mercantile expansion, the public houses and taverns, shops, bookshops, concert-rooms, theatres, street fairs and art galleries of London were the piecemeal response of a multifaceted society driven by the manifold social changes of the mid-nineteenth century.[2] As I shall contend in the following pages, such changes entailed a new negotiation of gender relations that was mirrored in Victorian classical burlesque.

The rich, bustling cultural milieu of early Victorian London was attracted by an overwhelming force which had been at the forefront of English literary and artistic tradition since the early years of Chaucer; that is, the classics of Greece and Rome. The manifest presence of antiquity in Victorian England has been the object of several highly influential books – for example, Richard Jenkins' *Dignity and Decadence*, Linda Dowling's *Hellenism and Homosexuality*, Norman Vance's *The Victorians and Ancient Rome*, Yopie Prins' *Victorian Sappho*, Christopher Stray's *Classics Transformed*, Isobel Hurst's *Victorian Women Writers and the Classics* and Jeffrey Richards' *The Ancient World on the*

Victorian and Edwardian Stage to name but a few. For the sake of brevity, I take the liberty here to summarize the all-pervasive influence of classical culture in the nineteenth century analysed in such a profuse bibliography with Goldhill's exhaustive and acute description:[3]

> Classics was an integral part of the furniture of the Victorian mind bolstered through the elite education system, spread parodically and aspirationally through popular culture, visible in the physicality of the architecture and sculpture of the capital; disseminated in opera, in theatre, in literature, and even in the battles over religion that dominated the spiritual crises that commentators loved to descry in the final years of the century.

Should one add, for example, ballet, the printing press, the advertising industry and the cultural commodities of the time, one would find the perfect backdrop against which classical burlesque materialized.

Though there are various surveying tactics available for introducing the plays collected in this volume, I propose first to walk the reader through some of the everyday stories and the countless expressions of classical antiquity that accommodated Blanchard's *Antigone* (1845), Talfourd's *Alcestis* (1850) and *Electra* (1859), and Brough's *Medea* (1856). Some cursory reflections upon the classical presences that haunted Victorian London only partially answer the question which opens this chapter, 'why classical burlesque?' The plethora of referents from Greece and Rome that flooded nineteenth-century Britain is a main cause for the profusion of the genre. Yet, as I shall contend, several factors which include the development of a complex stagecraft and the Victorian predilection for testifying to everyday life in the cultural commodities of the time contribute to the success of classical burlesque. A sneak peek at the classics in the lives of the Victorians is the starting point for understanding the texts and contexts of the four plays anthologized in this book. Then, I shall dig into the various theatrical histories of the plays selected to revisit and revise the texts, the performances and the people involved in them to add to the broader history of Victorian classical burlesque.

By the late eighteenth century the sale of Sir Robert Walpole's collection of paintings from his country house at Houghton had sparked off a public debate on the need for a site in Great Britain to house the great works of national art.[4] Yet it was not until 1838 – after the insistent calls by James Barry and other artists for the establishment of a national gallery to educate public taste in art – that Trafalgar Square sparkled with the paintings of the Old Masters at the National Gallery and the Royal Academy of Arts, both housed in the same building until 1869. Let us picture an average passer-by admiring the columns of the gallery, recycled from the demolished Carlton House anytime between the 1840s and 1859, the years that span the plays collected in this volume. Whether or not this person were acquainted with the heated controversy over the site of the building in Trafalgar Square, the scandal surrounding the picture-cleaning of the 1852 season, and the actual display of the paintings,[5] he or she would be invited, as a visitor, to cross the threshold of the gallery and marvel at the imprint left by the Greeks and Romans in European visual culture. The earliest examples acquired by the gallery that our visitor could admire belong to the Angerstein and the Beaumont collections and included, for example, Claude Lorrain's *Landscape with Cephalus and Procris* and *Landscape with Narcissus and Echo* as well as Richard Wilson's *The Destruction of the Children of Niobe*.[6] Encouraged to contemplate the latest acquisitions, said visitor would move from Titian's *Bacchus and Ariadne*, Correggio's *Venus with Mercury and Cupid* or Poussin's *Nymph with Satyrs*, to J. M. W. Turner's *Dido Building Carthage*, bequeathed to the nation by Turner after his death in 1851.

Should our new acquaintance be strolling through the streets of London in that same year, 1851, an obligatory stopover must have necessarily been the Great Exhibition at the Crystal Palace. Visited by over six million people, the Great Exhibition displayed manufactured products from over forty-four nations. A whole section of the exhibition was devoted to fine arts, sculpture, models, plastic arts, mosaics and enamels.[7] The watercolours painted before the event, which were reproduced as souvenir guides throughout the nineteenth century, manifest how the Exhibition still bore the imprint of a period when a love of art was inspired, among other things, by mythology and the classics of Greece and Rome.[8] Silver waiters from Donalds Wm. Jas & Charles in London with the engraved groups of *Triumph of Galatea* and *A compilation of Venus and Adonis* by Franciscus Albanus[9] a folding screen by James Howard Earle with encaustic painting illustrating the story of Cupid and Psyche,[10] and Onyx gem cameos with Cupid, Ariadne, Bacchantes and Medusa by the designer G. Brett were among the myriad examples from Greek and Roman myths that vied for attention in the Exhibition.[11] With an admission price of £3 for gentlemen, £2 for ladies and one shilling a head for the masses from 24 May, the 1851 Exhibition attracted visitors from all walks of life. Yet for those who could not relish all the beauties of the exhibition in person, and those who did and delighted in recalling the experience, extensive coverage of the event was provided by the press of the time which included illustrations from the exhibits.[12] This is but one example of how nineteenth-century newspapers and journals indoctrinated the general public on ancient Greece and Rome.

On some occasions antiquity also served as model for present concerns. In 1862 *The Englishwoman's Domestic Magazine* published the article 'The Women of Greece' which juxtaposed the Victorian ideal with classical women.[13] Newspapers also recommended to our visitor to London a wide range of entertainments of the period which, more often than not, revealed tantalizing glimpses of Greek and Roman mythology. Strolling around the city in 1846, for example, our acquaintance could enter the Ancient Hall of Rome at Great Windmill Street which exhibited *tableaux vivants* giving 'living representations of heroes and heroines of the antique' without 'the cold appearance of the Grecian statues'.[14] In July the same year, the Royal Academy presented *Diana surprised by Actaeon* by W. E. Frost, which was displayed in the *Illustrated London News* with the text from Ovid's *Metamorphoses* appended in the catalogue of the exhibition. Only three years later, in the summer of 1849, the room to visit was the sculpture room, and the work to admire E. H. Baily's *Group, in marble, of the Graces*, which was also illustrated in the *Illustrated London News*.[15] Yet Mr Foley's *Ino and Bacchus* at Lord Ellesmere's new house in Green Park, which was open to the public on certain days the same year, might have rivalled Baily's *Group* in admirers.[16] Not so far from Trafalgar Square and Green Park another kind of sculpture might have raised the interest of any visitor to London intrigued by the new advances of science in the 1850s. *The Florentine Venus* and the *Greek Venus*, displaying the muscular system at Reimer's Anatomical and Ethnological Museum, awaited the enquiring observer of the human body in Leicester Square. In the handbill for the 1854 exhibition, which boasted over five hundred waxworks exhibits, museum entry tickets for rich and poor alike were reduced to half-price as a nod to 'the great desire of the working classes to inspect the museum'.[17]

Operas and ballets were the elite spectacles where the privileged few could be awestruck by other Galatea-like celebrities who proved a fertile source for classical burlesque. It would be trite to highlight the presence of classical antiquity in opera and ballet, as copious research has been painstakingly conducted and published by specialists on the subject.[18] My sole intention here, therefore, is to endeavour to chart the classicizing texture which paved the way for classical burlesque in the growing nation. Glück's, Wagner's and Noverre's triumphant reinventions of the classics in the eighteenth and late nineteenth centuries embellish the period that concerns us here. Spurred on by responses to their work, the Victorian Drury Lane, Covent Garden and Her Majesty's theatres staged countless tragedies, ballets and operas based on classical antiquity. Against such a backdrop, it is no coincidence that Lumley commissioned Romani to write an opera based on Circe in his first years as manager of Her Majesty's Theatre,[19] and that, as we shall see, the production of Mendelssohn's *Antigone* in 1845 exerted such a profound impact on the intellectual circles of London.

Some other profitable performances of the period under discussion were, for example, Thomas Noon Talfourd's *Ion* (1836), Mademoiselle Rachel's *Les Horaces* in 1842, Fornasari's *Belisario* in 1843, the various productions of Bellini's *Norma* and Milton's *Comus* and a concert, for the first time in England, of Glück's *Orpheus and Eurydice* in 1860.[20] In 1846 the *pas des déesses* in *Le Jugement de Paris* at Her Majesty's featuring the renowned Marie Taglioni, Fanny Cerrito and Lucile Grahn was among the great ballet sensations of the year 'chronicled in enthusiastic terms, and pictured all over London'.[21] By way of an apologia for the *ballet d'action* a reviewer in the *Illustrated London News* extolled the movements of the three great ballerinas as those of the three rival goddesses, Juno, Minerva and Venus in Perrot's choreography.[22] Taking advantage of the craze sparked off by the *pas des deésses*, Charles Selby produced a burlesque extravaganza at the Adelphi that same year, *The Judgment of Paris; or, the Pas de Pippins*. A review of the play in the *Illustrated London News* offers a precis of the repercussion of the process of creation and production of burlesque which is key to our understanding of the genre:

> In a *pièce de circonstance* of this kind, which must of necessity be planned, written, and brought out with high-pressure haste, whilst the prototype is before the public, or fresh in their minds, acute criticism on its merits ought

not to be looked for. It is, however, filled with jokes upon passing topics and follies, and plays on words generally, some of which were received with the courtesy due to strangers, and others warmly welcomed as very old acquaintances indeed.[23]

As shall be discussed later in the book, considering Victorian burlesques *en masse* and as cultural products that chronicled the changes of an era is the only way to overcome the negative assumptions of genre criticism so often found in traditional approaches to the subject.

Returning to our stroll through the streets of London, the restoration of Covent Garden theatre in 1858 – with Aristophanes, Menander, Aeschylus, Bacchus, Minerva, Hecate and other heathen personages in and under the portico[24] – proved that it was not only the various forms of entertainment but also the very buildings which housed them that evoked a glorious and celebrated foreign but by no means alien past culture. The Neo-Palladian architecture and neo-classicism of the eighteenth century left the stamp of the ancients on numerous streets in London.[25] Nineteenth-century allusions include Benjamin Dean Wyatt's rebuilding of Drury Lane (1811–1812), featuring an interior with Corinthian columns. Furthermore, the early nineteenth-century Greek Revival architecture, with Sir Robert Smirke and William Wilkins at the forefront, inundated London with a deluge of iconic sites, enough to quench the thirst of any city-dweller captivated by the classical aesthetic of the time. Smirke's United Service Club, the Union Club and the Royal College of Physicians on Nash's promising Trafalgar Square, not to mention the British Museum, decorated the route of strollers who, in years to come, might well have attended any of the classical burlesques readily on offer in London.

On the streets, in museums and galleries and in the printed literature of the period, the trajectory of Greek and Roman mythological imagery in Victorian London reveals countless microhistories which prepare the ground for the success of classical burlesque. Imbued with topical jokes and references, tragic heroes, suffering heroines and epic deeds are revisited with a vengeance and transformed to showcase the anxieties of a growing empire. Hand in hand with such imagery, the average individual on the streets of London in the decades that paved the way for the birth of the genre would have realized that one of the most relevant direct sources for the spectacle in Victorian burlesque were the eighteenth-century fairground entertainments, where the plots and characters of the puppet shows, among others, reveal how the popularity of classical mythology went beyond high art.[26]

From the early years of the century, Martin Powell's adaptations of plays to the marionette theatre were based on legendary tales and ballads. They also came from other more sophisticated sources such as satire of topical issues and, more importantly, Italian opera. Some of his classical stories include *Hero and Leander*, *The Destruction of Troy* and *Venus and Adonis*.[27] Powell's approach to puppetry appealed to popular tastes where classical mythology was common ground. Later in the century, whilst Charlotte Charke, Colley Cibber's daughter, programmed her first season in London according to the 'high dramas' that were put on at the time,[28] Charles Dibdin was reviving classical myths and themes such as Pandora and Ulysses.[29] The most important puppet show based on classical myths was Kane O'Hara's *Midas*, which opened at Covent Garden in 1764,[30] and became the model for burletta in early nineteenth-century debates on the comic genres. The revival of *Midas* with Madame Vestris as Apollo inspired Planché's first classical burlesque,[31] and the spirit of classical burlesque also entered the nineteenth century with the aid of Lord Byron's parodies of Euripides' *Medea*, *Maid of Athens* and *Don Juan*.[32]

The re-opening of theatres by the late seventeenth century gave rise to the emergence of a wide variety of genres which eventually became a potential source for burlesque. One year after the first performance of John Gay's landmark piece of eighteenth-century comic theatre, *The What D'Ye Call It*,[33] Richard Leveridge, singer, composer and a minor playwright,[34] made incursions into the burlesque of Italian opera with *The Comick Masque of Pyramus and Thisbe* (1716), an afterpiece which satirizes Colley Cibber's *Venus and Adonis* (1715) and John Hughes' *Apollo and Daphne* (1715) in its prologue. Notwithstanding Leveridge's debt to Shakespeare, what is at issue here is the development of the audiences' taste for seeing classical myths on stage.[35]

The growing interest in classical mythology which developed throughout the eighteenth century is manifested in the numerous reworkings of the fables of Apollo, Daphne, Perseus and Andromeda that were produced from 1716 to 1730.[36] The 1730s witnessed a rebirth of Greece and Rome in the arts, literature and leisure of wealthy, highbrow Britain. The Society of Dilettanti's sponsorship of classical archaeology encouraged a significant body of literature on Greek antiquities,[37] and numerous private collections of Greek sculpture and art were built up in England between 1732 and 1786 (e.g. those of Thomas Coke and Sir Robert Walpole). In addition, the development of travel literature, which idealized the landscape of Greece, and the rise of Hellenized aestheticism exerted a powerful influence on the creation of a Grecian taste that was reflected on stage and reigned throughout. Moreover, the decline in the production of satire after the 1737 Licensing Act —which excluded political satire from the stage— might have turned the attention of the playwrights towards mock classical burlesques.[38]

Yet from Duffet's late-seventeenth-century *Psyche* to F. C. Burnand's late Victorian reworking of the myth, the concept and function of classical burlesque on the English stage bears out the truism that there is a correlation between the modern reworkings of Greek and Roman myths and the social history and politics of the target audience. The depiction of Queen Caroline as Dido by Theodore Lane in the etching *Dido in Despair* (1821) and the representation of Queen Victoria as Hermione in *Punch*,[39] show how humour and classical mythology can well account for the archetypal construction of society whether through caricatures, puppet shows, tavern singing or burlesque.

Nineteenth-century classical burlesque contains allusions to the industrial and social changes which underpinned the Victorian imagination, and the relationship between topical references and Greek and Roman mythology is the key to an aesthetic reinterpretation of prescribed roles. These anachronistic links between classicism and modernity round off the answer to my initial question 'why classical burlesque?' The analysis of classical burlesques *en masse* allows us to unravel the interplay between the social codes, cultural commodities and Greek and Roman myths which are juxtaposed in the texts. As a consequence, Talfourd's *Alcestis* and Blanchard's *Antigone*, far from being solitary cases, exemplify in conjunction with Robert Reece's *Cassandra* and others the social correlation of collective imaginaries and articulate cultural and social realities.

The histories of Victorian classical burlesque

James Robinson Planché was the driving force behind mid-nineteenth-century classical burlesque with *Olympic Revels; or Prometheus and Pandora*, which was first performed at the Olympic Theatre under the management of Madame Vestris in 1831.⁴⁰ Planché's *Olympic Revels* laid the foundations of the humour, costume and language of Victorian classical burlesque, which followed the performance conventions of the genre that Schoch summarizes thus:

> rhymed couplets in a parody of the original text; the transposition of characters from high to low; ... the contemporanization of past events ...; the ludicrous reenactment of classic scenes; ... a pronounced theatrical bias, with an emphasis on stage business, sight gags, and special effects ...; relentless puns; ... and soliloquies and set pieces rewritten as lyrics to contemporary songs, whether popular, operatic, or even minstrel ... Above all, burlesques trafficked in topical allusions.⁴¹

Other common performance conventions of classical burlesque were dance routines, tableaux, spectacular visual stunts, metatheatrical allusions and an anachronistic aesthetics. The four plays anthologized in this volume all represent such conventions to varying degrees.

Talfourd's *Alcestis* is perhaps the most anachronistic with a policeman of the famous '*Hτα division*', Polax, '*habited in a classic dress, with the exception of his hat, cape, and staff, which are those of a modern policeman*'. Yet topical allusions to everyday objects and Victorian customs abound in the four plays: Antigone alludes to an advertisement in the *Sunday Times* (l.134), and Creon in Brough's *Medea* intends to send her offspring to a Blue Coat School (1.1.1.71). The latest songs from operas and shows deflate some of the most tragic and well-known passages of the hypotexts of the four plays: Orestes closes Talfourd's *Electra* with an air from William Balfe's celebrated *Satanella* (1858) and Alcestis' famous own *rhesis* in Euripides' l.280–325 is partly rewritten as a song. Dance routines are explicitly introduced in Talfourd's *Electra,* where the famous Leclerqs took part in a classic divertissement. Gods, heroes and heroines come on and off stage with stunning spectacular effects, which are also inserted to imitate the idiosyncrasies of the latest popular productions; for example, Brough's *Medea* ends with the impressive discovery of the statue of Madame Ristori. Transvestite and breeches roles also contributed to the success of many of the performances which, in the case of the plays in this volume, featured, for example, Miss Ternan in breeches as Orestes in Talfourd's *Electra* and Frederick Robson as Medea, one of the most acclaimed transvestite roles of the mid-nineteenth century.

Another standard feature of classical burlesque was the display of Greek inscriptions of a transliterated English phrase. An inscription in a placard carried by Medea's children reads 'Φαθερλεσσ, ORPHELINS, ORFANI, FATHERLESS' (1.1.160) and upon the door plate of Admetus' house is read 'Mr. Admetos' and 'Please to ring the bell' in Greek characters. Puns in Latin as well as occasional quotations from classical authors were also common: Talfourd's *Electra* includes quotations from Virgil's *Aeneid*, V.320 in the Lacy's paratext, and the character Pylades cites from Diogene Laerci.

If Planché created the formula at the Olympic, the first burlesque of a Greek tragedy was Edward Leman Blanchard's *Antigone Travestie*, which opened at the New Strand Theatre in 1845. Other attempts had been made before Blanchard's *Antigone* to burlesque classical tragedy, but it was only he who 'discovered in the form and conventions of performed Greek tragedy itself an inspirational source for the popular stage.'[42] After Planché, classical burlesque was performed well into the 1880s. The mainstays of classical burlesque were Gilbert à Beckett, Francis Talfourd and the Brough brothers, all men of education who exerted a powerful influence on their contemporaries;[43] and later, Francis C. Burnand, Henry James Byron, and Robert Reece.[44] William Schwenck Gilbert was also inspired in the genre to create some of his well-known pieces, for example, *Pygmalion and Galatea* (1871) and *Thespis; or the Gods Grown Old* (1871). The staples of classical burlesque were Homer's *Iliad* and *Odyssey* and Ovid's *Metamorphoses*, but Virgil's *Aeneid*, Apollonius' *Argonautica* and the Greek tragedies – Aeschylus' *Agamemnon*, Sophocles' *Antigone* and *Electra* and Euripides' *Alcestis* and *Medea* – were also burlesqued.[45] Even though burlesque shared much Aristophanic laughter, it seems that only Planché's *The Birds of Aristophanes* (1846) was based on one of his comedies.[46]

The plays selected for this anthology were first performed at the New Strand, the Olympic and the Haymarket theatres to audiences that might have been acquainted with the mythological figures through education, through new cultural commodities, or through the numerous entertainments and publications with Greco-Roman themes available at the time.[47] Two such publications were Lemprière's dictionary and Millington's *Characteristics of the Gods of Greece*. The former was the standard reference work of this kind in mid-nineteenth-century England.[48] A review of Talfourd's *Electra in a New Electric Light* (1859) alludes to the reliance of burlesque on the dictionary,[49] and F. C. Burnand's *Paris, or, Vive Lemprière* licensed to be performed at the Royal Strand Theatre in 1866 explicitly mentions Lemprière as an authoritative text.[50] Yet the section of current literature in the *Illustrated London News* on 18 April 1868 advertised Ellen J. Millington's *Characteristics of the Gods of Greece: A Manual for School-Girls* which provided 'a tolerable acquaintance with the graceful deities of the Hellenic Olympus...to understand the frequent allusions to their personal history in poetry and general literature'.[51] The book was advertised as surpassing Lemprière's dictionary and was aimed at young people who did not read 'Ovid and Homer'.[52]

By the mid-nineteenth century, a formal education in Greek and Latin was a realm of a male-dominated elite culture. From the nobility of the eighteenth century, to the bourgeois groups seeking distinction in the nineteenth, classical education was a means of maintaining class identities and cultural authority. Certain social practices, such as the use of classical allusions and quotations in the speeches of the Houses of Parliament, consolidated an education in Greek and Latin as a status marker. Yet by the 1870s, and coinciding in time with the last years of splendour of classical burlesque, the socio-cultural authority of an education in Classics began to wane. This, Stray argues, gave way to curricular pluralism and to a more democratic access to Greek and Latin.[53] Furthermore, the expansion of female schooling in the second half of the century brought about the access of women to a formal education in Classics in private schools, colleges for women and universities.

There, then, arises the question recently posed by Richards of 'how far the audiences understood and appreciated what was being burlesqued'[54]. Following Schoch's terms, an ideal or 'competent' audience would certainly have had sufficient knowledge of the sources to fully comprehend the classical allusions in them. Hall describes such an ideal as the 'lower middle-class male who enjoyed the topical satire in *Punch*; his education in the Classics would have been similar to that inflicted on one theatregoer during his childhood in the 1840s, when a governess made him merely learn "parrot-wise" from the old Eton Latin grammar and from a couple of books on ancient myth and history'.[55] Yet, considering the various demands of 'knowingness' of classical burlesques (that is to say, a knowingness of Greek to understand the various inscriptions in the placards used in *Medea*, for example; of Greek tragedy to recognize the Sophoclean structure in Talfourd's *Electra*; or merely of the plots of the plays and the personal histories of their characters) one must also suppose certain levels of competency and incompetency in the various audiences who attended classical burlesques. Therefore, when classical burlesques toured minor theatres with less learned audiences, topical allusions and cultural clichés of the time might also have been the source of more amusement in the performance rather than the classical hypotexts. As shall be discussed in the next section of this introduction, reviews of the performance of Talfourd's *Alcestis* by the Infantry Brigade at Colchester certainly manifest how the play was more appealing to its spectators for its allusions to the police force than for its classical sources.

The ambivalence of the politics of burlesque favoured the recurrence of certain myths on stage; the debates on divorce prompted the emergence of a large number of Alcestis and Medeas burlesqued.[56] Moreover, classical myths frequently served theatrical purposes, so figures which could be easily depicted through songs and music – such as Orpheus and Eurydice – were as regular on stage as those which served as showcases for new stage effects. Francis Talfourd's *Atalanta, or the Golden Apples*, for example, which was first staged at the Haymarket Theatre on 13 April 1857, displayed a flying Cupid performed in breeches by the much acclaimed Mary Wilton. When Cupid descends from above to mesmerize the Paidagogos and change his character (f. 14), Talfourd is not only developing the line but is also showing off the stage machinery of the Haymarket under the management of Buckstone and not to mention the acting style of the famous Compton in the role of the Paidagogos. Another aspect which had a considerable influence on the selection of the classical themes was their topicality. Venus had been a major figure in the arts and literature of Romanticism, and the nineteenth-century casts of the Venus de Milo, together with the various sculptures which were inspired by it, turned it into a recurring character of burlesque.[57]

In general, nineteenth-century classical burlesque lacks a deep political discourse. Nonetheless, the ambivalence of the politics of burlesque with regard to women gives voice to transgressive moulds which remained concealed in other cultural representations. Whilst recent approaches to the genre reflect upon it as a major vehicle for the ideas proffered by the so-called New Women,[58] previous studies emphasize the shallowness of the plays as opposed to the in-depth parodies of late eighteenth-century creations. Yet the plays collected in this volume map out major features of the life of Victorian burlesque as the backdrop against which prominent figures of Greek tragedy deliver a deeply rebellious view of the roles of women in society. Therefore, the voices of Antigone, Alcestis, Medea and Electra render burlesque apt testimony to the social progress of women throughout the 1840s and 1850s.

The development and decay of classical burlesque, between the 1830s and the late 1860s, witnessed social and political changes that were mirrored on stage through the lens of humour.[59] During the 1830s, the Great Reform Bill (1832) enlarged the franchise and restructured representation in Parliament, and huge advances in social issues were made with the Factory Act (1833), the abolition of slavery in the Empire (1834) and the fights of the Anti-Corn Law League and the Chartists. The 1840s saw the establishment of the Royal Commission on Health of Towns and the passing of the Public Health Act in 1848, which improved the sanitary conditions of the country. The first step for the liberalism of the following decades was the repeal of the Corn Law in 1846, whilst the beginning of the potato famine in Ireland, together with the outbreak of railway mania, prompted an exodus which, by the 1870s, would result in an extensive urbanization of the British population. In 1851, the Great Exhibition inaugurated a period of liberalism which invaded mid-Victorian politics; free-trade, the development of a popular press and the industrialization of society are but a few examples of the results of such politics, which span the latter years of the century. The 1850s also witnessed a major boost for the rights of women. Individual champions like Caroline Norton, who had pressed for drastic reforms with the Infants Custody Act (1839),[60] began to receive the support of scores of followers.[61] The movement for women's rights epitomizes the state of turmoil which characterizes the last decades of the century.

The social and political changes described above were echoed in the arts and literature of the time. Charles Dickens' *Pickwick Papers* (1837), for example, reflected the high levels of electoral corruption after the enlargement of the franchise and Charlotte Brontë's *Jane Eyre* (1847) developed a critique against mid-nineteenth-century bourgeois patriarchal authority. Classical burlesque, in comparison with other expressions of Victorian humour, is rife with political ambivalence. Except for a few isolated cases, the topical references of the texts lack the denunciation of Dickens, Brontë, and even John Leech's caricatures in *Punch*. Nevertheless, allusions to contemporary issues such as the Woman

Question and the Health and Educational System, for example, showcase the mindset – and therefore the preoccupations and criticism – of the full gamut of society. Moreover, the aesthetic codes of burlesque entail an implicit criticism which is reflected in a subversion of Victorian morale.

With regard to the Woman Question which underpins the plays selected for this volume, two of Planché's most acclaimed classical burlesques, *The Golden Fleece* (1845) and *Theseus and Ariadne* (1848), develop the theme of the abandoned wife and are strongly related to the historical context in which they were first performed.[62] Divorce was a highly topical subject in the early 1840s after Caroline Norton's trials, and married women's inequality was at the centre of articles to the *Morning Chronicle* (1846–1850) written by John Stuart Mill and his wife, Harriet Taylor.[63] Planché's burlesques were groundbreaking and foreshadowed the spirit of social criticism which timidly lay behind contemporary allusions of classical burlesque in subsequent decades. As a consequence, only a year after Planché's reappraisal of the myth of Ariadne, the Brough brothers' *The Sphinx* was first put on at the Haymarket Theatre, bringing to the fore Jocasta's refusal of an arranged marriage and her displeasure with the domestic duties which dominated the lives of upper-class Victorian women.[64] In this sense, the play anticipates the open criticism against the lack of legislation protecting women in general and wives in particular which permeates Brough's *Medea* in 1856.

As we shall see, the 1857 Divorce and Matrimonial Causes Act's legalization of divorce in England was much discussed on the comic stage of the 1850s and 1860s. As an example, the anonymous *Apollo and the Flying Pegasus or the Defeat of the Amazons* (1858) alludes to the new plea allowed by the law which permitted women to allege domestic brutality in Court.[65] Yet, besides the Woman Question, other issues raised in the burlesque concern social microhistories related to the construction of Victorian Britain with allusions to the educational system, the Public Health Act (1848) and the repeal of the Corn Laws (1846), for example. In *Atalanta, or the Three Golden Apples* (1857), to cite but an instance, Talfourd aligns himself with the intellectual undercurrent which demanded a reform of the British educational system and rejected the study of classics.[66]

Considering these issues and the topics discussed above, several factors concur, therefore, in response to my initial question, 'why classical burlesque?' The lack of a deep political discourse in nineteenth-century burlesque cannot be denied. In addition, topical allusions, easy both to recognize and to forget, had condemned nineteenth-century popular theatre to oblivion. Nonetheless, as Hall points out, the fact of burlesquing – or subverting – a classical text embodies an act of transgression which, in this case, entails strong ideological concerns on the cultural division of the classes and a stagnant educational system which was based on Classics as a status marker.[67] Therefore, at a time when the position of the individual in society was being questioned, the function of humour carried wider socio-political concerns which went beyond mere entertainment.

The four plays collected in this volume span the years of the flourishing and decay of classical burlesque. Their corresponding hypotexts are either Greek tragedies or well-known nineteenth-century adaptations that foreground multiple models of women. Recurrent allusions to microhistories related to topical events in everyday life coexisted in burlesque with major social concerns such as comments on agreed marriages, divorce courts and erudite women, for which the popular stage became a forum for discussion. Yet the cultural codes transmitted with regard to women were indeed ambivalent and whilst they are depicted as irrepressible chatterboxes in H. J. Byron's *Orpheus and Eurydice* (1864), they rebel against a dictatorial government in E. L. Blanchard's *Antigone* (1845). With the purpose of reconstructing such historical contexts, and as a complement to the commentary and the textual notes of the plays, the next section of this introduction focuses on the anachronistic interplay between the social codes, the cultural commodities and the Greek and Roman myths which are juxtaposed in the texts selected.

Revealing the hidden substrata of the theatrical contexts in which the texts and performances were first received means digging into various historical layers of Victorian England. Therefore, this edited anthology not only aims at offering textual archaeology but also at revisiting the various theatrical histories at play when a modern reader approaches Victorian classical burlesque. Editing, then, becomes the means by which the historical and aesthetic networks between the plays selected and the theatrical scene of the time are uncovered. Furthermore, it is also the means to understand the microhistories silenced in the canonical histories of Victorian England. As such, the high topicality of classical burlesque serves as a mirror for the extra-textual histories of the period. This is illustrated in Blanchard's *Antigone*, which reflects a major financial fraud that took place in England in the 1840s which had been widely forgotten.

Some other extra-textual histories at issue in this edition bring together the performances of the plays selected with amateur productions of the shows, as is the case of Talfourd's *Alcestis* and the charity performance by the Infantry Brigade at Colchester. Others, such as the allusions to Richardson's popular shows in Blanchard's *Antigone*, are annotated in terms of the interplay between the metatheatrical references. Another group of parallel theatrical and extra-textual histories are disclosed by looking at the biographies of the people involved in the productions as recorded in the Lacy's printed editions. As exemplified in *Alcestis* and the Farren family, the annotations of the List of Roles in the plays selected testify to the involvement of the performers in various venues in London and in the provinces. Last but not least, the commentary of the plays in this anthology also manifests the connections between the texts collated, the performances and the visual culture of Victorian England. One of the most relevant example cases is that of *Medea* and the various examples of pictorial evidence of both the performances of Ristori and Robson.

With regard to the intra-textual histories, in the four plays selected, the collation of the pre- with the post-production texts brings to light textual additions and cancellations that ultimately affect the performance and the various theatrical histories at play here. The absence of most of the songs in the licensed manuscript copy of *Electra*, for example, prompts questions like by whom, why and for what purpose were the airs introduced in the performance. Furthermore, annotations on the source of the songs, as evidenced in *Electra*'s 'Satanella', from William Balfe's homonymous opera, unveil the links between classical burlesque and other highbrow forms of entertainment. An added element is the effect of censorship which, even if it is not so self-evident in the four plays of this anthology, indeed influenced the performance of Williams' *Medea* at the Adelphi in 1856, where allusions to the Eastlake controversy and the National Gallery were censored by the Lord Chamberlain's office.[68]

As we shall see, the annotations of the four plays in this volume provide information on popular fairground shows, fashions, customs and microhistories little regarded in the books of history. Digging into the textual and performance histories of the plays for any anthology of Victorian classical burlesque also means posing questions on the process of creation and production of the plays which ultimately means digging into theatrical histories. Editing classical burlesque allows theatre historians to revise and to write these histories even though, as argued by Davis (2012), the resulting edition – text – will never reconstruct the original performance of the play. Nonetheless, it might serve as a complementary artefact to the broader historical and semiotic picture; as a theatrical microhistory within the all-encompassing history of Victorian classical burlesque yet to be written.

Texts and contexts

Amid the cornucopia of plays that lampoon classical mythology on the Victorian stage, the burlesques anthologized in this volume share various characteristics which may be approached under the prism of Bratton's and Davis' foundational ideas of 'intertheatricality' and 'repertoire'. Bratton defines the 'intertheatrical' as 'an awareness of the elements and interactions that make up the whole web of mutual understanding between potential audiences and their players, a sense of … knowingness, about playing that spans a lifetime or more, and that is activated for all participants during the performance event'.[69] Finding the interconnecting vectors that provide a meaningful background for the semiotic webs at play here implies posing questions such as, how do these burlesques relate to their corresponding hypotexts? What are the interactions between players, dramatists and venues? How do the topical issues they address, criticize and ridicule fulfil the horizon of expectations of the audiences? As Davis argues, 'repertoire' understood as 'associational, polytextual, intertheatrically citational, recombinant patterns that sustain intelligibility'[70] narrows the wide intellectual scope of 'intertheatricality' drawing attention to the connections between the 'texts and their users'. The annotations that accompany Blanchard's *Antigone* (1845), Talfourd's *Alcestis* (1850) and *Electra* (1859), and Brough's *Medea* (1856) in this anthology aim to unveil some of the hidden connections. The pages that follow present the texts in their contexts as a threshold to understanding the reception of the classical myths in question. The focus is on the tragic heroines and Victorian negotiations with gender.

The lack of significant English models for *Antigone* during the seventeenth and eighteenth centuries, and the impeccable performance of the title role of the play by Charlotte Vandenhoff and later Helen Faucit were crucial for the success of Mendelssohn's *Antigone* in Victorian England (see fig 1.1). Hall and Macintosh's analysis of the repercussions both of the Covent Garden and the Dublin performances of the tragedy in 1845 identifies how Sophocles' *Antigone* suffused the intellectual, aesthetic and theatrical production of the subsequent decades. Responses to Mendelssohn's *Antigone* ranged from Margaret Sandbach and Thomas De Quincey to John Gibson and George Eliot. By and large, the Victorian Antigone draws attention to the virtuous and dutiful sister who sacrifices herself for the sake of her family and religious obligations. Yet Elizabeth Stuart Phelps' refiguration of the myth in 1891 points to the lack of a proper education and binding moral obligations as the social foundation of Antigone's sacrifice. A late-century example of the coexistence of the selfless and defiant Antigone in relation to the Woman Question is Julia Ward Howe's allusion to the myth in her lecture at The Congress of Women held in Chicago in 1893 and published in 1895. As Howe argues:

> In some of the comedies of Aristophanes the women's cause is presented in a light intended to provoke ridicule ... For ideal types we must go to those dramatists who deal with the historic and mythic traditions of the past ... My present limits will only allow me to speak of two of these characters, Electra and Antigone. Both of these women are rebels against authority. In both of them high courage is combined with womanly sweetness and purity ... And in these gracious and more purely feminine types presented by Sophocles, we admire the union of a womanly tenderness with womanly courage.[71]

Prior to Howe's restoration of the subversive voice of the heroine, E. L. Blanchard staged *Antigone Travestie* in 1845. Blanchard's burlesque depended on the staging of Mendelssohn's *Antigone*, whose spirit was recaptured by the playwright and transposed to the aesthetics of Victorian popular entertainment. Blanchard worked on the audience's memory of the original Sophoclean play and the production at Covent Garden. The humour of the burlesque relied, accordingly, not only on the classical hypotext but also on the intertheatricality of the play; on the unseen constellations of meanings established between the audience and the performance. One such constellation involved the setting of the play, which parodied an old Greek theatre 'in the shape of the outside of

Richardson's show', Richardson being a well-known impresario associated with fairground theatre.[72] Charles Dickens immortalized Richardson's show in *Sketches by Boz* (1836) with an 'immense booth, with the large stage in front … brightly illuminated with variegated lamps, and pots of burning fat' and actors in 'Roman dresses'.[73] Perhaps the bombastic style of acting and the shortness of the plays associated with Richardson's fairground theatre might have influenced other aspects of the performance.[74] What is true is that Richardson's popular setting and the title of the play establish the comic stance of Blanchard from the very outset. *Era* sets down the wise choice of the scenery as follows:

> The booth of the immortal Richardson … the Smithfield itinerant, was the scene of action; there was no mistake, there could be no mistake. The *Clown*, the fire-eater, and the jaded *Columbine*, had completed the outside business, and the sanctum was laid open with its triple curtained doors …[75]

Licensed on 1 February,[76] *Antigone Travestie* was first staged at the New Strand Theatre in London on 3 February 1845 sharing the bill with Blanchard's own *The Road of Life*, which had been first staged at the Olympic in October 1843.[77] Reviews of the play confirm the performance of the burlesque at the New Strand in March the same year, and the touring of *Antigone Travestie* to the Queen's Royal Theatre in Dublin in December 1845, where the Mendelssohnian *Antigone* had been performed by Helen Faucit with great success at the Theatre Royal earlier in the year.[78]

In February 1845, and only for a few remaining months, Henry Ball Roberts was still the manager of the New Strand.[79] In May 1845 Coplestone Coward Hodges would take charge of the theatre after a season of disagreement with the staff and unpaid salaries.[80] *Antigone* was widely acclaimed by the audience and the critics, who saw in Blanchard's burlesque the perfect comic imitation of the Covent Garden heroes: Vandenhoff, Macready, O'Connell and Macfarren.[81] The title roles were interpreted by Harry Hall as Creon and George Wild as Antigone, who, as Blanchard himself owns, had collaborated with the playwright on numerous occasions.[82] George Wild had been manager of the Olympic between September 1843 and November 1844, a period when Blanchard's *The Road of Life* and the farces *The Artful Dodge*, *Pork Chops*, and *Angels and Lucifers* were produced at the said theatre.[83] *The Road of Life* reached its hundredth night at the Olympic on 6 May 1844,[84] before moving to the New

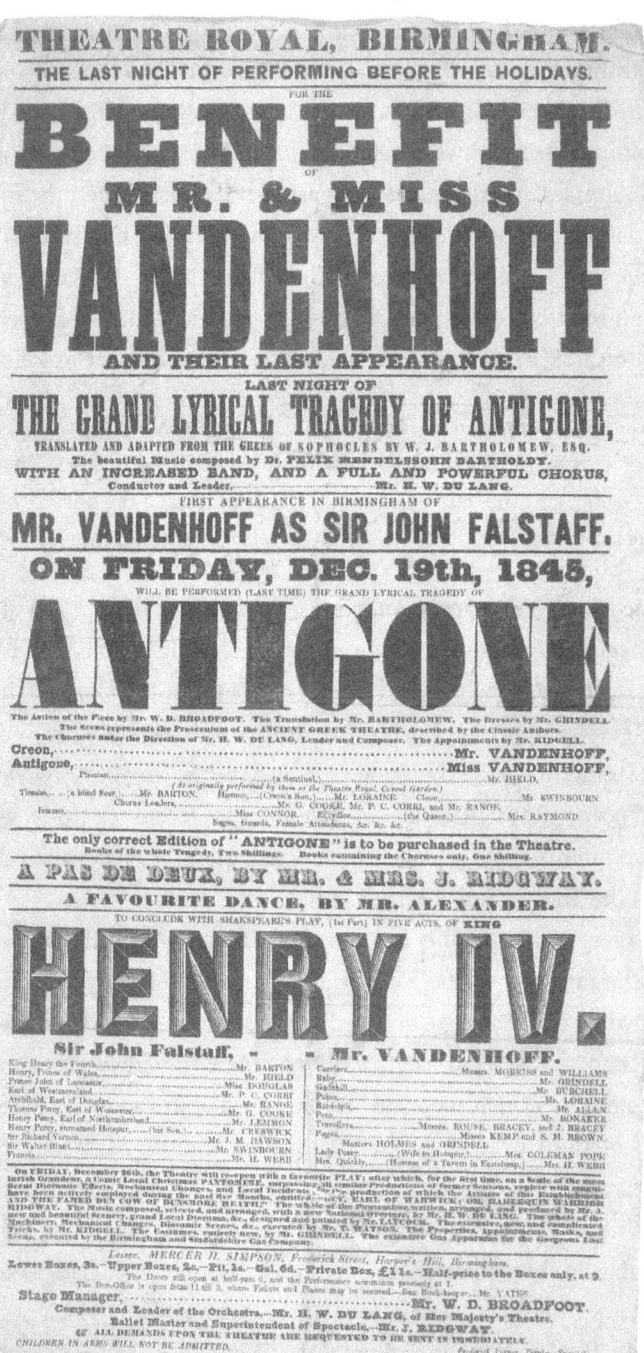

Figure 1.1 Playbill of Mendelssohn's *Antigone* at the Theatre Royal Birmingham (1845) © Laura Monrós-Gaspar.

Strand, where it inaugurated Wild's new engagement at the theatre and shared the bill with *Antigone Travestie*.[85] The plot of Blanchard's *Antigone* is in many ways related to *The Road of Life*, where six hundred pounds alter the life and career of a cabman and a poor debtor is represented in Whitecross Street Prison.[86] The debtor character is by no means alien to the Victorian stage as Booth underscores the transformation of the traditional role of the evil aristocrat in melodrama into fraudsters.[87] In Blanchard's *Antigone* the character was embodied by the minor role of Polynices.

Serving the purposes of humour, the fortunate conjunction of the two plays and two key historical facts impinge upon the burlesqued plot of the Sophoclean tragedy: the swindle of the 'Independent and West Middlesex Insurance Company' and the passing of the Bank Charter Act, known as Peel's Act, in 1844. Moody contends that the 'growth and collapse of capital markets proved a dramatic subject with strong appeal at the Victorian box-office'[88] and supports her arguments with substantial examples which cover the full theatrical panorama of the nineteenth century.[89] Indeed, literary works, particularly novels, were influenced by the role of paper money and the problem of giving substance to a paper currency by the early nineteenth century.[90] Blanchard's *Antigone*, therefore, is by no means an isolated case in showcasing the financial concerns of the Empire in the form of burlesque and must be therefore read against such 'intertheatricalities'.

In 1837 the lower and middle classes in England entrusted their properties and savings to a flourishing new company which eventually became one of the biggest frauds ever known in Victorian England: the 'Independent and West Middlesex Insurance Company'. In the early months of 1841 the company collapsed dashing the hopes of subscribers who watched the evaporation of their money. The illegal activity of the company had been persistently denounced by Frank Mackenzie, editor and proprietor of the Scottish *Reformers Gazette*, to no avail.[91] Finally, after five years of intense activity, the detection of the fraud and the downfall of those involved in it were widely echoed in the press of the time.[92] Sir Peter Laurie, as one of the Aldermen of the city of London, launched a fierce campaign in defence of those defrauded which won him wide popularity and recognition.

Blanchard refers to the West Middlesex swindle in the play in lines 63–70 when Creon directly alludes to the action taken by Laurie in aid of the nation.

Polynices' crime in the burlesque is an unpaid debt of £5 which has thrown him into Whitecross Street Prison,[93] the debtor's jail which the managing director of the 'Independent' company, Thomas Knowles, had already frequented some years before the fraud. An added touch of humour is Antigone's allusion to the debt as a 'five pound note ... from Threadneedle Street' (l.37–38). Peel's Act in 1844 restricted the issue of bank notes to the Bank of England's gold reserves and established a separate department for the issue of promissory notes, which granted special privileges to the company. At the time, it meant to secure the position of the Bank of England as the central bank of the nation, yet recent theories demonstrate a retrogression in such development in the decades that followed.[94] In any case, the limitation of provincial banks increased their dependence on the central bank for cash supplies, which inevitably strengthened the monopoly and control of the Bank of England.[95] Within the backdrop of a massive fraud and a financial crisis, new meanings imbue the significance attributed to Antigone in Victorian England.

Blanchard's Antigone embodied at the same time the sacrificial and obedient sister who upheld Victorian family values and the strong-minded woman involved in 'male'-made politics. In line with Florence Nightingale's *Cassandra*, Antigone's resolution to relate her truth was in tune with the political voice of the Victorian sage who scrutinized the legitimacy of ethical, political and financial institutions. Consider that in 1831 John Stuart Mill had published *The Spirit of the Age*, and in 1845 Benjamin Disraeli published *Sybil: or the Two Nations* and Fredrich Engels' *Die Lage der arbeitenden Klasse in England* came out in Leipzig. The dialogue between Hermon and Antigone on the relation between kings and subjects draws attention to issues of the sources of power and authority and reflects the socio-ideological crisis of the contemporary individual. The clash between free-thinking and reliance on authority was an acute dilemma in Victorian England. And the criticisms of the play which deal with hierarchical structures of society parallel Mill's approach to the right of private judgement and the free inquiry by all in moral and political conduct. An added point to this issue is the function of humour as a catalyst for debating social concerns.

Any scrutiny of the system of intertextualities at play in Blanchard's *Antigone* must necessarily ponder over the role of the venue in which it was first staged: the New Strand Theatre. Bratton's analysis of the making of the West End signals the Strand as the hub of burlesque featuring the latest iconic images in the cultural entertainment of the 1840s, where mainstream thoughts cohabited with caustic humour.[96] As a burlesque of the Strand, Blanchard's *Antigone* responded to topical concerns and inaugurated a new tendency which was successfully disseminated in the following decades: the burlesque of Greek tragedy.[97] As a topical product of the time, *Antigone* was in dialogue with other more conventional forms of entertainment. Therefore, intertheatrical connections of *Antigone*, inevitably prompt thoughts about productions in the Christmas season preceding Blanchard's premiere where robberies and financial debts were tackled through wit and humour. Sadler's Wells *Robin Hood and Little John, or Merrie England in the Olden Time* features various episodes of stealing[98] and, according to a review in *The Northern Star*, one of the most effective scenes and tricks in the 1844 Christmas pantomime at Drury Lane[99] 'was that of the exterior of the Insolvent Debtors' Prison', with the act of Parliament abolishing imprisonment for debt pasted on the wall.[100] This coincided in time with the publication of *Perry's Bankrupt and Insolvent Gazette*, regular accounts of debtors in contemporary newspapers, and anecdotes of escapes from debtors' prisons.[101]

With regard to gender dynamics, Antigone's words are well ahead of her time: she rebukes male oligarchy and chides the state for financial centralism. Furthermore, as Moody argues, the 'emergence of women as financial agents made possible a variety of comic scenarios in which women heal a crisis of capital' by the second half of the nineteenth century.[102] Moody uses Tom Taylor's *Settling Day*, which was first performed at the Olympic in 1865 as an example, yet Blanchard's *Antigone* predates the staging of the active involvement of women in financial crises. For that reason, even though it might be argued that George Wild's cross-dressed interpretation might dissipate any possible gender criticism, it should be noted that transvestism was one of the staples of Victorian burlesque, and on some occasions the characters less in tune with the Victorian ideals of femininity were precisely the ones performed by mature, well-known actresses and men. In fact, Brough's subversive and acclaimed *Medea* was also impersonated by a male actor, the celebrated Frederick Robson.

Robert Brough's *Medea* has been widely read against the backdrop of the Matrimonial Causes Act and the divorce legislation of the mid-nineteenth century.[103] Within such a context, and as part of a general upsurge of interest in the myth which pervaded the British stage between 1845 and the late

1850s (see fig 1.2),[104] *Medea; or, the Best of Mothers, with a Brute of a Husband* was first performed at the Royal Olympic Theatre on 14 July 1856, under the management of Alfred Wigan.

The performance was a massive hit from its premiere due to Frederick Robson's faithful and comic impersonation of Adelaide Ristori's Medea. Brough's burlesque is based on Ernest Legouvé's *Medea*, first performed at the Théâtre Italien in Paris in an Italian translation by Joseph Montanelli in April 1856.[105] In June the same year, the audiences at the London Lyceum enjoyed the performance of the diva, who was called before the curtain no less than four times on the night of the first performance.[106] Ristori's Medea was considered the 'great event of the theatrical year',[107] and such was its success that the Queen, the Prince Consort, the Princess Royal and Prince Frederick William of Prussia attended the show on Monday 9 June the same year.[108] As noted by one reviewer at the *London Daily News*, Legouvé's *Medea* appealed to the modern audiences more than the Medea of preceding poets for 'her feelings as a mother and a wife' rather than for 'the marvellous power of her incantations'.[109] Yet all of these passions were crucial for the neat impersonation of emotions achieved by Madame Ristori. Contemporary reviewers describe Ristori in the role of Medea as a 'a tall, finely-formed woman, with dark hair and large lustrous eyes, a noble contour being still further ennobled by the classic drapery and the grace and dignity of the attitudes.'[110] Both the physical characterization and the pathos of the prima donna were rendered faithfully by Robson verbatim in his comic impersonation.

William Farren, manager of the Olympic between 1851 and September 1853, had trusted Robson to replace the great comedian Henry Compton for his theatre when he moved to the Haymarket in March 1853.[111] Farren's investment was truly profitable for Wigan, as Robson's acting had become all the rage soon after his performance of Shylock in Talfourd's *Shylock; or, the Merchant of Venice Preserved* in July 1853.[112] In 1854, prefiguring many of the gestures which catapulted him to fame with Medea, Robson interpreted the title role in J. R. Planché's *The Yellow Dwarf* to great acclaim.[113] Robson's portrayal of the cunning passions of the monster was praised by none other than Planché himself and G. A. Sala,[114] and prepared the audiences at the Olympic for his Medea.[115] The necromantic tricks of the dwarf as well as his changing passions, which were later applauded by Henry Morley,[116] were

Figure 1.2 Playbill of J. R. Planché's *The Golden Fleece* at the Theatre Royal Haymarket in London (1865) © Laura Monrós-Gaspar.

undoubtedly recalled when he first set foot on the stage of the Olympic as the heroine from Colchis. Yet in Brough's *Medea*, Robson also 'made it his business to study the attitudes and elocution of Madame Ristori'[117] to such an extent that there 'was no occasion here for any man to regret that he had not seen Ristori' (see fig 1.3 and 1.4).[118] Dickens, who was inspired by Robson for some of his comic characters,[119] George Henry Lewes, Lewis Carroll and E. L. Blanchard were among his many devotees.[120] Dickens himself wrote of him to Macready: 'He has a frantic song and dagger dance, about ten minutes long together, which has more passion in it than Ristori could express in fifty years'.[121] Robson had interpreted the role of Macbeth with much success in Talfourd's *Macbeth Travestie* at the Olympic in 1853 and reviews of the play highlighted his comic enactment of the dagger scene, which was undoubtedly recalled in Brough's *Medea*.[122] A critic from *Reynolds's Newspaper* provides an acute precis of Robson's revolutionary acting: 'He so artistically blended the comic with the tragic, that scarce had the audience finished laughing at some telling repartee, than they found themselves thrilling with emotion at the deep, terrific, wild ravings of anger, hatred, and despair which convulsed the features and distorted the form of the great actor before them'.[123] As an example, the much acclaimed leopard scene as interpreted by Ristori was re-enacted as a cat leaping upon a rat by Robson producing a ludicrous effect praised both by the critics and the audiences.[124]

Robert Brough followed Thomas Williams' translation into English from the Italian version by Joseph Montanelli of Legouvé's *Medea*. Even though the burlesque includes sneering epithets which at some points accentuate Medea's savagery, the piece adheres to Legouvé in attenuating Medea's responsibility for killing her offspring. Furthermore, Brough's coda situates Medea at the 'forefront of the early campaign for women's independence',[125] for indeed she actively struggles against bigamy and for the rights of married women. Therefore, Medea's words in the final speech 'What can a poor, lone, helpless woman do – / Battled on all sides – but appeal to you?' (1.3.149-50) were addressed to the same audience which sympathized with Legouvé's dejected Medea, and the readership of the reviews of the Lyceum *Medea*, which condemned the 'perfidious conduct of her husband' and pitied 'the desolate unhappiness of the mother begging food for herself and her perishing children'.[126] Brough's *Medea* shared the bill of the premiere with *Delicate*

Why Classical Burlesque? 27

Figure 1.3 'Madame Ristori as Medea' (*Illustrated Times* 14 June 1856, p.433) © Laura Monrós-Gaspar.

Figure 1.4 'Frederick Robson as Medea (from a Photograph by Herbert Watkins)' (1856) © Laura Monrós-Gaspar.

Ground and *A Conjugal Lesson*, with which it was for some time performed, allowing Robson to display his magisterial range of stage passions.[127] The complete bill, together with the staging earlier in the same year of *The Jealous Wife*,[128] permitted the audience to see on stage some of the questions on marriage which were at the centre of the social debates: bigamy, infanticide and divorce.

In 1850 a Royal Commission on the Divorce Law was appointed to re-evaluate the regulations concerning marriage and divorce. The result was a three-volume report published in 1853 which became the basis for the Divorce Bill in 1854 and finally the Matrimonial Causes Act in 1857. The 1857 Act, though still perpetuating patriarchal structures, increased the availability of divorce for the middle classes in general and for women in particular. Public debates concerning divorce in the mid-nineteenth century span the years 1850 to 1857 and coincide in time with the first staging of Talfourd's *Alcestis* (1850) and the reception of Brough's *Medea* (1856). Yet the two plays are far from being isolated literary mirrors of such debates.

Between 1850 and 1851 John Stuart Mill and Harriet Taylor Mill decried the light sentences given to wife-beaters in a series of essays sent to the *Morning Chronicle*, and in 1854 the protofeminist Caroline Norton privately circulated her *English Laws for Women in the Nineteenth Century* denouncing the laws governing the rights of married women.[129] Furthermore, the mutual relationship between the Woman Question, marital discontents and the courtship plot resonated in mid-nineteenth century novels as much as did the bliss of matrimonial unions.[130] Indeed, in the decades when the burlesqued *Alcestis* and *Medea* were staged, William Thackeray wrote *The Newcomes* (1853–1855) and Charles Dickens published *Hard Times* (1854), both novels with plots involving the failure of marriages.[131] Yet, even though it is not until the 1880s that divorced characters figure significantly in the novel, many of the themes that late nineteenth-century novels explore are foreshadowed in earlier narratives which focus on the inequality of women in marriage.[132] Indeed, in 1851, for example, Caroline Norton fictionalized the well-known story of her unfortunate marriage in *Stuart of Dunleath*. Moreover, as noted by Hall and Macintosh,[133] only a few years after the first performance of the failed-marriage plot in *Alcestis* and *Medea*, sensation novels and their corresponding dramatizations hinging on bigamy and adultery for their plots were flooding the market (e.g. Ellen Wood's *East Lynne* (1861) and Mary Elizabeth Braddon's *Lady Audley's Secret* (1862)). As Eltis argues,[134] even though adultery was rare in melodramatic plots, accidental bigamy, particularly after the debates of the 1857 Matrimonial Causes Act, was not so infrequent, as it complied with the moral mandates of the genre.

Furthermore, press coverage of the debates on the divorce legislation and sensationalist accounts of the best-known divorce and bigamy cases of the period inevitably influenced the reception of the two plays and nurtured the literary imagination of the playwrights and novelists who in turn boosted the public's desire for and consumption of sensation.[135] Accounts of cases of bigamy were a recurring theme in the press of the time. Coincidentally, a fortnight before the premiere of Brough's *Medea* the case of a woman abandoned by her husband and left to beggary with her children was reported in the *Westmorland Gazette*[136] and on 16 July 1856, two days after the début of Robson as Medea, the case of Mr Charles Short, who had abandoned his wife and left her chargeable to the parish in order to marry a certain Ann Morgan, was brought to light by the press of the time.[137] In 1850, and for the whole decade, the Forrest divorce case filled the international gossip columns of the press.[138] The well-known actor Edwin Forrest had accused his wife, Catherine Forrest, of adultery before a court and jury in Philadelphia. The case implicated various names among both the English and the American intelligentsia and on the day before *Alcestis*' first night, the provincial press in England were promising to divulge new details of the case, pandering to their readers' baser instincts.[139]

Yet adultery and bigamy were not the harshest side effects of the lack of legal protection of women in Victorian England. Sadly, cases of infanticide – 'wilful child murder' to use contemporary phraseology – were counted in hundreds and it was only during the 1860s that public sensitivity to the issue reached its zenith.[140] Action was taken by organizations such as The National Association for the Promotion of Social Science,[141] and several laws on bastardy were passed to safeguard the lives of newborn babies. Infanticide was associated with double moral standards which could not be publicly accommodated in the Victorian mindset, and also with sexual practices diametrically opposed to what was expected from the 'angel-in-the-house' stereotyped women who were promoted in the conduct books of the period. Yet reasons behind such dreadful crimes were many and diverse as the well-known case of the domestic servant Elizabeth Duff confirms. Duff, who put an end to the life of her child Kate owing to her financial circumstances, raised the social awareness of the vulnerable condition of single working mothers and aroused people's sympathy towards their situation.[142]

Similar cases from the 1850s undoubtedly influenced the reception of Brough's *Medea*.[143] For example, that of Maria Tarrant, a twenty-five year old woman abandoned by her husband with a child, was being given widespread coverage in July 1856, when Brough's *Medea* was put on stage.[144] Tarrant, who was convicted and sentenced to execution for murdering her child through strangulation, raised the public's awareness of the lack of legal protection for abandoned women. A petition for clemency was signed and presented to the court; in the end, Tarrant was reprieved and an article on the case published in the *Morning Chronicle* drew attention to the disparate legal system which convicted one of the progenitors, the mother, whilst protecting the other, the father:

> We are aware that much diversity of opinion exists upon the question, and that cases of suspected destruction of illegitimate children are but too frequent; but it must be remembered that there are often two parties implicated, although one of them escapes without the slightest tarnish, but from whose sensual and unfeeling conduct the terrible result has originated.[145]

Public awareness of the issue raised by this case and others,[146] together with the framework devised by intellectuals such as John Stuart and Harriet Taylor Mill, and Caroline Norton prompted yet more debate on the various remedies for the social problems possibly underlying child murder. A legislative change and a formal cataloguing of stillbirths, for example, were suggested.[147] William Burke Ryan, who was to have an essential impact on the laws of infanticide in the 1860s with the publication of *Infanticide – Its Law, Prevalence, Prevention and History* (1862), suggested that fathers' names should formally appear on birth certificates so that they could be compelled to pay maintenance and ease the burden on the mother.[148] Ryan was awarded the Fothergillian Gold Medal of the Medical Society of London for his essay entitled 'On infanticide in its Medico-legal Relations' in 1856, when Brough's *Medea* was put on stage.

Yet Brough's *Medea* was not the only classical burlesque which reflected the problems of women in Victorian England. As discussed earlier in the chapter, by the end of the century, prophetic voices who debated on marriage legislation and women's suffrage were invoked in numerous newspapers and magazines devoted to the Woman Question.[149] Furthermore, uneasy questions about marriage were at the centre of the politicized works of suffragette drama by the early twentieth century. The theatre of the 1890s with revivals of Ibsen's *A Doll's House*, the premiere of Oscar Wilde's *A Woman of No Importance* and Pinero's *The Second Mrs Tanqueray*, for example, had opened a Pandora's box and, by the turn of the century, wifehood and motherhood were being overtly questioned. Marriage was being debated in the popular press and theatre of the time, resulting in a sub-genre of 'condition of marriage plays', as coined by Stowell, which exposed one of the most inflammatory issues of the Edwardian era.[150] As we shall see, the denunciation implicit in Talfourd's *Alcestis*, as weak and private as it might have been, anticipated Cicely Hamilton's agitprop in *Marriage as Trade* (1909) and illustrated the subversive voice of Victorian classical burlesque heroines.

Foreshadowing the success of Brough's *Medea*, and coinciding in time with the inauguration of the Royal Commission on Divorce and the first performance of Jack Wooler's *Jason and Medea* in August 1850, Francis Talfourd's *Alcestis, the Original Strong-Minded Woman* was first put on at the Strand Theatre on 4 July 1850 with Mrs Elizabeth Leigh Murray in the title role. Talfourd's *Alcestis* was revived in the London theatres, the provinces, Dublin and New York well into the 1860s.[151] Yet, unlike Blanchard's *Antigone* and Brough's *Medea*, the success of the play was not tied to any particular production but to its interplay, to its 'intertheatricality' with the topical repertoire which added to the influence of other classically inspired productions.[152]

On some occasions it was the setting and stagecraft that were intimately related to the plays with which *Alcestis* shared the bill; on some others, topical references in the burlesque favoured its revival by certain companies and for specific audiences. For example, after its first performance at Farren's New Strand, Talfourd's *Alcestis* was revived in May 1853 at the Theatre Royal in New Hall, Reading, sharing the bill with *The Vampire: or, the Bride of the Isles and the Feast of Blood* and *The Practical Man* in a benefit performance for Mr Sheridan Smith.[153] Planché's *The Vampire*, based on a French melodrama staged in Paris in the same year, was first performed at the Lyceum in 1820.¹⁵⁴ The play entered the provincial circuit and enjoyed much success. One of the key sensations of Planché's romantic melodrama was the famous 'vampire trap' which was purposely designed for it and later used by Orcus to travel to Hades in Talfourd's burlesque. As the Lacy's acting edition of the play makes explicit, the first lines of 'My skiff is on the shore' are deliberately sung by Orcus and then by Alcestis on a trapdoor centre stage through which they gradually descend (l.412-417):

> My trap is in the floor,
> And waiting for thee:
> I can't allow no more,
> You must travel with me;
> And as we're sinking down my song shall be
> My dearest Alcestis I love but thee!

Reviews of the first performance of *Alcestis* at the Strand in 1850 describe Orcus' costume as following that of a modern devil 'horns and tail inclusive'.¹⁵⁵ The conjunction of *Alcestis* and *The Vampire* the same evening in Reading undoubtedly provided *Alcestis* with cultural intertexts beyond the classical references and connected the heroine with popular notions of the underworld and Planché's vampire marriage.

Similarly, it is no coincidence that various military regiments chose Talfourd's *Alcestis* for the performances of their theatre groups.¹⁵⁶ For example, the Infantry Brigade at Colchester put on fragments of Talfourd's *Alcestis* for its charity amateur performance in 1865.¹⁵⁷ References to the police force in London abound in the play and reach their apogee in the character of Polax, 'inspector of Pellise', who was widely acclaimed by the audience.¹⁵⁸ The performance of the officers was received with merriment in Colchester: '"the strong-minded woman" being very creditably performed by Mr. Rich of the 34th Regiment, while Mr. Hamilton, of the 84th, as Polax, provoked frequent rounds of laughter and applause'.¹⁵⁹

Beyond such anecdotal allusions to contemporary facts and customs, Talfourd's *Alcestis* should be read, as observed earlier, in the light of the divorce laws of the mid-nineteenth century. The title of the burlesque – *Alcestis, the Original Strong-Minded Woman* – manifests how Talfourd's *Alcestis* departs significantly from the Euripidean prototype, which is reinforced by the subtitle of the 1850 Lacy publication which referred to the burlesque as 'a most shameless misinterpretation of the Greek Drama of Euripides'[160] and Talfourd's allusion to Euripides as the 'injured poet' in the summary of his plot.[161] Unlike his father, Frank Talfourd was not an active campaigner for the rights of women. However, Alcestis' 'classical soliloquy' must have unequivocally heightened the female audience's empathy with the heroine. Alcestis evokes the disillusionment of arranged marriages, the legal vulnerability of children and the unequal opportunities for women to overcome their mind-numbing existences. Alcestis' appeal to the audience is more easily identified with than that of Brough's Medea. The words of Admetus' wretched wife could well have been articulated by the women campaigners for the regulation of marriage.[162]

Unlike Brough's *Medea*, Alcestis' 'voice' is timid, even melodramatic. Talfourd's title, however, raises an important question regarding the reception of the play by the Victorian audience. The identification of Alcestis with 'strong-minded women' evoked a whole semiotic construct which pointed to a highly marked socio-political referent in which Talfourd's Electra and Macbeth, and Reece's Clytemnestra also participated.[163] As argued above, women questioned the institution of marriage in contemporary novels and short stories throughout the nineteenth century. Yet the immediacy of theatre and the wide scope of Victorian burlesque audiences attached considerable significance to the denunciations made by Alcestis as a 'strong-minded' woman.

By the end of the nineteenth century, the stereotyped image of Sarah Grand's New Woman was associated with the student at Girton College who rode a bicycle, smoked and rejected the conventional dress codes for women.[164] Yet beyond the physical cliché, the New Woman was an emerging new citizen who fought for a voice in the social, political and economic framework of the late nineteenth century. The emancipation bells had been ringing since the early Victorian period, when another 'race' of women was monopolizing the discussion in intellectual coteries with their 'strong-mindedness'. Whilst the common meaning for the epithet 'strong-minded' is to have a 'strong, vigorous, or determined mind',[165] the *OED* records a particular denotation for the nineteenth century which disparagingly refers to 'women who have or affect the qualities of mind and character regarded as distinctively masculine, or who take up an attitude of revolt against the restrictions and disabilities imposed on their sex by law and custom.'[166] Indeed, the clichés associated with

New and strong-minded women were analogous and the latter became immediate forerunners of Grand's archetype.

As a consequence, 'strong-minded women' were at the centre of topical debates until the publication of Grand's article, when the signifier changed.[167] The archetype was aestheticized in the literature of the time; for example, Dickens refers to them as a woman with 'a dreary face and bony figure and a masculine voice' in *Martin Chuzzlewit* (1844), and Mary Elizabeth Braddon as the one who 'writes books and wears spectacles' in *Lady Audley's Secret* (1862).[168] A real life well-known impersonation of the character was Barbara Bodichon, an ardent campaigner for the rights of women in Victorian England. Bodichon, who was founder and benefactor of Girton College and numerous other educational institutions, was herself excluded from the executive committee for the establishment of the College for being publicly associated with 'strong-minded' campaigners for the rights of women.[169] Together with Bodichon, it would not have been difficult to imagine other well-known women such as Harriet Taylor or Emily Davies, as 'strong-minded women', surrounded by the books and attired in the clothes by means of which the 28 April 1894 number of *Punch* ridiculed the figure of the emerging New Woman.

The mid-nineteenth-century press is deluged with such examples of 'strong-minded' women giving lectures to their peers and being criticized for neglecting their duties as mothers, wives and daughters. An article published in *Woolmer's Exeter and Plymouth Gazette* on 14 August 1847, for example, summarized the portrayal of strong-minded women within the patriarchal mindset as follows:

> The strong-minded woman is generally a spinster. If she be married, it is invariably to a husband the reverse of strong-minded. In nine cases out of ten she is a raw-boned sinewy creature designed after the scrag-of-mutton order of architecture ... Her great point is, that the weaker vessel is not the weaker. Women have been trampled on. Let them assert their native dignity, and have meetings at the Crown and Anchor. The rights of woman! Down with the base usurper man! Is not woman his equal? Of course she is. The 'strong-minded' will demonstrate it to you anatomically, physiologically, metaphysically and historically ... The husbands of strong-minded women frequently sup out.

Meetings 'at the Crown and Anchor' and public lectures forged public opinion for and against 'strong-mindedness'. As an example, the reviewer in the *West*

Middlesex Advertiser and Family Journal of a lecture by Mrs Emilius Holcroft held at the Pimlico Literary Institute in February 1859 endorsed the ideas defended by 'strong-minded women' as long as they did not interfere with their social obligations in the female sphere of action.[170] Conversely, the *Paisley Herald and Renfrewshire Advertiser* provided a full account of Miss Lucy Stone's lecture on the rights of woman given at the Metropolitan Hall, Boston (US), in 1853 sparing no details on the need for emancipation.[171]

Being a highly topical issue, strong-minded women could not escape the burlesque pen and soon became an easy target for satirical drama. From the 1850s on, the epithet turned into a stock character representing a woman who was the complete opposite of the 'angel-in-the-house'. Strong-minded women were related to a wide range of emerging professional women such as governesses, artists and nurses as well as bluestockings, philanthropic women and intellectuals.[172] On stage, they also prefigured independent, self-assured women, often opposed to weak ladies and effeminate male leading roles. The 'strong-minded woman' referent was, therefore, easily recognizable to the audiences of *Alcestis* and *Electra* at the Strand and the Haymarket. Examples of strong-minded women characters in Victorian theatres abounded: in 1853 Miss Woolgar played the 'strong-minded' Mrs Portia Lucrecia Green in *Bloomerism; or, the Follies of the Day* at the Adelphi;[173] in 1868 Miss Julia Mathews was 'the original strong-minded' Clytemnestra in Robert Reece's *Agamemnon and Cassandra*,[174] and in 1873, Marion Halcombe from Wilkie Collins' *The Woman in White* was being interpreted as a strong-minded woman at the Theatre Royal in Hampshire.[175] Furthermore, they were commonplace in Talfourd's burlesque writing. In 1847, for example, Talfourd's *Macbeth Travestie* was first put on at the Henley-on-Thames Regatta; a year later the play moved to the Strand, whose audience witnessed *Alcestis* in 1850. Even though Talfourd does not explicitly employ the term 'strong-minded' to depict the Shakespearean heroine, on several occasions Macbeth wonders whether his wife is a 'female woman', prompted by the strength and determination of her character. Following in the line of Macbeth, Talfourd's 1859 burlesque of Electra presents a very resolute Clytemnestra, and Electra herself is identified in the Lacy's edition of the play as 'the strong-minded daughter'.

Against such a backdrop, Alcestis' resolve to escape the bonds of marriage for an unfeminine adventure through Hades is synonymous with neglecting her duties as a wife and, therefore, equals the actions of certain strong-minded women. Yet she is not the only 'strong-minded' woman in this anthology; with rather more radical overtones, and not simply rejecting the set structures of matrimony, Talfourd's strong-minded Electra comes on stage for the first time in April 1859 at Buckstone's Haymarket.[176] Talfourd's work retains the framework of the Sophoclean tragedy, adding topical allusions to popular entertainments and to the installation of electric carbon arc lamps in London theatres. The fifth act of *Electra* exemplifies the high topicality of the genre: the audience faces a stage where, in imitation of a street fair, the characters see a Punch and Judy show, engage with street games and witness a performance on a Thespian cart. Moreover, The title of the burlesque hints at Taglioni's ballet *Electra: the Lost Pleiade* which was first put on at Her Majesty's in April 1849.[177] Reviews in the *Illustrated London News* refer to the staging of the *Pleiade* with embodied stars that 'are seen to rise in the azure firmament as they are represented in the allegorical creations of the great masters of Italian pictorial art [which] . . . decorate the ceiling of Her Majesty's Theatre.'[178] (See fig. 1.5)

Indeed, Talfourd was relying on a boom in entertainment that year to attract the audiences to the Haymarket rather than on one of the tragic works of Sophocles: in March, electric light was the subject of the Grosvenor College Lectures;[179] experimental cars with electric lighting in Paris were highly advertised throughout;[180] the summer *Bilston Exhibition of the Fine Arts, Curiosities and Manufacturers* included 'electric light and telegraph';[181] and electric light was one of the most popular inventions of the year highlighted in Blackwell's *Great Facts*.[182]

Reviews of the play show that Talfourd's *Electra* shared the bill on its premiere with John Palgrave Simpson's comedy *The World and the Stage*, which was first performed at the Haymarket on 12 March 1859,[183] and the farce *A Daughter to Marry*.[184] The whole bill manifested two main conflicts in Talfourd's burlesque: the contrasting characters of Electra and Chrysothemis – cousins and not sisters in Talfourd's work to facilitate the love plot – and their respective marriages. Reinforcing the classical antagonism between Electra and Chrysothemis, Simpson's comedy developed the theme of two abandoned sisters who found opposing ways in life: one through a respectable marriage and complying with the mainstream mindset, and the other by defiantly becoming an actress. Analogies with other pairs of female

Figure 1.5 'Scene the Last from the New Ballet of "*Electra, or the Lost Pleiad*" at Her Majesty's Theatre in London' (*Illustrated London News* 5 May 1849, p.293) © Laura Monrós-Gaspar.

characters who illustrate the nineteenth-century aesthetic construction of women are drawn from the outset. Elinor and Marianne in Jane Austen's *Sense and Sensibility* (1811), Lady Isabel Vane and Barbara Hare in Ellen Wood's *East Lynne* (1861), and Laura and Lizzy in Christina Rossetti's *Goblin Market* (1862), to name but a few, all evince both sides of the same struggle: whether or not to stray from Victorian mainstream standards. For Talfourd's Electra, besides the Sophoclean conflict, it meant becoming involved in politics and rejecting the norms set for women in the conduct books of the period.

The second issue to consider in Talfourd's portrayal of Electra and Chrysothemis is their marriage plot against the backdrop of the mid-nineteenth-century Surplus Women Question. The Census of 1851 brought into focus a majority of unmarried women among the adult population in England. This was perceived not only as a demographic crisis but also as a political and social predicament, and the Surplus Women Question soon became the object of public lectures, newspaper articles and pamphlets. The limited career opportunities for women sparked off a debate in which the married versus the strong-minded woman models were re-examined.[185] Unmarried women were forced to look for an income in a variety of trades thus increasing the threat for the male labour market, which soon endorsed the pejorative connotations associated with the new independent, forceful, strong-minded woman. The Electra-Pylades and Chrysothemis-Orestes marriage plots in Talfourd's burlesque undoubtedly respond to generic issues; yet read against such wider social concern they infer new meanings to the tragic heroines which are easily recognizable by the audiences at the Haymarket.

The two cousins in Talfourd's burlesque are of marriageable age yet remain unattached: Chrysothemis' suitor, Orestes, is believed to be abroad and deceased, as any English young man fighting in the Crimean War might have been; and Electra has devoted herself to a higher cause in life than marriage, politics. As members of the Royal family in Mycenae the two remain at home without an occupation and therefore represent, in turn, a haunting menace to the sovereign authority. Furthermore, the farce staged on the premiere of the burlesque, *A Daughter to Marry*, reinforces the focus on their spinsterhood. Electra's Sophoclean endeavour to dethrone Aegisthus in revenge for the death of her father is transplanted to the wilful attempt of a Victorian strong-minded young lady to be involved in politics. As a consequence, the rags and the slovenly appearance that mark her mourning become pejorative signs of the clichéd nineteenth-century strong-mindedness. Chrysothemis, on the contrary, represents the 'angel-in-the-house' trope that threatens both Electra's ideals and the domestic stability of the house of Clytemnestra, a domineering strong-minded wife. Nonetheless, the domestic wanderings of the two young ladies, unlike those of coeval Victorian women, will be rewarded with an Aristotelian happy ending: marriage.

Talfourd's Electra is the last stopover on our stroll around the theatrical appropriations of gender and Classics in mid-Victorian London. As regards gender politics, even though the play undermines mainstream tenets, it lacks a deep feminist hue. Contrasting it with Blanchard's *Antigone* and Brough's *Medea*, Electra's protest does not explicitly raise contentious issues yet it reflects topical concerns which bring the plot closer to modern middle-class audiences. Therefore, considering the intertheatricalities which surround its production and reception, we can safely argue that it both mirrors and contests the patriarchal mindset which was being disputed by avant-garde voices in favour of the rights of women.

The four burlesques collected in this book manifest how humour provides the perfect backdrop for the coexistence of old codifications with new sign systems that prefigure women in the arts and culture of the time. Such binary structure reflects silenced and subversive, derided and esteemed classical heroines who syncretize with the modern female voices of the Victorian era. Emancipated women and bodies coexisted with reified subjectivities which struggled to abandon the periphery. The semiotic and historical substrata which construct the identity of women throughout the nineteenth century set the ground for an analysis of the changing perceptions of women in consumer culture. Unveiling the images behind such perceptions with the aid of intertheatricality entails understanding the shifting social mores which allow for modern refigurations in classical burlesque. As a consequence, reflecting the unavoidable dichotomies which permeate an exceptionally fast-changing society, classical burlesque linked arts with life, Greek tragedy with popular culture and the past with the present of women's life in Britain.

Note on the texts and this edition

The plays selected for this volume all survive in the Lord Chamberlain's Plays collection of manuscripts (henceforth referred to as *LC*) held at the British Library. Three of them – Talfourd's *Electra* and *Alcestis*, and Brough's *Medea* – were published in Lacy's Acting Plays Collection soon after their first staging, yet no printed copy was ever published of Blanchard's *Antigone*.

The present edition is based on the most authentic acting edition of the plays collated with *LC* manuscript (see fig 1.6). In the case of *Antigone*, it is the only printed edition of the text. The volume includes a full commentary and textual notes to the plays selected. The principal aim of the apparatuses is to revisit the historical background and to convey something of the popular cultural milieu of the original contexts by providing information on topical allusions which facilitate their understanding. The purpose of the collations is to show the alterations made on the texts from their first versions sent for licence to the Lord Chamberlain's office to the staging and final publication of the texts. No omissions from the manuscripts are recorded in the *Lord Chamberlain's Office Day Books* or in the *Lord Chamberlain's Plays Supplementary Papers*.[186] Passages which are commented on in the introduction are only annotated with reference to the pages in which they are mentioned. Two burlesques, Blanchard's *Antigone* (1845) and Brough's *Medea* (1856) are based on the performances of their corresponding hypotext. Therefore, an account of significant comic refigurations of celebrated passages is provided where appropriate.

With regard to *Antigone*, the set of 9 folios in the bound manuscript BL Add. Ms. 42982 ff. 165–173 is in good condition though slightly worn on the edges. The folios are written on both sides of beige paper in black ink and measure about 24.5 × 18.5 centimetres. The script is regular and legible and the hand is presumably the same throughout. The manuscript is not signed by the copyist and no alterations are marked from the Lord Chamberlain's office. In the present edition, emphatic capitals from the manuscript have been silently reduced to lower case. Initial capitals are not used when the full title is not given. When the title alone is a recurrent appellation identifying a role (e.g. the King), the capital is adopted. Also, the ampersand has been silently transformed into 'and' and the *virgulae* into commas, full stops and exclamation marks to make the text as intelligible as possible to the modern reader. Punctuation has been silently modernized unless it involves changes in rhetorical effects.

The present edition of Talfourd's *Alcestis* is based on the 1850 printed copy published at Thomas Hailes Lacy collated with the bound *LC* manuscript, BL Add MS 43028 ff. 633–653 (see fig 1.7). The set of 21 folios is in good condition except for f. 653, where the beginning of the three lines above the last is missing, and only slightly worn at the margins. The manuscript is signed on f. 633 by the manager of the theatre, William Farren. The folios are written on one side of a beige paper in black ink and measure about 26.3 × 19 centimetres. The script is regular and legible and presumably by the same copyist. The 1850 Lacy edition was probably published after the first performance of the play and includes a detailed list of characters, and information on the plot, scenes, props and music. In contrast with Brough's *Medea* and Talfourd's own *Electra*, no blank space is left on the folios for the addition of the songs.

The edition of Brough's *Medea* is based on the 1856 printed copy published at Lacy's collated with the *LC* unbound manuscript, BL Add MS 52960, K (see fig 1.8). The set of 48 folios is in good condition except for folios 43 and 48, which are slightly cut at the bottom. The manuscript is signed on folio 48b by Robert B. Brough. The folios are written on one side except for ff. 11, 21, 30, 35, 36, 41, 44 and 47, which are written on both sides (f. 11b and f. 35 are written upside down). The paper is beige throughout except in ff. 10–13, 18, 20, 21 and 32–37, which are written on a grey paper. Folios 16, 19, 43 and 48 are written on a beige paper of a higher weight.

The folios are written in black and blue ink and pencil; the three alternate for corrections and revisions. The script is irregular; a second hand seems to have rewritten in black ink passages in pencil on folio 28. The same second hand writes in blue ink the second part of the song on f. 8, and on ff. 44b, 47b and at the bottom of f. 48. Folios 22, 24, 31, 47 and 48 include footnote cues referring to corrections and alterations within the same manuscript that testify to the various revisions of the text. A plausible hypothesis for the variations on the script and ink is that Brough was first burlesquing the tragedy from Thomas Williams' translation and then from attending Ristori's performance. Evidence of Brough's reliance on the text for a first draft is in the stage directions, which on some occasions follow Williams' translations verbatim (e.g. 1.1.0.1–5), and in the blank spaces left for songs (e.g. f. 27), which are completed with script in a different ink on, for example, folio 8. Subsequent revisions of the manuscript include cuts and amended passages in black and blue ink (e.g. ff. 11, 22, 21b, 42 and 41b). The 1856 printed edition was probably published after the first staging of the play and includes a detailed description of the scenes and costume.

The present edition of Talfourd's *Electra* is based on the 1859 printed copy published by Thomas Hailes Lacy collated with the *LC* unbound manuscript, BL Add MS 52982 C (see fig 1.9). The set of 32 folios in BL Add MS 52982 C is also in good condition and only slightly worn on the top and bottom edges; particularly on folios 21 and 23 which are stained both with black ink in the top right corners and folio 23 also at the bottom of the page. On folio 14 the script starts only by the middle of the folio as if the copyist had left a blank space for a song. On folio 18 there is also a blank space at the end of scene three and before the beginning of scene four probably for the same reason. The folios are written on one side of a watermarked blue paper in black ink and measure about 21.4 × 33.6 centimetres. The manuscript is signed on folio 32b (the only folio which is written on both sides) by the prompter; the script is regular and legible throughout yet looser and more accelerated from folio 27 onwards. Another sign of the acceleration of the copyist is that folio 30 numbers the scene as 'Scene 8' where it should be 1.7. The 1859 Lacy edition was probably published after the first staging of the play. Following the patterns of nineteenth-century publications, it includes a detailed description of the plot, the characters and the scenes of the play before the text. Notable differences between the published text and the manuscript lie in the songs and the stage directions. The notes on the List of Roles account for variations in speech prefix designations.

Conventions of textual notes

In songs and long passages, textual notes (t.n.) aim at reproducing the layout of the text in the collated manuscripts. Therefore, the standard t.n. follows this pattern: line reference, lemma ('the reading quoted from the present text'), closing square bracket, and siglum of other readings (usually *LC*) followed by the reading. Unless otherwise stated, the lemma come from the 1850, 1856 and 1859 printed texts (hereafter *1850*, *1856*, and *1859*). The textual notes, therefore, allow the reader to keep track of the variation from *LC* to the printed edition of the text.

Speech prefixes are sometimes variable in *LC* and almost always abbreviated. This edition follows the speech prefixes of the base text except in *Alcestis* 595 SP, where the duplication of PHOEDRA is emended. In this edition, speech prefixes have been silently expanded and the names of the speakers are written in small capitals. In SDs and SPs, the characters' names that vary throughout *LC* have been regularized. Decisions as to the chosen forms are explained in the corresponding commentary notes to the List of Roles. Only significant variations in the stylings of the speech prefixes are collated.

Stage directions are italicized and placed within brackets when they are written after the name of the characters or interspersed within the text. I have followed the traditional line numbering by scene and stage directions are numbered decimally according to the line of the text in which they begin. Both in *LC* and in the base texts stage directions use various abbreviations which have been systematically preserved (see **Glossary of stage terms** below)

Most modernizations of spelling and punctuation are as trivial as altering '&' to 'and' and as modernizing apostrophes, and therefore are unworthy of record. Therefore, only departures from the punctuation and spelling from the base text which affect syntax or meaning are annotated. Underlined words in *LC* are interpreted as italics. Noteworthy spellings from the base text are given in italic parentheses.

Undeciphered words and letters in *LC* are marked by an asterisk. Emendations are identified by line number. Emphatic italics from the printed editions which indicate word puns have been adopted. Cancellations in the manuscripts are indicated with a continuous line through the letters. Underlining in *LC* is kept in t.n.

Glossary of stage terms

C.	Centre
L.	Left from the actor's point of view
L.C.	Left centre from the actor's point of view
L.H.	Left of the House
L.U.E.	Left upper entrance
L.1 E.	Left first entrance. 'The English system of grooves in which pieces of scenery moved established a standard position for entrances to the stage. Left 1st entrance was the entrance nearest the audience on the actor's left side, L.2 E. the next entrance upstage, & c. Entrances were numbered consecutively up to L.U.E. – left upper entrance, the farthest upstage' (Rowell 1972: 14)
R.	Right from the actor's point of view
R.C.	Right centre from the actor's point of view
R.H.	Right of the House
R.U.E.	Right upper entrance
R.1.E.	Right first entrance from the actor's point of view (R.2.E, the next entrance upstage)

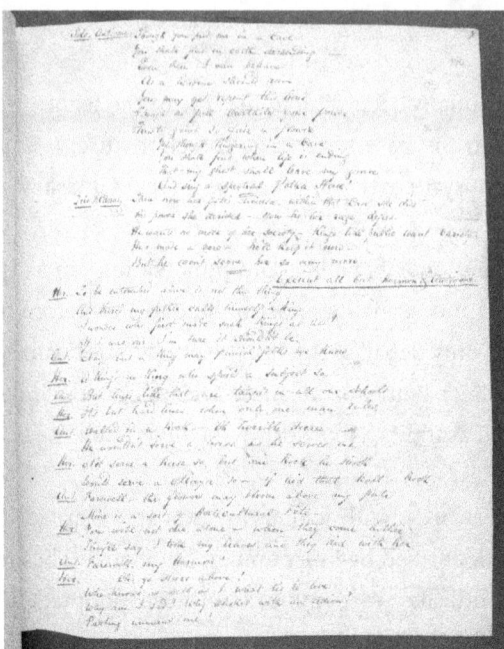

Figure 1.6 Folio 170 of the Manuscript of E. L. Blanchard's *Antigone Travestie* © The British Library Board, BL MS 42982 ff.165–173.

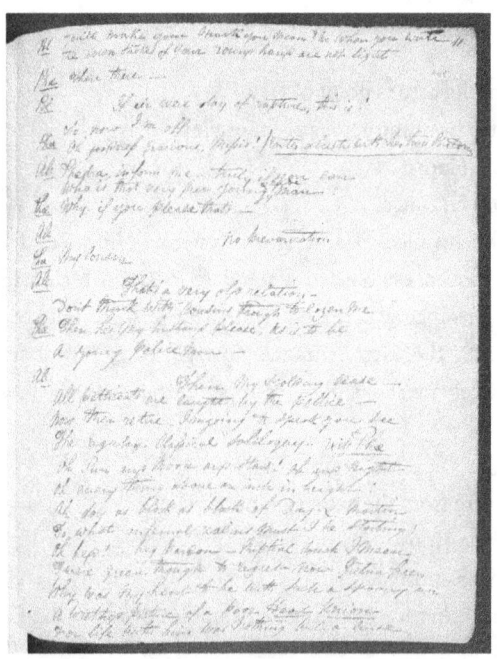

Figure 1.7 Folio 645 of Francis Talfourd's *Alcestis, the Original Strong-Minded Woman* © The British Library Board, BL MS 43028 ff.633–653.

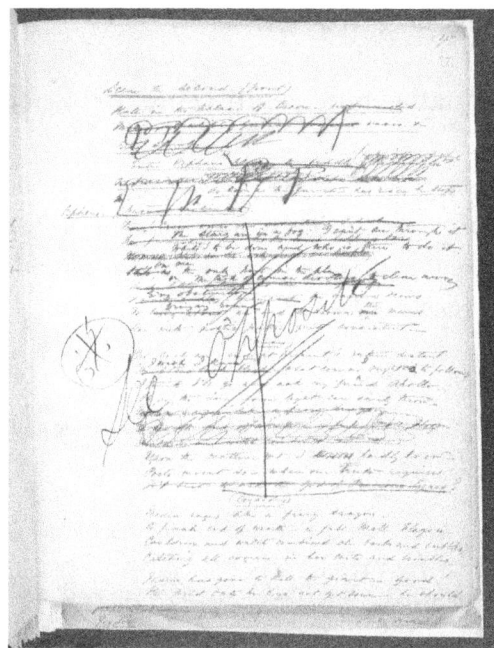

Figure 1.8 Folio 22 of Robert Brough's *Medea; or, the Best of Mothers, with a Brute of a Husband* © The British Library Board, BL MS 52960, K.

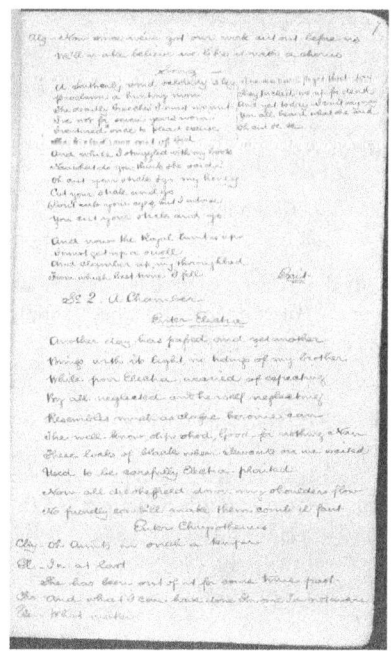

Figure 1.9 Folio 7 of Francis Talfourd's *Electra in a New Electric Light* © The British Library Board, BL MS 52982.

List of representative nineteenth-century classical burlesques

(Unless otherwise stated, all theatres are in London. Where no venue in round brackets appears it should not be assumed that there was no theatrical production. I have provided details of the venues only when I discovered them in original manuscripts or in reliable authorities.)

A' Beckett, G. A.
    Caught Courting; or, Juno by Jove! (Royal Victoria Theatre, 1834)
    The Three Graces: a Classical and Comical, Musical and Mythological Burlesque (The Princess's Theatre, 1843)

Addison, J. and J. Howell.
    Jason and Medea: A Ramble after a Colchian. A Classical Burlesque (1878)

Amcotts, V.
    Ariadne: or, The Bull! The Bully!! And The Bullion!!! (1870, Oxford)
    Pentheus: A Burlesque in Three Acts. Founded to a Certain Extent on the 'Bacchae' of Euripides (1866, Oxford)

Bayly, N. T. H.
    Cupid (Olympic, 1832)

Blanchard, E. L.
    Antigone Travestie (Strand, 1845)

Brough, R. B.
    Medea; or, the Best of Mothers, with a Brute of a Husband. A Burlesque, in One Act (Olympic, 1856)
    The Siege of Troy (Lyceum, 1858)
    The Sphinx (with W. Brough) (Haymarket Theatre Royal, 1849)
    The Twelve Labours of Hercules (Strand, 1851)

Brough, W.
    Endymion; or, the Naughty Boy Who Cried for the Moon (St James's, 1860)
    Hercules and Omphale; or the Power of Love (St James's, 1864)
    Pygmalion or the Statue Fair (Strand, 1867)

Burnand, F. C.
    Acis and Galatea; or the Nimble Nymph and the Terrible Troglodyte (Olympic, 1863)
    Arion; or The Story of a Lyre (Strand, 1871)
    La Belle Hélène (Alhambra, 1873), a revised version of *Helen* (Adelphi, 1866)
    Cupid and Psyche; or Beautiful as a Butterfly (Olympic, 1864)
    Dido, the Celebrated Widow (St James's, 1860); acted as *The Widow Dido* (Royalty, 1865)
    Helen, or Taken from the Greek (Adelphi, 1866)
    Ixion; or, the Man at the Wheel (Royalty, 1863)
    Ixion Rewheeled (Opera Comique, 1874)
    Paris, or, Vive Lemprière (Strand, 1866)
    Patient Penelope; or, the Return of Ulysses (with M. Williams) (Strand, 1863)
    Pirithous, or the Son of Ixion (Royalty, 1865)

Ulysses; or The Ironclad Warriors and the Little Tug of War (St James's, 1865)
Venus and Adonis; or, the Two Rivals and the Small Boar (Haymarket, 1864)

Byron, H. J.
Orpheus and Eurydice; or, The Young Gentleman who charmed the Rocks (Strand, 1863); acted as *Eurydice; or, Little Orpheus and his Lute* (Strand, 1871); revised as *Pluto; or Little Orpheus and his Lute* (Royalty, 1881)
Pan; or, The Loves of Echo and Narcissus (Adelphi, 1865)

Cooper, F. F.
Ion Travestie (Garrick Theatre, 1836)

George, G. H.
King Jupiter or the Freaks of the Graces (Effingham Salon, 1856)

Gilbert, W. S.
Thespis, or the Gods Grown Old (Gaiety, 1871)

Graves, J.
Olympic Frailties or the Magic Zone (Olympic, 1841)

Hawtrey, G.
Atalanta (Strand, 1888)

Lemon, M.
Medea; or a Libel on the Lady of Colchis (Adelphi Theatre, 1856)

Metcalfe, C.
Hecuba à la Mode; or, The Wily Greek and the Modest Maid (Vestry H. Anerley, 1893)

Nolan, E.
Agamemnon at Home; or, The Latest Particulars of that Little Affair at Mycenae (St John's College Amateurs, Oxford, 1867)
Iphigenia; or, The Sail!! The Seer!!! And the Sacrifice!!! (St John's College Amateurs, Oxford, 1866)

O'Neil, J. R.
The Siege of Troy; or, the Miss-Judgement of Paris (Astley's Amphitheatre, 1854)

Oxberry, W. H.
Acis and Galatea (Adelphi, 1842)

Planché, J. R.
The Birds of Aristophanes (Haymarket, 1846)
The Deep Deep Sea; or, Perseus and Andromeda; an Original Mythological, Aquatic, Equestrian Burletta (Olympic, 1833)
The Golden Fleece; or, Jason in Colchis and Medea in Corinth (Haymarket, 1845)
Olympic Revels; or, Prometheus and Pandora (Olympic, 1831)
Olympic Devils; or, Orpheus and Eurydice (Olympic, 1831)
Orpheus in the Haymarket (Haymarket, 1865)
The Paphian Bower; or, Venus and Adonis (Olympic, 1832)
Telemachus; or, the Island of Calypso (Olympic, 1834)
Theseus and Ariadne; or, The Marriage of Bacchus (Lyceum, 1848)

Rede, W. L.
  Conquest of Cupid or Lucre against Love (Strand, 1842)

Reece, R. (E. G. Lankester)
  Agamemnon and Cassandra; or, the Prophet and Loss of Troy (Prince of Wales, Liverpool, 1868)
  Our Helen (Gaiety, 1884)
  Prometheus; or, the Man on the Rock (New Royalty, 1865)
  Romulus and Remus, or the Two Rum'uns. A New Classical Burlesque (Vaudeville, 1872)
  The Very Last Days of Pompeii; or, a Complete Bulwer-tement of the Classical Drama (Vaudeville, 1872)

Selby, Ch.
  The Judgement of Paris; or, the Pas de Pippins (Adelphi, 1846)

Spedding, B. J.
  Ino; or, The Theban Twins (Prince of Wales's, Liverpool, and Strand, 1869)

Stephens, H. P.
  Cupid; or, Two Strings to a Beau (Royalty, 1880)
  Galatea; or, Pygmalion Reversed (Gaiety, 1883)

Suter, W. E.
  Jupiter's Decree and the Fall of Phaeton or the Fiery Courses of the Sun (Astley's Amphitheatre, 1853)
  Perseus; or, a Rocky Road to Travel (Queen's, 1864)

Talfourd, F.
  Alcestis, the Original Strong-Minded Woman: a Classical Burlesque in One Act (Strand, 1850)
  Atalanta, or the Three Golden Apples, an Original Classical Extravaganza (Haymarket, 1857)
  Electra in a New Electric Light (Haymarket, 1859)
  King Pluto and Proserpine; or the Belle and the Pomegranate. An Entirely New and Original Mythological Extravaganza of the 0th Century (Haymarket, 1858)
  Thetis and Peleus (with W. P. Hale) (Strand, 1851)

Trail, F. T.
  Glaucus; or, a Fish Tail (Olympic, 1865)

Unknown authors.
  Apollo and the Flying Pegasus or the Defeat of the Amazons (Astley's Amphitheatre, 1858)
  Calypso and Telemachus (Sadler's Wells, 1865)
  Dido and Aeneas (Strand, 1893)
  Endymion (1881)
  Orpheus and Eurudice (Strand, 1871)

Wooler, J.
  Jason and Medea: A Comic, Heroic, Tragic, Operatic Burlesque-Spectacular Extravaganza (Grecian Saloon, 1851)

Notes

1 See Jacky Bratton, *The Making of the West End Stage: Marriage, Management and the Mapping of Gender in London 1830–1870* (Cambridge: CUP, 2012).
2 Ibid.
3 See Simon Goldhill, *Victorian Culture and Classical Antiquity: Art, Opera, Fiction, and the Proclamation of Modernity* (Princeton and Oxford: Princeton University Press, 2011), p. 23.
4 See Charles Saumarez Smith, *The National Gallery: A Short History* (London: Frances Lincoln, 2009), p. 13.
5 Christopher Whitehead, *The Public Art Museum in Nineteenth Century Britain: The Development of the National Gallery* (Aldershot: Ashgate Publishing, 2005), p. 132.
6 Ibid. 33–34.
7 Jeffrey A. Auerbach, *The Great Exhibition of 1851: A Nation on Display* (New Haven: Yale University Press, 1999), p. 94.
8 See for example John Absolon, 'Part of the French Court, No 2' (1851). Watercolour and gouache over pencil on paper (Victoria and Albert Museum no. E.7-2007), and 'Part of the China Court' (1851), Watercolour and gouache over pencil on paper (Victoria and Albert Museum no. E.9-2007).
9 Anon., *Great Exhibition of the Works of Industry of all Nations. Official Descriptive and Illustrated Catalogue by Authority of the Royal Commission* (London: Spicer Brothers, vol. II, 1851), p. 822.
10 Ibid. 823.
11 Ibid.
12 See for example *ILN,* 21 June 1851, p. 1 for the illustration of Kiss's sculptured Amazon and *ILN,* 5 July 1851, p. 32 for Freccia's Psyche.
13 See also Isobel Hurst, 'Ancient and Modern Women in the Woman's World', *Victorian Studies* 52 (2009), pp. 42–51, for a detailed analysis of the series published in *Woman's World* by the late years of the century with articles such as Julia Wedgwood's 'Woman and democracy' and 'A Pompeian Lady'.
14 *Blackwood's Lady's Magazine and Gazette*, Vol. 20, 1846, p. 89; *ILN* No.195. Vol. VIII, 24 January 1846, p. 62.
15 *ILN* No.376. Vol. XIV, 16 June 1849, p. 412.
16 *ILN* No.361. Vol. XIX, 10 March 1849, p. 152.
17 Pamela Pilbeam, *Madame Tussaud: and the History of Waxworks* (London, New York: Hambledon and London, 2003), p. 140.
18 See for example Joshua Billings, Felix Bundelman & Fiona Macintosh, *Choruses Ancient & Modern* (Oxford: OUP, 2013); Peter Brown & Suzana Ograjenšek, *Ancient Drama in Music for the Modern Stage* (Oxford: OUP, 2010); Goldhill,

Victorian; Robert C. Ketterer, *Ancient Rome in Early Opera* (Urbana: University of Illinois Press, 2009); Marianne Macdonald, *Sing Sorrow: Classics, History and Heroines in Opera* (Westport: Greenwood Press, 2001); and Fiona Macintosh (ed.), The Ancient Dancer in the Modern World. Responses to Greek and Roman Dance (Oxford: OUP, 2010).

19 Benjamin Lumley, *Reminiscences of the Opera* (London: Hurst and Blackett, 1864), p. 3.

20 Henry Saxe Wyndham, *The Annals of Covent Garden Theatre From 1732 to 1897* (London: Chatto & Windus, 1906), p. 231; See also Lumley, *Reminiscences*, p. 5.

21 Lumley, *Reminiscences*, p. 151. See also Laura Monrós-Gaspar, *Cassandra the Fortune-teller: Prophets, Gipsies and Victorian Burlesque* (Bari: Levante Editori, 2011), pp. 150–151.

22 *ILN*, 25 July 1846, p. 59.

23 *ILN*, 22 August 1846, p. 122.

24 See Wyndham, *Annals*, p. 223.

25 Robert Taylor's wings for the Bank of England, Robert and James Adams's street designs in Portland Place, Stratford Place, the Adelphi and Fitzroy Square, and Chambers' Somerset House are but a few examples of the monumental architecture of the period which was inspired by classical antiquity. See Albert E. Richardson, *Monumental Classical Architecture in Great Britain and Ireland* (New York: W. W. Norton & Company, 1982).

26 Edith Hall, 'Classical Mythology in the Victorian Popular Theatre', *International Journal of the Classical Tradition* 5 (1999), pp. 336–366, p. 341.

27 George Speaight, *The History of English Puppet Theatre* (London: Hale, 1990), pp. 94–95.

28 In April the comedy, *Amphitryon*, by Dryden, was announced as in preparation, but it never seems to have been performed. Ibid. 113.

29 Ibid. 117.

30 See Speaight, *History*, pp. 118–119: 'The play opens with the heathen deities seated amid the clouds in full council; Apollo has given offence, and Jupiter darts a thunderbolt at him and casts him from Olympus; the gods all ascend together to the rolling of thunder. Meanwhile the clouds part to reveal the earth, with a scene of "a champaign country with a distant village"; shepherds sleeping in the field are roused by a violent thunderstorm, and run away frightened; "Apollo is seen whirling in the air, as if cast from heaven; he falls to earth with a rude shock, and lies for a while stunned; at length he begins to move, rises, advances, and looking upwards, speaks". This play was given over seventy performances'.

31 William Davenport Adams, *A Book of Burlesque. Sketches of English Stage Travestie and Parody* (London: Whitefriars Library, 1891), p. 45.

32 Hall, 'Classical', pp. 341–342.
33 Ibid. 43–47.
34 Olive Baldwin and Thelma Wilson, 'Leveridge, Richard (1670–1758)', *Oxford Dictionary of National Biography*, Oxford University Press, Sept 2004; online edn, January 2008, http://www.oxforddnb.com/view/article/16536 [accessed 14 March 2013].
35 See William J. Burling, *A Checklist of New Plays and Entertainments on the London Stage 1700–1737* (London: Fairleigh Dickinson University Press; Associated University Presses, 1993) for a full account of the theatrical shows put on stage throughout the eighteenth century. Burling's catalogue comprises the lists on *The London Stage, ESTC* – the online *Eighteenth Century Short-Title Catalogue*, and on Allardyce Nicoll, *A History of English Drama. 1660–1900. Vol. IV* (Cambridge: CUP, 1955); Robert D. Hume, *The Development of English Drama in the Late Seventeenth Century* (Oxford: Clarendon Press, 1976) and other major catalogues of the eighteenth century.
36 John Hughes' *Apollo and Daphne* was first staged at Drury Lane as a *masque afterpiece* in 1716. In 1723, Theophilus Cibber wrote a version of *Apollo and Daphne* which was subtitled as a 'Dramatick Entertainment of Dancing' and was first put on in 1723 at Drury Lane. In 1725 the pantomime *Apollo and Daphne: or, Harlequin Metamorphoses* by John Thurmond, Richard Jones and Henry Carey was first seen at the same theatre. In 1726 another pantomime, *Apollo and Daphne; or, the Burgo-Master Trick'd*, by John Rich and Lewis Theobald and music by J. E. Galliard was staged at Lincoln's Inn Fields. In 1729, the anonymous pantomime *The Scene of Apollo and Daphne* was put on at Drury Lane. See Burling, *Checklist*.
37 Bernard Herbert Stern, *The Rise of Romantic Hellenism in English Literature 1732–1786* (New York: Octagon, 1969), p. 18.
38 George Rowell, *Theatre in the Age of Irving* (Oxford: Blackwell, 1981), p. 67.
39 *Punch*, 23 September 1865, p. 117.
40 Nicoll, *History*, IV, p. 379.
41 Richard W. Schoch, *Victorian Theatrical Burlesques* (Aldershot: Ashgate, 2003), p. xx. See Hall, 'Classical' for a full account of the particulars of classical burlesque.
42 Edith Hall and Fiona Macintosh, *Greek Tragedy and the British Theatre 1660–1914* (Oxford: OUP, 2005), p. 339. Hall and Macintosh refer to Frederick Fox Cooper's *Ion Travestie*, which burlesqued T. N. Talfourd's *Ion* and opened at the Garrick Theatre in London in 1836. Unlike Blanchard's, Cooper's burlesque lacked many of the conventions of Greek tragedy.
43 For example Charles Selby, William Henry Oxberry, Albert Smith, Kenny and Shirley Brooks, Leicester Buckingham and Andrew Halliday. Other minor authors of the period were Leman Rede, Stirling Coyne and Tom Taylor.

44 Other burlesque playwrights of the late Victorian period were Mr H. B. Farnie, Mr Alfred Thomson, Mr Conway Edwardes, Mr G. A. Sala, and Herman Merivale.
45 Hall, 'Classical', pp. 341–350.
46 Christopher Stray, *Classics Transformed: Schools, Universities, and Society in England, 1830–1960* (Oxford: Clarendon Press, 1998), p. 83.
47 Jeffrey H. Richards, *The Golden Age of Pantomime: Slapstick, Spectacle and Subversion in Victorian England* (London: I. B. Tauris & Co), p. 78.
48 Hall, 'Classical', p. 339.
49 See J. Michael Walton, 'Aristophanes and the Theatre of Burlesque', in Stratos E. Constantinidis (ed.), *Text & Presentation 2005* (London: McFarland and Co., 2006), pp. 3–14 for an analysis of Planché's *The Birds of Aristophanes* (1846). See Edith Hall and Amanda Wrigley, *Aristophanes in Performance 421 BC–AD 2007. Peace, Birds, and Frogs* (Oxford: Legenda, 2007), for a performance history of Aristophanes.
50 See *Penny Magazine*, 25 May 1839, pp. 194–195 for an account of Aeschylus' tragedies; See John C. Kendrew, *Penny Books* (York, 1826), p. 13, p. 19 for the Penny fables 'The Waggoner and Hercules' and 'Mercury and the Tortoise'. See Jim Davis & Victor Emeljanow, *Reflecting the Audience: London Theatregoing, 1840–1880* (Hatfield: University of Hertfordshire Press, 2001) for a close analysis of the audiences of Victorian London, and Jim Davis ' "They Shew Me Off in Every Form and Way": The Iconography of English Comic Acting in the Late Eighteenth and Early Nineteenth Centuries', *Theatre Research International* 26 (3) (2001), pp. 243–256 for a close analysis of the relation of the visual and the verbal in the creation of contemporary myths on the Victorian culture.
51 See Martin Lowther Clarke, *Greek Studies in England 1700–1830* (Cambridge: CUP, 1945), p. 172. The 35th English edition of Lemprière's *Classical Dictionary* appeared in 1824. The dictionary was compiled while Lemprière was still an undergraduate at Oxford (1788) and Lord Byron accused Keats of 'versifying Tooke's *Pantheon* and Lempriere's *Dictionary*'. Ibid. 172 n. 4.
52 'The half-price, the brains that have ached at college, will doubtless find a savage joy in "taking their change" out of Mr. Talfourd's witty interpretation of Sophocles, and the large class who know nothing of the subject will be gratified at finding a page of Lemprière instinct with flesh and blood.' *Lloyd's Weekly Newspaper*, 1 May 1859, p. 7.
53 See Francis C. Burnand, *Paris or Vive Lemprière. A New Classical Extravaganza* (British Library Add. MS 53049N, 1866), p. 42. See also Henry James Byron's *Weak Woman*, a comedy first performed in 1875 at the Strand.
54 *ILN* Nos. 1478, 1479. Vol. LIL, 18 April 1868, p. 390.
55 Ibid.

56 See Fiona Macintosh, 'Medea transposed: burlesque and gender on the mid-Victorian stage', in E. Hall, F. Macintosh and O. Taplin (eds), *Medea in Performance: 1500–2000* (Oxford: Legenda, 2000).
57 See Bernard Denvir, *The Early Nineteenth Century: Art, Design and Society 1789–1852* (London: Longman, 1984), p. 146 and Elizabeth Prettejohn, 'Reception and Ancient Art: The Case of the Venus de Milo', in Ch. Martindale and Richard T. Thomas (eds), *Classics and the Uses of Reception* (Oxford: Blackwell Publishing, 2006), pp. 227–249. See Adams, *Book,* p. 48: 'Venus and Adonis have always been great favourites with the producers of travestie. Among those who have made them the central figures of burlesque are Mr. Burnand, whose work was brought out in 1864, and Mr. Edward Rose, whose *Venus,* written in collaboration with Mr. Augustus Harris, and first performed at the Royalty in 1879 (with Miss Nelly Bromley as the heroine), was re-written for revival, and finally taken as the foundation of a third production in 1880.' Other burlesques inspired by Venus are, for example, *The Paphian Bower or Venus and Adonis* by J. R. Planché and C. Dance (1832) and *Venus versus Mars* by J. T. Douglas (1870).
58 See Macintosh, 'Medea', pp. 75–99.
59 Adams divides burlesque into these two periods the first covered by Planché's literary production and the second until Miss Kate Vaughan and Mr Edward Terry retired from the Gaiety (Adams, *Book,* p. 33).
60 K. D. Reynolds, 'Norton, Caroline Elizabeth Sarah [*other married name* Caroline Elizabeth Sarah Stirling Maxwell, Lady Stirling Maxwell] (1808–1877)', *Oxford Dictionary of National Biography*, Oxford University Press, 2004, http://www.oxforddnb.com/view/article/20339 [accessed 7 November 2013].
61 Ray Strachey, *The Cause. A Short History of the Women's Movement in Great Britain* (London: Virago, [1928] 1989), p. 64.
62 Macintosh in 'Medea' demonstrates the connections between Planché's redemption of Medea and the marriage/divorce debates in mid-nineteenth-century England.
63 Ann P. Robson, 'Mill, Harriet (1807–1858)', *Oxford Dictionary of National Biography*, Oxford University Press, 2004, http://www.oxforddnb.com/view/article/38051 [accessed 7 November 2013].
64 Ibid.: 'Less patriotically I'm inclin'd; / To *marier pour la patrie* I've no mind'.
65 A mythological burlesque in one act. To be performed at the Astley's Royal Amphitheatre on Monday April 1858.
66 British Library Add. MS 52965 S, 11.
67 Hall, 'Classical', pp. 350–354.
68 See *Lord Chamberlain's Office Day Books*, Add Ms. 1852–1865: Add Ms 53703, ff.184b–185.
69 Jacky Bratton, *New Readings in Theatre History* (Cambridge: CUP, 2003), p. 37.

70 Tracy C. Davis, *The Broadview Anthology of Nineteenth Century Performance* (Peterborough: Broadview Press, 2012), p. 14.
71 Mary Kavanaugh Oldham Eagle, *The Congress of Women Held in the Woman's Building*. World's Columbian Exposition (Chicago), 1895. *The Gerritsen Collection of Aletta H. Jacobs*. College University Library. http://gerritsen.chadwyck.com [accessed 15 October 2013], pp. 102–103.
72 Hall & Macintosh, *Greek*, p. 339.
73 Charles Dickens, *Sketches by Boz. Illustrative of Every-Day Life and Every-Day People* (London: Chapman & Hall, [1836] 1895), p. 84 and p. 95.
74 See Pierce Egan, *The Pilgrims of the Thames in Search of the National* (London: W. Strange, 1838), pp. 78–120 for a detailed account of Richardson's shows. Note that Blanchard wrote for the stage with T. L. Greenwood under the pseudonym 'the Brothers Grinn'. Greenwood was the grandson of the famous scene painter Tom Greenwood associated with Richardson's shows.
75 *Era*, 9 February 1845, p. 6.
76 Nicoll, *History*, IV, p. 268. See also *LC's Day Books*, Add Ms 53702, f.7.
77 Nicoll dates the premiere of the play on 4 February yet reviews of the time point to 3 February instead (e.g. *Era*, 2 February 1845, p. 4).
78 *Era*, 2 February 1845, p. 4; *Era*, 7 December 1845, p. 6.
79 Diana Howard, *London Theatres and Music Halls 1850–1950* (London: The Library Association, 1970), p. 230.
80 An anecdote chronicled in *The Morning Post*, 17 March 1845, p. 5 accounts for the discrepancy between Roberts and Mr Marble, the leading actor in *Yankee Land* to be performed on the same day after Burnand's burlesque. The uproar also involved Harry Hall, stage director of the New Strand and Creon in *Antigone*, and it tackled the payment of the salaries of various members of the company.
81 *London Standard,* Tuesday 4 February 1845, p. 3.
82 Edward L. Blanchard, *The Life and Reminiscences of E. L. Blanchard* (London: Hutchinson, 1891), p. 28.
83 Ibid. 44,156.
84 *Morning Post*, 7 May 1844, p. 5.
85 *Era*, 26 January 1845, p. 6.
86 *Examiner,* 23 December 1843, p. 806.
87 Michael Booth, *Theatre in the Victorian Age* (Cambridge: CUP, 1991), pp. 164–167. See Barbara Weiss, *The Hell of the English: Bankruptcy and the Victorian Novel* (Lewisburg: Bucknell University Press, 1986) for an analysis of bankruptcy in the Victorian novel.
88 Jane Moody, 'The Drama of Capital: Risk, Belief, and Liability on the Victorian Stage', in F. O'Gorman (ed.), *Victorian Literature and Finance* (Oxford: OUP, 2007), p. 92.

89 e.g. *Payable on Demand* by Tom Taylor (1859) at the Olympic Theatre.
90 Nicholas Shrimpton, '"Even these metallic problems have their melodramatic side": Money in Victorian Literature', in F. O'Gorman (ed.), *Victorian Literature and Finance* (Oxford: OUP, 2007), pp. 21–22.
91 John Francis, *Chronicles and Characters of the Stock Exchange* (London: Longman, Brown, Green and Longmans, 1855), p. 350.
92 See for example the *Worcestershire Chronicle*, 24 March 1841, p. 4 and *Devizes and Wiltshire Gazette*, 15 April 1841, p. 2.
93 Both in 1826 and in 1833, two Bank Acts forbade the issue of notes of less than £5. See Shrimpton, 'Money', p. 23.
94 Philip Barrett Whale, 'A Retrospective View of the Bank Charter Act of 1844', *Economica*, New Series 11 (43 A) (1944), pp. 109–111, p. 109.
95 Shrimpton, 'Money', pp. 23–24.
96 See Jacky Bratton, *The Making of the West End Stage: Marriage, Management and the Mapping of Gender in London 1830–1870* (Cambridge: CUP, 2012).
97 Hall & Macintosh, *Greek*, pp. 336–341.
98 *Morning Chronicle*, 27 December 1844, p. 3
99 The pantomime was *Puck's Pantomime, or Harlequin and Robinson Crusoe*.
100 *Northern Star,* 28 December 1844, p. 8.
101 See for example the anecdote of the escape from Kidderminster debtor's prison in *Hereford Times*, 3 August 1844, p. 123.
102 Moody, 'Drama', p. 99.
103 See for example Shanyn Fiske, *Heretical Hellenism: Women Writers, Ancient Greece, and the Victorian Popular Imagination* (Athens: Ohio University Press, 2008), Macintosh, 'Medea'; Edmund Richardson, 'A Conjugal Lesson: Robert Brough's Medea and the discourses of Mid-Victorian Britain', *Ramus Critical Studies* 32.1 (2003), pp. 57–83 and Edmund Richardson, *Classical Victorians: Scholars, Scoundrels and Generals in Pursuit of Antiquity* (Cambridge: CUP, 2013).
104 The myth was refigured in *The Golden Fleece; or, Jason in Colchis and Medea in Corinth*, James Robinson Planché (1845); *Jason and Medea,* Jack Wooler (1851); *Medea,* adaptation of E. Legouvé (1856); *Medea; or, A Libel on the Lady of Colchis,* Mark Lemon (1856); *Medea in Corinth,* John Heraud (1857). See Macintosh, 'Medea', pp. 75–100.
105 *Medea; or, A Libel on the Lady of Colchis*, Mark Lemon (1856), another burlesque based on the Legouvé-Ristori Medea was put on at the Adelphi coinciding in time with Brough's. Nonetheless, Lemon's *Medea* never exceeded Brough's adaptation of Legouvé's text and Robson's rendering of Ristori.
106 *Era*, 8 June 1856, p. 10.
107 *London Daily News,* 5 June 1856, p. 5.

108 *Era*, 15 June 1856, p. 5.
109 *London Daily News*, 2 June 1856, p. 2.
110 *London Standard*, 5 June 1856, p. 1.
111 Mollie Sands, *Robson of the Olympic* (London: The Society for Theatre Research, 1979), p. 42.
112 Craven Mackie, 'Frederick Robson and the evolution of realistic acting', *Educational Theatre Journal* 23 (2) (1971), pp. 160–170, p. 163. As Mackie argues, 'During his eleven season at the Olympic, Robson acted in over seventy pieces, most of which were successful in terms of both critical reception and audience appeal. The most popular pieces initially ran, uninterrupted, from three to six months and were frequently revived. The Olympic's bill generally consisted of three or four pieces, of which Robson usually acted in the mainpiece and at least one afterpiece. Robson maintained an active repertory of approximately fifteen roles' ('Frederick', p. 179). See also George Augustus Sala, *Robson: A Sketch* (London: John Camden Hotten, 1864), p. 18.
113 'His acting was inimitable, combining tragic and comic emotions with the completest success, and to the immense delight of the audience', *Reynolds's Newspaper,* 31 December 1854, p. 12. 'The principal weight of the acting fell on Mr. Robson, who had numberless opportunities, in the extremes of love and hate which agitate the yellow dwarf, to exhibit his genius for mock tragedy', *London Standard*, 27 December 1854, p. 4. See also Sala, *Robson*, pp. 47–48.
114 George Taylor, *Players and Performances in the Victorian Theatre* (Manchester: Manchester University Press, 1989), p. 76.
115 Note that some of the topics cursorily touched upon in Planchés' fairy extravaganza – such as bigamy and arranged marriages – which were so masterly dealt with on stage by Robson are developed in Brough's *Medea*.
116 Henry Morley, *The Journal of A London Playgoer. From 1851 to 1866* (London: George Routledge & Sons, 1866), p. 159.
117 *London Standard,* 15 July 1856, p. 1.
118 *Morning Chronicle*, 15 July 1856, p. 5.
119 Taylor, *Players*, p. 77.
120 Richard Foulkes, *Lewis Carrol and the Victorian Stage: Theatricals in a Quiet Life* (Aldershot: Ashgate Publishing, 2005), pp. 150–154; Sands, *Robson*, p. 79.
121 Charles Dickens; Graham Storey, Madeline House and Kathleen Tillotson, *The Letters of Charles Dickens: the Pilgrim Edition* (Oxford: OUP, 1995), p. 170.
122 See *Examiner*, 30 April 1853, p. 6. For an account of Robson's rendering of Macbeth see Bratton, *Making,* pp. 198–199; Sands, *Robson,* p. 52; Sala, *Robson*, p. 18; Richard W. Schoch, *Not Shakespeare: Bardolatry and Burlesque in the Nineteenth Century* (Cambridge: CUP, 2002), pp. 979–982; Schoch, *Victorian*, pp. 95–106; Taylor, *Players*, pp. 75–6; xiv–xvii.

123 *Reynolds's Newspaper*, Sunday 20 July 1856, p. 13. See Mackie, 'Frederick' for a full analysis of Robson's acting style.
124 *Morning Chronicle*, Tuesday 15 July 1856, p. 5. See *Caledonian Mercury*, Friday 6 June 1856, p. 2 for a précis of Ristori's re-enactment of the scene. Note that the same scene was also burlesqued in Williams' *Medea* at the Adelphi ff.9–10.
125 Macintosh, 'Medea', p. 97.
126 *London Standard*, 5 June 1856, p. 1. See also *Caledonian Mercury*, 6 June 1856, p. 2: 'a tall and handsome woman carrying one child and leading another, appeared on the mountains at the back of the stage. This was the Ristori – this was Medea, in whom the maternal principle was at once made prominent to heighten the horror of the catastrophe.'
127 Sands, *Robson*, p. 79. See also, *London Daily News*, 4 July 1856, p. 4; *London Standard*, 14 July 1856, p. 2.
128 *Lloyd's Weekly Newspaper*, 6 January 1856, p. 6.
129 Mary Lyndon Shanley, *Feminism, Marriage and the Law in Victorian England 1850–1895* (Princeton, NJ: Princeton University Press, 1989), p. 38. See also Mary Poovey, 'Covered but Not Bound: Caroline Norton and the 1857 Matrimonial Causes Act', *Feminist Studies* 14 (3) (1988), pp. 467–485.
130 Kelly Hager, *Dickens and the Rise of Divorce: The Failed-Marriage Plot and the Novel Tradition* (Aldershot: Ashgate Publishing, 2010).
131 Ibid. 5.
132 Anne Humphreys, 'Breaking apart: the early Victorian divorce novel', in N. D. Thompson (ed.), *Victorian Women Writers and the Woman Question* (Cambridge: CUP, 1999), p. 42.
133 Hall & Macintosh, *Greek*, p. 422.
134 See S., Eltis, *Acts of Desire: Women and Sex on Stage 1800–1930* (Oxford: OUP, 2013), p.47.
135 See Arvel B. Erickson & Fr. John R. McCarthy, 'The Yelverton Case: civil legislation and marriage', *Victorian Studies* 14 (3) (1971), pp. 275–291; and Jeanne Fahnestock, 'The rise and fall of a convention', *Nineteenth-Century Fiction* 36 (1) (1981), pp. 47–71, for a full account of the Yelverton case in the 1860s and its influence on the account of bigamy in the sensation novels of the decade.
136 *Westmorland Gazette*, 5 July 1856, p. 7.
137 *Taunton Courier, and Western Advertiser*, 16 July 1856, p. 12, and *Exeter and Plymouth Gazette*, 19 July 1856. For similar cases see, for example, *Northampton Mercury*, 26 July 1856, p. 4; *Leeds Times*, 12 July 1856, p. 8.
138 e.g. *Era*, 23 June 1850, p. 12; *Manchester Courier and Lancashire General Advertiser*, 29 June 1850, p. 3. The end of the case was reported in *Wells Journal*, 7 January 1860, p. 2, for example.

139 e.g. *Derby Mercury*, 3 July 1850, p. 3. As stated in *Cork Examiner*, 6 September 1850, p. 2, Forrest accused his wife of adultery with George Jameison at Cincinnatti, Ohio, with N. P. Wills, Samuel Marsden Raymond, Clacraft, John B. Rich, Henry Wykoff and W. H. Howard in New York and other unknown persons. The Westmeath scandal was a further well-known paradigm. See, for example, 'The Interesting Westmeath Case', *Morning Post*, 18 December 1826, p. 1, for an early example of the wide press coverage of the case.

140 Lionel Rose, *The Massacre of the Innocents: Infanticide in Britain, 1800–1939* (London: Routledge, 1986), p. 41. Between 1852 and 1856 as many as 616 cases of infanticide are registered in the *Annual Report of the Registrar-General of Births, Deaths and Marriages in England* (London: George Eyre and William Spottiswoode, 1858), p. 173. See also Ann Higginbotham, '"Sin of the Age": Infanticide and Illegitimacy in Victorian London', *Victorian Studies* 32 (3) (1989), pp. 319–337, and Ann Marie Kilday, *A History of Infanticide in Britain C. 1600 to the Present* (Basingstoke: Palgrave, 2013).

141 As argued by Rose, in 1864 it started to focus on the caring of the offspring of single working mothers (Rose, *Massacre*, p. 41).

142 Cathy Sherryl Monholland, *Infanticide in Victorian England, 1856–1878: Thirty Legal Cases (England)*. Masters Thesis (Rice University, 1989), http://hdl.handle.net/1911/13382 [accessed 15 December 2013], p. 25.

143 For a detailed account of the cases see Patrick Wilson, *Murderess: A Study of the Women Executed in Britain since 1843* (London: Joseph, 1971); Mary S. Hartman, *Victorian Murderesses: A True History of Thirteen Respectable French and English Women Accused of Unspeakable Crimes* (New York: Schocken Books, 1977); Monholland, *Infanticide*; Jennifer Thorn (ed.), *Writing British Infanticide: Child-Murder, Gender, and Print, 1722–1859* (Newark: Delaware University Press, 2003); Nicola Goc, *Women, Infanticide and the Press, 1822–1922: News Narratives in England and Australia* (Aldershot: Ashgate Publishing, 2013).

144 *Reading Mercury*, 26 July 1856 p. 5; *London Daily News*, 10 July 1856, p. 6; *Newcastle Journal*, 12 July 1856, p. 7.

145 *Morning Chronicle*, 22 July 1856, p. 6.

146 See Monholland, *Infanticide*, for further information.

147 Kilday, *History*, p. 147.

148 Ibid. Ryan was a member of *The National Society and Asylum for the Prevention of Infanticide* founded in 1863.

149 See *Women's Penny Paper*, 23 March 1889, p. 6; *Woman's Herald*, 7 January 1893, pp. 6–7; *Woman's Signal*, 17 January 1895, pp. 7–8; *Woman's Signal*, 4 June 1896, pp. 360–361.

150 Sheila Stowell (ed.), *A Stage of Their Own. Feminist Plays of the Suffrage Era* (Manchester: Manchester University Press, 1992), p. 105. Also see Elaine

Showalter, *A Literature of their Own. From Charlotte Brontë to Doris Lessing* (London: Virago, [1977] 2009) pp. 174, 207–209 and Stowell, *Stage*, pp. 71–99.

151 In 1851 it was put on for a charitable amateur performance at the Royal Soho Theatre in London with F. Talfourd in the role of Alcestis (Hall & Macintosh, *Greek*, p. 437, p. 576); in 1853 it was advertised at the Marylebone Theatre (*Reynolds's Newspaper*, 13 November 1853, p. 8). In 1850 it was staged at Burton's Olympic Theatre and Brougham's Theatre in New York (Helene Foley, *Reimagining Greek Tragedy on the American Stage* (Berkeley: University of California Press, 2012), p. 29. See also Hall & Macintosh, *Greek*, p. 436 n.12.

152 Hall & Macintosh, *Greek*, p. 435.

153 *Berkshire Chronicle*, 21 May 1853, p. 8.

154 Donald Roy, *Plays by James Robinson Planché* (Cambridge: CUP, 1986), p. 6.

155 *Era*, 7 July 1850, p. 12.

156 See for example the amateur theatricals by the Officers of the Garrison at the Theatre Royal George's Street in Cork in aid of the Indian relief fund, *Cork Examiner*, 9 October 1857, p. 2.

157 *Norfolk Chronicle and the Norwich Gazette*, 23 December 1865, p. 5.

158 e.g. *Era*, 7 July 1850, p. 12.

159 See n.156.

160 Francis Talfourd, *Alcestis, the Original Strong-Minded Woman: a Classical Burlesque in One Act* (London: Thomas Hailes Lacy, 1850), p. 2.

161 Ibid. 4.

162 Ibid. 16–17.

163 See Monrós-Gaspar, *Cassandra*, pp. 194–204.

164 Carolyn Christensen Nelson, *A New Woman Reader: Fiction, Articles, and Drama of the 1890s* (Peterborough: Broadview Press, 2000), p. ix. The term 'New Woman' was first used by Sarah Grand in an essay published in the *North American Review* in 1894 to refer to the reawakening of women in society. As argued in 'The New Aspect of the Woman Question,' *North American Review* 158 (March 1894), p. 448 as edited in Nelson, *New Woman*, p. 142, New Women were women who perceived 'the sudden and violent upheaval of the suffering sex in all parts of the world. Women were awakening from their long apathy, and, as they awoke, like healthy hungry children unable to articulate, they began to whimper for they knew not what. They might have been easily satisfied at that time had not society, like an ill-conditioned and ignorant nurse, instead of finding out what they lacked, shaken them and beaten them and stormed at them until what was once a little wail became convulsive shrieks and roused up the whole human household.'

165 *OED* 'strong-minded' *adj.* a.

166 *OED* 'strong-minded' *adj*. b.
167 See Harriet Taylor and John Stuart Mill, 'The Enfranchisement of Women', *Westminster Review* 55 (1851), pp. 189–311. The polemical Irish dancer Lola Montez, for example, who was famous both for her art and her scandalous life, reflected upon such a stereotype in a series of lectures published in 1858 and presented worldwide in *The New York Times,* 16 February 1858, p. 5.
168 Charles Dickens, *Martin Chuzzlewit* (Ware: Wordsworth, [1844] 1994), p. 42; Mary Elizabeth Braddon, *Lady Audley's Secret* (London: Penguin, [1862] 1998), I.xxxiv, p. 330.
169 See Pam Hirsch, 'Bodichon, Barbara Leigh Smith (1827–1891)', *Oxford Dictionary of National Biography*, Oxford University Press, September 2004; online edn, May 2007, http://www.oxforddnb.com/view/article/2755 [accessed 7 November 2013]
170 *West Middlesex Advertiser and Family Journal*, 5 February 1859, p. 2.
171 See *Paisley Herald and Renfrewshire Advertiser*, 20 August 1853, p. 4.
172 Ellen Jordan, *The Women's Movement and Women's Employment in Nineteenth-Century Britain* (London: Routledge, 1999), pp. 87–144.
173 *London Standard,* 3 October 1851, p. 3.
174 See Monrós-Gaspar, *Cassandra*, p. 230.
175 *Hampshire Telegraph*, 2 April 1873, p. 3.
176 See Edith Hall, 'Sophocles' Electra in Britain', in J. Griffin (ed.), *Sophocles Revisited. Essays Presented to Sir Hugh Lloyd-Jones* (Oxford: OUP, 1999) for a full account of the myth of Electra in Britain.
177 Hall, 'Electra', pp. 285–286.
178 *ILN,* 5 May 1849 p. 293.
179 *Bath Chronicle and Weekly Gazette*, 17 March 1859, p. 3.
180 *Wells Journal*, 25 June 1859, p. 3; *Hereford Times,* 3 September 1859, p. 14.
181 *Birmingham Journal*, 4 June 1859, p. 4.
182 See *Great Facts; a Popular History and Description of the most Remarkable Inventions during the Present Century*, Frederick C. Blackwell. London: Houlston and Wright as advertised in *Bradford Observer*, 28 April 1859, p. 7.
183 Nicoll, *History*, V, p. 567. See *London Standard,* 25 April 1859, p. 3; *Morning Post,* 19 May 1859, p. 5
184 *Era,* 24 April 1859, p. 10.
185 See Tracy C. Davis, *Actresses as Working Women: their Social Identity in Victorian Culture* (London: Routledge, 1991) for the consequences of the Surplus Question for the theatre industry.
186 Two lines from the Adelphi *Medea*, however, are recorded as being omitted from the manuscript in representation. *LC's Day Books* 1852–1865: BL Add Ms 53703, f.185.

2

Antigone Travestie

Edward L. Blanchard

(1845)

Antigone Travesie by Edward L. Blanchard was first performed at the Strand Theatre in London on 3 February 1845 with the following cast:

ANTIGONE	George Wild
CREON	Harry Hall
CONDUCTOR	Mr F. Romer

Mr Attwood, Mr Dean, Mr Cockwill, Mr Morris, Mrs C. Melville were also involved in the play, yet so far in my research I have not found evidence of the specific roles they performed.

The text of *Antigone Travestie* is taken from the bound manuscript BL Add. Ms. 42982 ff. 165–173, held at the Lord Chamberlain's Plays Collection at the British Library.

Edward Litt Leman Blanchard

Edward Litt Leman Blanchard (1820–1889), born in London, was the son of William Blanchard, a comic actor in the Kembles' Covent Garden company. Edward Blanchard edited various periodicals, such as *Chambers' London Journal* (1841) and the *New London Magazine*, and pursued a career as a writer of illustrated books and novels. Blanchard's most important work, however, was for the stage. He was manager of The Royal Manor House Theatre (1838–1841) and a regular contributor to *Fun*, the *Illustrated Times* the *Era Almanack and Annual*, *The Observer* and the *Daily Telegraph*. Blanchard's descriptions of his work as manager at The Royal Manor House Theatre provide an insight into the theatrical background where extraordinary enthusiasm for classical burlesque abounded. For the stage he wrote pantomimes, farces, dramas, entertainments and comic songs, either under his own name or the pseudonyms Francesco (or Francisco) Frost and the Brothers Grinn (with T. L. Greenwood). From 1852 to 1888 he wrote annual Christmas pantomimes for the Drury Lane Theatre. Some of his burlesques include *The Merchant of Venice* (Olympic, 1843), *Robinson Crusoe* (Strand, 1845) and *The Cricket on our own Hearth* (Olympic, 1846).

Manuscript paratext

f. 165

To be performed on Monday Next

1/28/45

2/1/45

<u>Antigone Travestie</u>

<u>In One Act.</u>

<u>New Strand Theatre.</u>

<u>January 1845.</u>

f. 166

<u>Antigone.</u>

<u>Travestie.</u>

<u>Dram. Pers.</u>

Creon.

Hermon, his Son.

Phocian, a Guard.

Tiresias, an Astrologer.

Leader of Chorus.

Conductor of Band.

======

Antigone.

Ismene.

==========

<u>Chorus &c &c</u>

List of Roles

CHORUS
ANTIGONE
ISMENE
CREON
PHOCIAN   *a Guard*   5
LEADER   *of Chorus*
HERMON   *Creon's Son*
TIRESIAS   *an Astrologer*

CONDUCTOR   *of band*

Court   10

---

1 **CHORUS** Whereas the chorus is a group of Theban elders in Sophocles' *Antigone*, here they are young men (1.1.1), probably soldiers or courtiers, who facilitate the natural outcome of the dramatic situations with a strictly neutral attitude. See Hall & Macintosh (2005: 322–324) for a detailed account of the chorus in the Covent Garden 1845 production of Mendelssohn's *Antigone*.

2 **ANTIGONE** Antigone is the daughter of Oedipus and Iocasta and sister of Eteocles, Polynices and Ismene in Sophocles. Sophocles' *Antigone* deals with events after the Theban War in which Eteocles and Polynices killed one another. The new king of Thebes, Creon, has issued an edict forbidding anyone to bury the body of Polynices. Antigone defies the edict. Here Polynices' crime is an unpaid debt of £5 which has thrown him into prison. Antigone is performed in a travesty role by Mr G. Wild.

3 **ISMENE** Antigone's sister in Sophocles. Here Creon's daughter (1.1.45). Being sisters, like Chrysothemis and Electra, the contrast between the two models of women is stronger in Sophocles.

4 **CREON** Brother of Iocasta. After Oedipus' fall and the death of Eteocles he became king of Thebes. Here the character is interpreted by Harry Hall. Reviews and memoirs of contemporary playwrights show that Hall's performance was much acclaimed. See Blanchard (1891), i. 202, n.2 as qtd in Hall & Macintosh (2005: 340).

5 **PHOCIAN** takes the name from the Greek region of Phocis. In Sophocles' tragedy the guard keeps watch over the corpse of Polynices under orders from Creon.

6 **LEADER** Coryphaeus. In Greek tragedy the Coryphaeus spoke for the chorus when it took part in the action.

7 **HERMON** Son of Creon. Haemon in Sophocles' *Antigone*. In the tragedy he takes his own life after the death of Antigone. Some critics relate the name of Haemon with αἷμα, blood, for his death with a sword. Here Phocian announces that Hermon has been strangled to death with a rope (l.319).

8 **TIRESIAS** Legendary seer and pivotal figure in the Theban plays of Sophocles and Euripides. Here a modern prophet. The identification of prophets and seers from Greek and Roman mythology with contemporary astrologers was commonplace in Victorian England. For a full discussion see Monrós-Gaspar (2011: 186–193).

9 **CONDUCTOR** Ghost character. Music was an important ingredient for Victorian burlesque. Even though there are no dialogues with the conductor of the band throughout the play, he could have participated in a comic sketch during the performance. Therefore, he is included in the dramatis personae of the manuscript.

10 **Court** Group of non-speaking characters.

[1.1] *Exterior of Richardson's Show. Enter* TWO DIVISIONS OF CHORUS.

FIRST DIVISION
    How now? what row are you going to make my boys?
    Oh, my! surely, there's meaning in that phiz.

SECOND DIVISION
    We're here, that's clear, so you've made no mistake, my boys,
    But hollo! Don't you know? we the Chorus is.

TOGETHER
    We fill up the dialogue when it a little porous is   5
    And let's slip the meaning which to you we will unfold,
    So when you do not understand just encore us choruses
    And then you will the cause of all immediately be told.

LEADER
    Break off in sticks, let each make his incision,
    We now must try a little long division.   10
    Here comes Antigone, for years she's sorrowed,
    So now stand back, and see what's going for 'ard.

Enter ANTIGONE *RD.*

ANTIGONE
    Ah me! What griefs are mine, much more I cannot bear!
    Perhaps Ismene wouldn't mind a share,
    So people take the sum of their distress   15
    Divide by two, and make that sum much less.
    I'll call and see my friend, Ismene, dear!

---

0 SD **Richardson's show** refers to the shows by John Richardson. Richardson's Theatre was an itinerant fairground theatre founded in 1798. Enjoying much success, Richardson's shows are described in Dickens' *Sketches by Boz* (1836) with a full account of his staging of tragedies. For a detailed description of the shows see, for example, *Harper's New Monthly Magazine*, XXXIII, June to November, 1866, p. 633.
    TWO DIVISIONS the entrance of the two divisions of the chorus in Mendelssohn's *Antigone* enjoyed much success as reviewed, for example, in *The Morning Post*, 6 January 1848, p. 6. 'Divisions' also refer to the execution of a rapid melodic passage in music (*OED*, *n.* 7a).

1 **row** line (*OED*, *n.* 1) and quarrel (*OED*, *n.* 5).
2 **phiz** face or countenance (*OED*, *n.*).
4–8 Metatheatrical reflection upon the function of the classical chorus.
11 Antigone's sorrow refers to the fate of Oedipus and the Theban saga.
14 **Ismene** sister to Antigone in Greek mythology. Here Creon's daughter. See List of Roles, 3n.

ISMENE
    Is that you, dear Antigone? I'm here.
ANTIGONE
    If not at work, one word to you I'd say.
ISMENE
    One word, nay, ten, on words' we mean to play.   20
ANTIGONE
    Oh, silly belle, your language is a fiction,
    The diction of our sex is Contra-diction.
ISMENE
    But say, what makes thy face so long?
ANTIGONE   Oh, bother!
    It will be longer ere I get another
    Joe Miller! Hem! A catalogue of woes   25
    With lots of evils, you may, love, suppose,
    And then suppose that case is mine so dark.
ISMENE
    Well then, what then?
ANTIGONE   You'd be about the mark,
    My heart is broken,
ISMENE   Well, but what communion
    Could give relief?
ANTIGONE   But one, that's the Art Union   30
ISMENE
    And this your grief, what cause so great can bring it?
ANTIGONE
    I cannot speak, so will try to sing it.
    Songs are the great infallible resource
    To which all sad stage heroines have recourse.

SONG

ANTIGONE
    Oh, he was a knight whom we all loved well,   35
    And he owed the King a small sum as they tell.

'Twas a five pound note with the worth complete
As ever was launched from Threadneedle Street,
A debt not light he must pay that day,
But his mind was set, and his heart was gay. 40

A bailiff flies through the streets close by,
What means that with despairing cry?
Farewell the joys and scenes of home
In Whitecross Street no friend can come.
Your father derides, he his claim won't waive, 45
And my brother in quod has a notion grave.

ISMENE

Your brother's then arrested by the king?

ANTIGONE

Just so, that 5£ note has done the thing.
But I'll be quits,

ISMENE   Why, what are you about?

ANTIGONE

He's let the King in, but I'll let him out. 50

ISMENE

Antigone!

---

20   Puns are one of the mainstays of Victorian burlesque (Schoch, *Victorian*, p. xx).

21–2 Manifest the rebellious character of Antigone regarding the Woman Question. Antigone was performed by a male actor, a common practice in Victorian burlesque. Vindictive words by classical female heroines interpreted by male actors are commonplace in classical burlesques as manifested in Robert Brough's *Medea* (1856) and Robert Reece's *Agamemnon and Cassandra; or the Prophet and Loss of Troy* (1868), for example.

25   **Joe Miller** a joke (*OED*, 'Joe' n. 2, 4b). Joe Miller was an actor at Drury Lane in the days of Hogarth. He was considered by his contemporaries to be chiefly remarkable for the gravity of his demeanour. (See, for example, a review in *Edinburgh Evening News*, 16 August 1881, p. 2.) In 1845, coinciding with the performance of *Antigone*, an edition of his book of jests came out and was widely acclaimed in the press.

30   **Art Union** the Art Union of London was established in 1836 to extend the love of the Arts of Design and encourage artists (King, 'Art Union', 1964).

32–4 **I . . . recourse** theatrical convention in opera and burlesque.

38   **Threadneedle Street** site of the Bank of England, which is often called 'the Old Lady of Threadneedle Street'. See pp. 21–2.

44   **Whitecross Street** site of a debtors' prison (Mayhew & Binny, *Criminal*, pp. 83, 536).

46   **quod** prison (*OED*, n.)

47–60 The whole dialogue is evidence of Antigone's determination which aligns her with the nineteenth-century trope of 'strong-minded women'. See pp. 22–3

50   In Sophocles, Antigone's rebellion is to bury the body of her brother Polynices.

ANTIGONE   I'm bent upon it.
ISMENE   Wait!
ANTIGONE
    Whene'er I'm bent I set about it straight.
ISMENE
    But recollect, my father's stern not kind.
ANTIGONE
    I should be stern to, if I stayed behind.
ISMENE
    But pause, how can you pass the guards in masses?   55
ANTIGONE
    Pshaw! Paws have made of late the greatest passes.
    Just ask Miss Martineau, or when you see'em
    Look o'er the numbers of the Athenaeum.
ISMENE
    Will nought prevail?
ANTIGONE   No! Arguments though stronger,
    Time's waste were greater if my stays were longer.   *Exit.* 60
ISMENE
    Alas, the King, if he should prove eaves-dropper,
    May turn her stern but never will he stop her.   *Exit.*

            Enter CREON *and Court.*

CREON
    Sage Senators of Greece, you've heard of late
    My kingdom has got in a fearful state.
    An insurrection would have cracked this Crown,   65
    Had not Sir Peter Laurie put it down.
    The leader of this vile rebellion known
    I, for a debt, have into prison thrown.
    And now I bid you list to this decree
    That Polynices never shall be free.   70

Enter PHOCIAN *hastily.*

Ha, ha, thy face is pale, speak, quick, what news?
Don't shake and shiver in thy trembling shoes,
But rise and set before me what's the matter.
Speak sooth, or else, by Jove, I'll make you flatter.

PHOCIAN

    Well, then, great King, know that our prisoner's bolted,   75

CREON

    The doors?

PHOCIAN   No, sire, himself, the bird has moulted,

CREON

    Who set him free? 'twas done, no doubt before you?

PHOCIAN

    I've not the least idea, sire, I assure you.

CREON

    There I believe you, Polynices fled!
    My vengeance baffled, curses on his head,   80
    Go! Take a cab! Find out who's done this deed,
    And ascertain how came the prisoner freed,
    If you should fail, you go yourself to prison.
    I'll have your life since I cannot have his'n.

---

56 **Paws** jocularly applied to the hand (*OED*, *n.*¹, 2).
    passes also an 'act of passing the hands over or across a person without touching, in a manner intended to have hypnotic or mesmeric effects' (*OED*, *n.* 4, 12). Pun to allude to the mesmeric practices of Harriet Martineau recorded in the Athenaeum in the 1840s.

57 **Miss Martineau** Harriet Martineau (1802–1876) was a British writer and social theorist. She examined all aspects of society, particularly the status of women.

58 **Athenaeum** the Athenaeum was a highly influential periodical during the Victorian period. In 1844 it published Martineau's 'Letters on Mesmerism' (Martineau, *Autobiography*, pp. 196–198).

63 **Greece** Creon was king of Thebes, one of the classical *poleis* or city-states of the region today known as Greece.

66 **Sir Peter Laurie** (1778–1861), politician. Lord Mayor of London and Chairman of the Union Bank (*ODNB*).

70 Note that Creon's decree in Sophocles is that no one should bury the corpse of Polynices.

81 **cab** a common practice in Victorian burlesque was to include topical references to daily life customs and objects.

84 **his'n** his (*OED*, *pron.*). Midland and southern form of the pronoun.

SOLO

CREON

 Be off at once, and don't delay,   85
 Your cab's expenses I will pay.
 But find the traitor on your way,
 Or else your head will forfeit pay. Ritooral looral &C.

  Exeunt Creon, Court and Phocian.

LEADER

 They've now gone off, each blustering and windy,
 To know who dared create this awful shindy.   90
 They here return, he well knew how to track her
 So clear your pipes and stand a little backer.

CHORUS

  Now you shall see what you shall see.
 This is Miss An—tig—o—ne.
 She's in a precious hobble, as the King will be recounting, 95
 So fare ye well our style of gal, you'll soon be o'er the mountain.

  Enter ANTIGONE, PHOCIAN— CREON— *and Court.*

CREON

 You've found the culprit then? He shall sing small
 Where is he?

PHOCIAN   Sire, it ain't a he at all.
 The person was a miss.

CREON   A miss indeed for me,
 Let me behold her then, Antigone!   100

ANTIGONE

 So I was christened.

CREON   Ah! You freed your brother!
 You have become a traitor!

ANTIGONE   You're another,
 You threw him into jail, I let him out,

CREON
>I don't know what you make this row about,

>A row! Odzooks, with rage I'm boiling over! 105
>No locomotive on the Rail to Dover
>Felt such high pressure as now goads me on.
>I shall blow up myself or else some other one,
>Where is my daughter? Who is there waiting?

PHOCIAN
>She's in her room, sire,

CREON
>What doing?

PHOCIAN
>Rumiwating. 110

CREON
>Go bid her hither.   *Exit Phocian.*
>Doubtless though you hid it
>She did assist you.

ANTIGONE
>No, alone I did it,
>What's done, is done, and cannot be denied
>You're done, own that, and done on the wrong side.

CREON
>Oh, woman! Woman!

ANTIGONE
>Don't insult our sex, 115
>Vivat Regina now, not vivat Rex.

Enter ISMENE *and Phocian.*

CREON
>The wrecks indeed of all my hopes I see

89	**windy** 'full of talk or verbiage' (*OED, adj.* 1, 6b).	106	Allusion to the mania of the 1840s for the Railway which linked London with the provinces.
92	**backer** further back (*OED, adj.*).		
95	**hobble** difficult situation (*OED, n.*).		
97	**sing small** to be silent (*OED*, 'small', *adv.*).	109	**daughter** departing from the classical tradition Ismene is here daughter of Creon. See List of Roles, 3n.
101	**christened** note that Sophocles' tragedy predates the tradition of Christening. Here the term is used as a synonym for naming.		
101–4	In Sophocles the betrayal is to breach Creon's decree to deny Polynices burial.	115–16	Antigone as a strong-minded woman. Reference to Queen Victorian who reigned in England between 1837 and 1901.
105	**Odzooks** exclamation expressing surprise (*OED*, 'od', *n.* 1 and *int.*).		

>   Say, girl, did you assist in setting free
>   This Polynices?
> ISMENE   Polly who, pa?
>   I've been you know, all day along with Ma.   120
> CREON
>   You've marred my vengeance, but go fetch my son,   *Exit Phocian.*
>   He loves but shall not wed so vile a one.
> ANTIGONE
>   Tyrant, I laugh at all such threats as these!
>   Love knows its cues, you cannot stick its P's.
> ISMENE
>   I told you that your conduct would be watched   125
> ANTIGONE
>   I reckoned not my chickens ere they're hatched,
>   So like Wellington's Statue, with horse fit to jolter, he
>   Turns his back on the Change and then looks up the Poultry.

Enter HERMON.

> CREON
>   My son, you love Antigone,
> HERMON   Yes, rather,
> CREON
>   Behold a sight to horrify a father.   130
>   She has proved false, to me,
> HERMON   To you, then till
>   We part, with all thy faults I love thee still.
> ANTIGONE
>   Beloved Hermon, you had best betimes
>   Try an advertisement in the Sunday Times,
>   Wanted a wife —An amiable young gent—   135
>   You know the usual style, ten shillings spent
>   In this way, will secure another bride,
> HERMON
>   Another one! Are you not at my side?
>   Marry come up, why should we further tarry?

ANTIGONE

    Come up you may, but never can we marry.   140

    In next Gazette, your father's mind revolved,

    We shall appear with a partnerships dissolved.

CREON

    When you have had your *conversazione*

    I've got a word to say to Antigone,

ISMENE

    Oh, ponder well, be not severe.

CREON   It late is   145

    To offer, but to take no advice gratis,

    Now, men of Greece who long have braved the storm,

    As dips of fashion, and the moulds of form,

    Who shine within the palace and enough

    Have left to light the kitchen,

ANTIGONE   Kitchen! Stuff!   150

CREON

    As men of letters you our kingdom dreads

ANTIGONE

    'Mongst men of letters he will find wise heads.

CREON

    Be witness, in what penetrating lingo

    I swear to punish,

ANTIGONE   Don't swear,

---

120 **Ma** no reference as to who her mother is throughout the play.

127 **Wellington's Statue** the statue was inaugurated on 26 June 1844 at its original placement, in front of the Royal Exchange. This had a high impact on the press of the time as exemplified by the numerous accounts of the inauguration (see, for example, *The Kentish Gazette*, 25 June 1844, p. 1; *Taunton Courier, and Western Advertiser*, 26 June 1844, p. 5).

128 **Change** at the Exchange. The change is the place for the transaction of business yet since 1800 the word was treated as an abbreviation of the Exchange (*OED*, *n.*).

Poultry the name of a street at the east end of Cheapside in London. Formerly the site of a market where fowl were sold (*OED*, *n.*).

134–8 Antigone plays on the deeply-rooted practice of advertising throughout the nineteenth century. *The Sunday Times* is a broadsheet newspaper founded in 1821 as *The New Observer*.

141 **Gazette** general noun for 'one of the three official journals entitled *The London Gazette*, *The Edinburgh Gazette*, and *The Dublin Gazette*, issued by authority twice a week, and containing lists of government appointments and promotions, names of bankrupts, and other public notices. Hence sometimes used generally for the official journal of any government' (*OED*, *n.* 2a).

143 *conversazione* assembly of an intellectual character from the late eighteenth century (*OED*, *n.*). Here 'conversation'. Blanchard uses the Italianized word for metrical reasons.

147 **Greece** Thebes in Sophocles. See 63n.

CREON   her, by jingo.
    I thus my vengeance breathe, though she defies it   155
  And say,

ANTIGONE   Say nothing.

CREON   Then I'll vocalize it.

ANTIGONE
  We'd better make a trio if you can,
  Two out of three, and, (*to Hermon*) you go the odd man.

                    TRIO

CREON
  My herald now proclaims, the morn
      When you so guilty found,   160
  Shall in a cave, a maid forlorn,
      Be taken under ground.
  There in this cavern deep confined,
      With horrors none can tell,
  Too late, alas, you, then will find   165
      My cave is not a sell,
  Heigho! Jiggy! I've sworn that I'll punish Antiggy

HERMON
  Oh dear, Jiggy, that's certainly awkward, Antiggy,

ANTIGONE
  Your sentence old chap, I don't value a rap.

CHORUS
  Her sentence old chap, she don't value a rap.   170

CREON
  I've sworn by Jove and Jingo too
  This day the girl shall die.

LEADER
  You now will learn from what he's going to do,
  A good receipt to make a family stew.
  First take your king, and pop him in hot water,   175
  Then when he boils you may serve out the daughter.

SOLO

HERMON

> My heart's in my high-lows, my heart isn't here,
> All through that wild buck who's collering my dear,
> I feel from my waistcoat it's gone down below,
> My heart's in my high-lows wherever I go. 180

SOLO

ANTIGONE

> Though you put me in a cave
> You shall find me in earth descending,
> Even there I can behave
> As a heroine should rave,
> You may yet repent this hour, 185
> Though no poll curtailed your power
> Thus to grind so fair a flower.
> > Yes, though lingering in a cave,
> > You shall find when life is ending,
> > That my ghost shall leave my grave 190
> > And sing a spectral Polka Stone!

TRIO AND CHORUS

> Then now her fate's decided, within that cave she dies,
> His power she derided, now he her rage defies,
> He wants no more of her society, kings like public want variety,

---

154 **by jingo** 'a vigorous form of asseveration' (*OED*, jingo *int.*, and *n.*, and *adj.*).

161 **cave** Creon's first sentence in Sophocles is to stone the culprit to death. The sentence changes to a less degrading death after finding out that it is Antigone. Blanchard follows Sophocles in Creon's second sentence. Caves were also recurring topoi in the nineteenth century and both women and enigmatic characters were entombed, concealed and silenced in caves and grottoes.

177 **high-lows** a boot laced (*OED*, *n.*). Pun.

178 **buck** 'A gay, dashing fellow; a dandy, fop, "fast" man' (*OED*, *n.* 1, 2b).
collering blushing (*OED*, 'colour | color', *v.*).

191 **Polka Stone** 'polka', as the lively dance which became popular in England after 1844 (*OED*, *n.* 1). Used as attributive as in 'polka music', 'polka step'. Word pun.

194 **variety** metatheatrical allusion to the wide range of spectacles available for the Victorian audiences.

    He's make a vow, he'll keep it now,   195
    But he won't serve her so any more.
                            Exeunt all but Hermon and Antigone.

HERMON
    To be entombed alive is not the thing,
    And there's my father calls himself a king,
    I wonder who first made such kings as he!
    If I was one I'm sure it shouldn't be.   200
ANTIGONE
    Nay, but a king may punish folks we know.
HERMON
    A king's no king who spoils a subject so,
ANTIGONE
    But lines like that are taught in all our schools,
HERMON
    It's but hard lines, when only one man rules.
ANTIGONE
    Walled in a rock! Oh horrible decree!   205
    He wouldn't serve a horse as he serves me.
HERMON
    Not serve a horse so, but one rock he shook
    Would serve a mayor so, if he'd that wall, rock,
ANTIGONE
    Farewell, the flowers may bloom above my pate,
    Mine is a sort of Horticultural Fête,   210
HERMON
    You will not die alone, when they come hither
    They'll say I took my leaves, and they did *with her*.
ANTIGONE
    Farewell, my Hermon!
HERMON   Oh, ye stars above!
    Who knows as well as I what 'tis to love?
    Why am I sad? Why choked with an adieu?   215
    Parting unmans me!
ANTIGONE   And unmans me too!

DUET

ANTIGONE
    Whilst the lads of the village shall drearily
HERMON   Ah!
ANTIGONE
    Share their labours to hand me along,
    I say unto thee that verily
HERMON   Ah!
ANTIGONE
    The King's come it rather too strong.   220
CHORUS
    All right and tight, they bid good night
    The monarch's spite has killed her quite.
HERMON, ANTIGONE
    Half dead with fright, in such a plight
    Deprived of light, she'll die outright.   *Exit Hermon.*
LEADER
    That he may join his rock imprisoned bride   225
    He's gone to book a place for one outside,
    Antigone, who finds she's lost her beau,
    Half cracked remain in Grecian status quo.
ANTIGONE
    Immured within a well, through earth a ducker
    None but a pump can give me any succour   230
    Shut up within a crib, three yards by two,
    Not knowing with my two feet what to do.
    What if wild beasts should come, and I am beaten,
    I'm in this ravine, ravenously eaten.

203–4 The lines manifest Antigone's involvement in the socio-political issues of her time. See pp. 22–3.
210 **Horticultural Fête** a common entertainment in Victorian England.
216 **unmans** to deprive of courage and of the qualities of a man. To effeminate (*OED*, *v.*). Note that the role of Antigone was interpreted by a male actor.
220 **come … strong** to act, to practise, to perform one's part excessively (*OED*, *v.* 29a).
229 **ducker** a diver (*OED*, *n.* 1).

No room to stand upright, my head gets acks, 235
I make an impression there with ceiling whacks.
No room to turn, see in that situation
A virgin verging upon desperation.
The cavern crumbles! Ah, my fear increases!
P'raps on that stage I'll tear myself to pieces 240
To pieces in one act, for there no doubt,
Only the miners then can bring me out
Stifled for want of air, but lost, perdition!
I'll grasp at all I can in this position.

DUET

ANTIGONE
 When time hath bereft me, 245
CHORUS
 Oh, look at her eyes,
ANTIGONE
 And lovers have left me,
CHORUS
 Just hear how she cries,
ANTIGONE
 In the midst of my sadness.
CHORUS
 You cannot be free. 250
ANTIGONE
 And the end of its madness,
CHORUS
 With that we agree.

SOLO

ANTIGONE
 What a capital lark, to steal out in the dark,
  From the place where they stow me away,
 To give them treats, by a chase in the street, 255

                    As swiftly as she darts away.
                'Tis plain I am done in the eyes of his son,
                    But an Irish howl I'll sing,
                And I'll keep my flight for another night
                    If once I could smuggle the King.   *Exit.*   260

LEADER

    You see Antigone has gone to perish,
    Unmindful of the long life let us cherish.
    Now here's the King, and where you find the Court,
    You know the game produces always sport.

            Enter CREON *and Court.*

CREON

    Methinks some poet somehow somewhere sings   265
    Of wondrous fallings off in earthly things,
    Of gorgeous empires going to decay,
    Of rapid rivers running all away,
    How mighty mountains shrink to mole hills small,
    And little hills become no hills at all,   270
    So now I find with vengeance I've gone through
    That nothing more is left a king to do.

            Enter PHOCIAN.

    How now, thy news?
PHOCIAN   The fortune-teller's come
    And wants to know, sire, if the King's at home.
CREON

    Then tell the juggler slave to call again,   275
    I'm busy, thou troublest me, I'm not in the juggler vein.

---

236 **whacks** a stroke (*OED*, *n.*).
242 **miners** also a reference to 'minor' theatres.
258 **Irish howl** in Ireland 'a lamentation for the dead, typically featuring unrestrained wailing, gesticulation, etc. (also in extended use) a cry, wail, or clamour raised by Irish people' (*OED*, *adj.* and *adv.* and *n.*).
273 **fortune-teller** See p. 81 n. 298.
275 **juggler** the association between jugglers, fortune-tellers and classical mythology was commonplace in Victorian England. 276 Allusion to William Shakespeare's *Richard III*, IV, ii 'not in the giving vein'.

PHOCIAN
>	But he declares he something has to say
>	Which being important must be said to day.

CREON
>	Well, let him enter. (*Exit Phocian.*) As he reads the stars,
>	He in a twinkling, can forsee the wars. 280
>	He knows full well what foe may prove a scorner,
>	So from his shell I may extract a warner.

>	*Enter* TIRESIAS.

CREON
>	What tale of wonder would'st unfold to me?

TIRESIAS
>	None are so blind as those who will not see
>	There is a spot that stains your country's peace. 285

CREON
>	I've read so, in the History of Grease.
>	Thou foolish knave, dost think I need be told
>	How well one works the Oracle with gold?

TIRESIAS
>	Dost think, oh King, I prophecy for pelf?
>	No sovereign left, you'll lose a crown yourself, 290

CREON
>	There's mischief in thy words, say what's the reason
>	That thus you blend low cunning with high treason?

TIRESIAS
>	You've been and cast one living in a tomb.

CREON
>	Aye, by St. Paul's she well deserves her dome.

TIRESIAS
>	In that yourself and kingdom dearly suffers. 295

CREON
>	So royal trains are stopped by railway buffers,
>	But what's the train of evils this will bring?

TIRESIAS

> A down train, hearken to the Gypsey King!

SONG

TIRESIAS

> Oh, I am the Gypsey King,
>   And not such a king as thee,   300
> Your conduct is not the thing
>   And that you will presently see.
> Your empire will be knocked down,
>   And your lands will your enemies seize.
> They won't leave the king half a crown,   305
>   So your Majesty do as you please.

BOTH

> For   you are
>   I am   the Gypsey King —ha! ha!
> Yes   he is
>   I am the Gypsey King!   *Exit Tiresias.*

CREON

> Oh scene distracting, well may poets say

---

281 **scorner** one who despises, shows contempt for you (*OED*, *n.*)

282 **warner** one or something that advises (*OED*, *n.* 1)

285 **spot** place (*OED*, *n.* 1, II.8a) and stain (*OED*, *n.* 1, I.1a)

286 **Grease** pun for Greece after stain.

288 **Oracle** 'In ancient Greece and Rome [the oracle was] the instrument, agency, or medium (usually a priest or a priestess) through which the gods were supposed to speak or prophesy; the mouthpiece of the gods. Also: the place at which such advice or prophecy was sought' (*OED*, *n.* I.1). Among the various forms of divination, the responses given at a precise oracular site were the most prestigious. Techniques by which responses were given also varied, 'inspired' prophecy being among the most important. Oracles, as related to fate, for example, play an important role in Greek tragedies.

297 **train** 'set of attendant things, circumstances or conditions' (*OED*, *n.* 1, 10. fig.) and railway carriages (*OED*, *n.* 2. II.21a).

298 **Gypsey King** it is no coincidence that the song chosen for Tiresias is related to the Gipsy King. Gipsies were often associated with classical seers as Tiresias and Cassandra in Victorian England. The gift of prophecy of Greek and Roman myths was linked with the art of fortune-telling of gipsies.

303–4 Thebes is later invaded by Lycus, who takes Creon's crown.

305 **crown** ornamental fillet, wreath (*OED*, *n.* I.1a) and coin (*OED*, *n.* II.8).

>   What must be must, each dog will have his day.   310
>   Did ever monarch pocket ills like mine?
>   Grief makes me dry, bring me some ale or wine.

Enter PHOCIAN.

PHOCIAN
>   All hail, my liege, but whine indeed you may.
>   Your son is dead, and there's the deuce to pay.

CREON
>   What, dead, defunct, gone, bolted, mizzled quite,   315
>   What, no life left?

PHOCIAN
>   Your majesty is right.
>   The prince stopped waiting at the cavern's side
>   Until he found Antigone had died
>   Then seized a rope, though crazed he never looked it
>   Twisted it round his neck,

CREON
>   And then he,

PHOCIAN
>   Hooked it.   320

CREON
>   Oh horror! Now to write up, I'll begin,
>   A kingdom to be let, enquire within,
>   No son, no joy, and no Antigone!
>   Ah me! Ah me! Ah me! Ah me! Ah me!
>   To keep my might I now no longer can,   325
>   Pity the sorrow of a poor old man,
>   I well these signs of royalty can spare,
>   Since thus I've lost my only son and heir
>   Oh Hermon, Hermon and beloved Antig!
>   (*Drops wig which is picked up by Chorus.*)
>   I'll thank you, sir, just to return that wig.   330
>   Against this sea of woes in vain I strove,
>   I feel myself a miserable cove,

A song may perhaps departed spirits raise,
Oblige me with the light of other days.

MEDLEY

CREON

 Oh, here's a pretty mess for a king to be in,   335
 It's enough to make a man like a Cheshire cat grin,
 To lose all my joys, but don't care a pin,
  For I'll soon prove an emigrant cutter,
 What do you think should a king have for supper,
  Who has lost all his teeth and has no bread and butter?   340
  So clar de Palace and old King Creon neber tire.

 I'll seek some distant sham rock
  That's close by New South Wales,
 And go as many a bankrupt leaves
  The country where he fails.   345
 I would not stay another night
  For diamonds, pearls or gold,
 But take my treasure there all right
  And live on what is sold,
 And thus I'll play a wiser part,   350
  And building farms around
 Will let none know what time I start,
  Or where I'm to be found.

---

310 **each ... day** everyone has his own time of action, period of influence or power (*OED*, *n*. 15).

315 **mizzled** 'decamp, disappear suddenly, vanish' (*OED*, *v*. 2).

330 **wig** the wig is taken here as a humorous sign of royalty. Note Cassandra's rejection of her robes as a priestess of Apollo in Aeschylus' *Agamemnon*.

338 **emigrant cutter** migrant ship. Emigration was a regular practice in Victorian England. The following lines refer to emigration to Australia as a consequence of bankruptcy.

341 Line adapted from the American blackface minstrel tradition song 'Clar de Kitchen' dated 1832 (*United States Songster*, 1936, p. 159).
neber at no time.

343 **New South Wales** site of migration in Australia during the nineteenth century. Between 1788 and 1853 New South Wales was populated with thousands of convicts from England with crimes mostly related to theft. Assisted migration to New South Wales was suspended between 1842–1843 and 1846–1847 due to a financial crisis in the area. Assistance was temporarily renewed in 1844 (Harper, *History*, pp. 77–79).

>   Yes, I'll take a train tonight
> >   By railroad down to Dover,   355
> >   Book a place all right
> >   And cross the Channel over,
> >   Then to Paris, I
> >   Will go when the weather cooler is,
> >   And call when passing by   360
> >   On Louis Phillippe at the Tuileries!
> >   Only say, when the train is slack again
> >   And from that day, you won't see me back again.

>   *Enter* HERMON, ANTIGONE— *and the rest.*

HERMON
>   The man whose grief is vented in a song
>   May hope that grief won't last him very long.   365

CREON
>   What, all alive again?

ANTIGONE   Yes, rocks teach curious trades.
>   I played my cards so well, they turned up spades,
>   With these we dug our way to light and glory
>   Ask him, sir, if you think I tell a story.

CREON
>   You didn't hang then, though the King's in check?   370

HERMON
>   Yes, pa, I did, but 'twas round her neck.

CREON
>   Odzooks, I am so glad being in the right of it,
>   I tell you what we'll do, we'll make a night of it,
>   If these good friends will join our social board
>   We'll nightly give the best we can afford.   375
>   Our house of entertainment isn't large,

ANTIGONE
>   Hearty the welcome, though a moderate charge,
>   Give then Antigone a frequent call,

CREON
>You'll own that she's been *Wild*,

ANTIGONE
>   And that is *Hall*.

FINALE

And now that our frolie's o'er we wait for your kind approbation.   380
> Give us but your smiles to night and we'll away with sorrow

Grant that Antigone's been in a pretty situation.
> Then, if you're satisfied, pray call again tomorrow.
>> Now to the end advancing,
>> Pleasure still entrancing,   385
>> Come for an hour,
>> Don't mind a shower,
>> Come, we say, now come!

Rain heard —Umbrella's held up by every body.

Curtain descends to "Long reign over us."

END

---

361 **Louis Philippe** Louis Philippe I, King of France between 1830 and 1848. He was the last king to rule France and he was forced to abdicate and live in exile.
Tuileries the Tuileries Palace in Paris, which was the residence of King Louis Philippe.

367 **spades** one of the four suits in a pack of playing cards (*OED*, *n*. 2) and a tool consisting of an iron blade used for digging (*OED*, *n*. 1).

370 **in check** 'under restriction of freedom of movement or action, under control' (*OED*, *int.* and *n*. 1, B.9b).

374 **good friends** audience. Final address to the audience following the conventions of burlesque.

376 **house of entertainment** in this case, the New Strand Theatre, where *Antigone Travestie* was first performed.

379 **Wild** George Wild, interpreter of Antigone.
Hall Harry Hall, interpreter of Creon.

Textual notes

1 SP] <u>1st Div.</u>
3 SP] <u>2nd Div.</u>
6 let's] let
48 £5] 5£
58 Athenaeum] *(*Atheneum*)*
60 SD] <u>Exit Antig.</u>
62 SD] <u>Exit Ismene</u>
95 recounting] *(*recountin*)*
124 its] it
227 Antigone, who] Antigone who
228 status quo] *(*statu quo*)*
231 three] *(*3*)*
two] *(*2*)*
236 ceiling] *(*cieling*)*
260 SD] <u>Exit Antigone.</u>
361 Tuileries] *(*Tuilleries*)*

3

Alcestis, the Original Strong-Minded Woman

Francis Talfourd

(1850)

Alcestis, the Original Strong-Minded Woman was first staged at the Strand Theatre in London on 4 July 1850. The present edition is based on the 1850 printed copy published at Thomas Hailes Lacy, collated with the bound LC manuscript, BL Add MS 43028 ff.633–653, held at the Lord Chamberlain's Plays Collection at the British Library.

Francis Talfourd

Francis Talfourd (1828–1862), son of the playwright and politician Thomas Noon Talfourd, was educated first at Eton College (1841–1845) and then matriculated at Oxford in 1845. Member of Christ Church, he founded, together with Brasenose graduate W. C. Bedford, The Oxford Dramatic Amateurs, by which many burlesques were put on. For example, while at Oxford, he staged *Macbeth Travestie* at the Henley Regatta of 1847, where he played the role of Lady Macbeth. The travesty was staged again in 1848 at the Strand Theatre and revived in 1849 at the Royalty Theatre in London, and at the Olympic in 1853. Frank Talfourd wrote for various theatres in London and some of his most representative classical burlesques are *Alcestis, the Original Strong-Minded Woman* (Strand, 1850) and *Electra in a New Electric Light* (Haymarket, 1859); he also produced *Thetis and Peleus* (Strand, 1851) with W. P. Hale, *Atalanta, or the Three Golden Apples* (Haymarket, 1857) and *Pluto and Proserpine; or, The Belle and the Pomegranate* (Haymarket, 1858).

Manuscript paratext

f. 633

License sent

June 30. 1850

WBD

Alcestis Travestie

A Classical Burlesque in One Act

Proposed day of Representation

Thursday July 4th 1850

New Strand Theatre

W. Farren

Manager

f. 634

Alcestis Travestie

A Classical Burlesque in one act

being a most shamelefs misinterpretation

of the Greek Drama of Euripides

By

Characters Misrepresented

Apollo—

Orcus—

Hercules—

Admetus—

Polax—

Alcestis—

Phoedra—

Two Children—

Lacy's edition paratext

ALCESTIS,
THE ORIGINAL
STRONG-MINDED WOMAN:
A CLASSICAL BURLESQUE
IN ONE ACT.
BEING
A MOST SHAMELESS MISINTERPRETATION OF
THE GREEK DRAMA OF EURIPIDES
[*First Performed at the Strand Theatre, July*, 4, 1850.]

BY THE AUTHOR OF
THE TRAVESTIES OF 'MACBETH', AND THE 'MERCHANT OF VENICE',
'MAMMON AND GAMMON,' 'NUMBER ONE A.,' BY SPECIAL
APPOINTMENT, '&C.

ALCESTIS,
THE ORIGINAL STRONG-MINDED WOMAN.

AS PERFORMED AT THE STRAND THEATRE.

CHARACTERS MISREPRESENTED.

APOLLO *the original 'Sir Oracle',* —Miss Adams.
ORCUS *or Death; his first appearance in so early a stage—an infernal god, and an infernal nuisance* —Mr. H. Farren.
HERCULES *a hero whose address was well known at his* club. —Mr. W. Farren.
ADMETUS *an individual weak in intellect, and not 'recommended by any Faculty.'* —Mr. Compton
POLAX *inspector of Pellise, and Petticoats, as usual of the 'Hτα division.* — Mr. W. Shalders.
ALCESTIS *the regular Greek Play heroine, rigidly correct, and perfectly Classical.* —Mrs. L. Murray.
PHOEDRA *a servant of all works, and no play; taken up by the Policeman aforesaid*—Mrs. A. Phillips.
TWO CHILDREN *very bad characters, as they have nothing to say for themselves*—Misses Sharp and Gilbert.

SCENE—*Pherea, in Thessaly*
TIME—*Old enough to know better.*

The PLOT, which has been thought an eligible plot for
building one story on, is therefore mainly referable to
the injured poet above mentioned, and may be thus
briefly described. Admetus, being due to Death, and as
such totally unprepared to take himself up, is about   40
to betake himself down, according to previous
arrangement, when Orcus, who had been meanwhile

15 STRONG-MINDED WOMAN see pp. 33–36.
16 The manager at the Strand was William Farren, who signed the manuscript to be sent to the Lord Chamberlain's office, and William B. Donne. Donne's initials are on f. 633 of the MS.
18 *Oracle* Apollo was the prophetic deity of the Delphic Oracle. See *Antigone*, 288n.
Miss Adams probably the same Miss Adams who in October the same year was performing farces and dramas at the Olympic Theatre, where the Farrrens moved after a period at the Strand.
21 **Mr. H. Farren** Henry Farren (1827–1860), actor. Son of the actor William Farren and his companion Harriet Elizabeth Saville, Mrs Faucit. Also father of Nellie Farren, a famous actress. Henry Farren made his début in London at the Haymarket in *The School for Scandal*. In the spring of 1849 he briefly managed the New Strand Theatre which was soon left to the hands of his father. His father William Farren was manager of the New Strand when *Alcestis* was put on stage in July 1850. In September, Henry moved to the Olympic with his elder brother, where he essayed some heavier roles in dramas and tragedies. He also managed the Theatre Royal at Brighton and acted at Sadler's Wells, London, before sailing to America. In the United States he was also successful as a performer and manager (*ODNB*, Lewes).
23 **Mr. W. Farren** (1825–1908) reviews of the play refer to W. Farren junior (i.e. *Bell's Life in London and Sporting Chronicle*, 7 July 1850, p. 3), Henry Farren's elder brother. In the spring of 1849 he was successfully acting at the Strand under the name Forrester until September 1849, when he used his own name. He also moved to the Olympic with his father and brother Henry in 1850. In 1853 he first appeared at the Haymarket, where he acted until 1867. He also acted for the Vaudeville, the St. James's Theatre and the Aquarium, among others (*ODNB*, Lewes).
25 **Mr. Compton** (real name Charles Mackenzie, 1805–1877), actor. In his early years he was apprenticed to a maternal uncle, a cloth merchant near London. His first theatrical engagement was at Lewes, then as a member of the Bedford circuit he adopted Compton as his stage name. He specialized in low-comedy roles and his first début in London was at the English Opera House (Lyceum) in 1837. In the 1840s he was renowned for his Shakespearian clown roles. In 1847 he performed at the Olympic, where he remained for three years and then migrated to the Strand. His best remembered engagement was at the Haymarket of John B. Buckstone (*ODNB*).
27 'Hτα *division* by the mid-nineteenth century the police forces divided the conurbation into divisions. This refers to the H division (ἤτα division), which became famous by the late 1880s because of the Whitechapel murders attributed to Jack the Ripper.
27 **Mr. W. Shalders** scene painter who worked with Compton and Leigh Murray at the Olympic under the tenancy of William Farren. He also specialized as a low comedian (*London as it is*, 216). His two abilities were seen in *Alcestis*.
29 **Mrs L. Murray** Elizabeth Leigh Murray (1815–1892) was the wife of the actor Henry Leigh Murray (Henry Leigh Wilson), and second daughter of the playwright Henry Lee. She first appeared on stage in her early childhood and her début in London was at Madame Vestris' Olympic. She played at Covent Garden and in many provincial theatres. In 1850 she was Apollo in Francis Talfourd's *Diogenes and his Lantern*, first performed at the Strand Theatre in February.
31 **Mrs. A. Phillips** Mrs Alfred Philips, actress and playwright, author of *An Organic Affection*. As a playwright she wrote 'quite specialized roles for herself' (Newey, 'Women', p. 198). She was Lady Macbeth in Thomas Talfourd's burlesque of *Macbeth* at the Olympic.
34 *Pherae* Admetus was king of Pherae, in Thessaly.
42 **arrangement** see List of Roles, 3n.

trying his mean wiles upon Alcestis (Admetus' very much better half,) expressed himself willing to receive her as a substitute; her husband, friends and relations, not feeling quite so dispossessed to be disposed of. Alcestis however consents, packs up her own traps, and then obligingly goes packing down those of Orcus. At this melancholy juncture, Hercules chances to be passing through Thessaly, on his return from his provincial engagements; and having a knack of turning up a trump at a *rub*, plays his club so judiciously as to retake the Queen, in spite of the deuce, and restores her to her family and friends.

The Scenes, being the work of Mr. W. Shalders, need but be seen to be appreciated, and will be all his fancy painted them. It is hoped that the piece will be no less in drawing. For the *Costumes*, Messrs. Nathan have undertaken to give all the characters a proper *dressing*. The (*special*) Appointments which have been made by Mr. Mc. Ginn, will be strictly kept –in the Property Room; and the effect of the Music will doubtless be electrical through so able a conductor as Mr. J. Barnard.

50-1 **provincial engagements** Herakles is fulfilling his labours in Euripides. Herakles shared the characteristics of a god and a hero and was a significant traveller.

58 **Messrs. Nathan** well-known costume designer in Victorian London (*Dickens's Dictionary*).

59 **proper** *dressing* burlesque was highly anachronistic. As exemplified with the character of Polax, the 'proper dressing' for this burlesque was probably a mixture of classically inspired costumes, following the tradition of the toga plays, and contemporary attires.

List of Roles

APOLLO	*the Oracle*	
ORCUS	*death*	
ADMETUS	*husband of Alcestis*	
ALCESTIS	*wife to Admetus*	
POLAX	*an inspector of police*	5
PHOEDRA	*a servant*	
HERCULES	*a hero*	

Two Children

---

1 APOLLO 'One of the chief gods of Greek mythology; Olympian god of prophecy, of the arts and sciences, of medicine, of shepherds and animal husbandry, and since the 5th century BCE also the sun god' (Grafton, Most, Settis, *Classical*, p. 54). The character is here performed in a transvestite role by Miss Adams.

2 ORCUS God of the underworld in Roman mythology.

3 ADMETUS King of Pherae and husband of Alcestis. At their marriage, Admetus forgets to sacrifice to Artemis and finds his nuptial chamber full of snakes, a sign of imminent death. Admetus obtains the concession that someone may die in his place, though when he makes his request of his closest relations, he finds only his wife Alcestis is willing to make the sacrifice. Herakles will save her from death. Admetus is also a model for Greek hospitality.

4 ALCESTIS Daughter of Pelias and wife of Admetus. Pelias promised her daughter to the man who would yoke a lion and a boar to a chariot. Admetus won her with the aid of Apollo. The myth is best known from Euripides' *Alcestis*. She has been considered a model for the dutiful, self-sacrificing wife.

5 POLAX Not in Euripides. Being an inspector of police, the name is probably a pun with 'poleaxe', 'poleax'. Originally, a poleaxe was a weapon for use in close combat; later it also referred to weapons of this kind used ceremonially by the bodyguard of a monarch or great personage (*OED*, *n*. 1). It also referred to the axe used by loggers, carpenters, firefighters and butchers (*OED*, *n*. 2, 3). Polax is also an inspector of 'pellise', petticoats, young women.

6 PHOEDRA Alcestis' servant in Euripides. The two servants in the Greek tragedy are reduced here to the comic characters of Polax and Phoedra to emphasize the humorous nature of the play.

7 HERCULES The Latin for Herakles, the greatest of Greek heroes. He shared the characteristics of a hero and a god. Chief events of Herakles' life are the Twelve Labours (see 446n.). As an infant he killed the two serpents which were sent by Hera to attack him in Thebes. Later she drove him mad causing him to kill his wife, Megara, and their children. He also took part in the expedition to Troy and founded the Olympic games.

8 TWO CHILDREN Alcestis' children. Eumelus is a speaking character in Euripides yet they are both mute characters in the burlesque.

[1.1]

Before the house of Admetus. A modern area practicable (L.H.) Practicable door and steps. (R.H.) Upon the door plate in Greek characters is seen Μρ Αδμητος —and also 'πλεασε τὸ ῥιγγ θὲ βελλ.'

Enter APOLLO *L.*

APOLLO

    Ladies and Gentlemen, I am Apollo—   1
    Although I frankly own it doesn't follow
    From my costume; no matter, let that be,
    Although in hat and hessians, I am he.
    The fact is, 'twixt ourselves, I plainly see it is   5
    All up with us—this age don't care for deities.
    And with our attributes there's no deceiving it,
    My lyre for instance—people don't *believe* in it.
    The vulgar rabble's wiser than the sages
    Of those delightful green old middle ages.   10
    Then they respected altars! ah! things I trow
    In every respect are altered now!
    My oracles don't get, upon my word,
    A common hearing from the common herd—
    Not e'en a votive kid, much less a nice   15
    "Go-in at a tremendous sacrifice."
    Our temples, which were crowned in former day
    With leaves of laurel, now they leaves, and say
    They won't *give laurel* where they can't *o-bey*.
    With votaries the shrine's no longer thronged,   20
    And grievously our sacred rites are wronged,
    By men who, changing all their vows to cursings,
    Begin to talk about the "rights of persons"—
    If this goes on much longer, for myself, I
    Must really give up trade, and shut up Delphi.   25
    But who comes here? Ah! Orcus, how d'ye do?

Enter ORCUS *L. U.*

ORCUS

    I'm pretty well, and who the deuce are you?

APOLLO

    Not know Apollo! have you lost your eyes?

ORCUS

    If you're Apollo I apologize.

APOLLO

    Well, and what brings you here? for I must say   30
    That Death should walk in the broad face of day,
    And chat in a familiar off-hand way,
    Really appears to me an impropriety
    Which would be scouted in genteel society.

ORCUS

    Of what's correct all know Apollo's nice sense,   35
    But being *Orcus* I've a *'Awker's* licence.

APOLLO

    And what's the object that you have in view?

0.1 SD 'Mr Admetos' and 'Please to ring the bell' in Greek characters.
     practicable 'usable, as opposed to painted on' (*OED*, *adj.* and *n.*).
0.2 SD 'Please to ring the bell' in Greek characters.
1–26 Apollo's soliloquy reflects upon the deeply rooted Victorian practice of prophesying and fortune-telling. The god regrets how gipsies and popular sages of the time, such as Old Moore and Zadkiel, have replaced old beliefs and customs. His going against 'the rights of persons' (l.23) represents the reactionary circles of the mid-nineteenth century which resist social reforms. The function of Apollo's prologue in Euripides' *Alcestis* is to introduce the plot to the audience.
3 **From my costume** Victorian burlesque was highly anachronistic. Apollo here alludes to a costume which probably puts together elements of the classical toga plays with contemporary outfits.
4 **hessians** short for 'Hessian boots'; boots from Hesse in Germany (*OED*, *adj.* and *n.*[1]). They were popular both in military and civilian fashion by the late eighteenth century and eclipsed by Wellington boots by the 1820s (Moore and Haynes, *Clothing*, pp. 190–191). References to 'Hessian boots' abound in the literature of the time; they are mentioned, for example, in William Makepeace Thackeray's *Vanity Fair* (1847).
8 **lyre** the lyre, the quiver and arrows are common attributes of Apollo. The lyre represents Apollo as the patron of poets.
13 **oracles** see *Antigone*, 288n.
23 **"rights of persons"** treatises on education, the law, and on the rights of the individual abound in the eighteenth and nineteenth centuries. An influential text, for example, was Sir William Blackstone's *The Commentaries on the Laws of England* (1765–1769), which included a section on the rights of persons that was later reprised by nineteenth-century thinkers such as James Stewart in 1839.
25 **Delphi** see 13n.
36 **'Awker's licence** licence for selling goods in the street. *''Awker'*, hawker unaspirated as mispronounced missing off the 'h'; a street vendor (*OED*, *n.*[2]).

ORCUS
>   Well, as a friend, I don't mind telling you—
>   I— I am in love!

APOLLO   You take away my breath!
>   Is love a "ruling passion strong in death?"   40
>   And might I venture to enquire her name?
>   *Blonde* or *Brunette*?

ORCUS   Well, *lightish* for a *flame*.

APOLLO
>   Another? well—opinions differ so—
>   I thought that you had flames enough below.
>   But, pardon me, proceed to revelation   45
>   Of the fair maid's cognominal appellation.
>   In plainer words, you have forgot her name.

ORCUS
>   Alcestis.

APOLLO   Not Admetus' wife?

ORCUS   The same.

APOLLO
>   What, is she due already?

ORCUS   No, not yet
>   But if she choose to pay her husband's debt   50
>   In *propriâ personâ*—eh—dy'e see?
>   I'll take her down instead of him, with me.
>   Else, like a detonator, down he goes,
>   To pay the *debt o'natur* which he owes! —
>   Don't interrupt—my mind's made up—I've sworn it,   55
>   And, for the weakness that relents, I scorn it.

APOLLO
>   Forgive him.

ORCUS   What would of my word be thought then?

APOLLO
>   You'd *let him off* were't not for the *report* then?

ORCUS
>   Mind your own business, and leave me to mine,
>   Or, since it seems you can't refrain from prying   60

    Where you're not wanted—know, I mean to carry her
    To my domains, where, spite of you, I'll marry her.

APOLLO

    If you persist in these uncouth expressions
    I'd not for something occupy your hessians.
    However we won't quarrel—there's my hand,   65
    But, if I can I foil you—understand.

ORCUS

    The friendly strife I'm ready to begin,
    With all my heart, and may the best man win!

SONG

Standard Bearer.

    Though you appear the model minstrel knight,
        I'm King of Night, and you won't catch me sleeping,   70
    So, interfering with my vested right,
        I'll see if I can't make you pay for peeping!
    The lady owns to me a higher claim,
        You shan't redeem for nought that long pledged token,
    And e'er you put me out, and win my flame,   75
    My compact or your head shall first be broken   *Exeunt severally.*

Enter ADMETUS, *very dejected, from the house;*
he has a long pipe in his hand, and slowly advances to the front.

---

40 **"ruling … death"** quoted from Alexander Pope's *Moral Essays* (1731–1735) (Ep. I, l.262).
44 **below** the underworld.
46 **cognominal** having the same name (*OED*, *adj.* and *n.*).
51 *in propriâ personâ* in one's own person or character.

68.2 SD Common song of the period usually sung in military contexts. Later versions include, for example, 'The Standard Bearer Quadrille', composed by Jullien on Herr Pischer's songs from the 'Deutche Lyra' (M&N Hanhart, ca.1860), and 'The Standard Bearer', composed by Phillip Fahrbach Junr (London: Riviere & Hawkes, ca. 1890). In the United States, 'The Standard Bearer' became a Civil War song.
76 **compact** 'a covenant or contract made between two or more people or parties' (*OED*, *n.*¹).

ADMETUS

    Oh what a night of mourning I have passed;
But, thank the stars, they've disappeared at last.
I thought with light my heaviness would cease,
Yet the day's *broken* and I find no *peace*.   80
My pipe's my only consolation now,
And I will clear my pipes and tell you how.

(*Sings.*)

AIR

Billy Nutts the Poet.

    On all hands be this truth allowed,
        Experience must show it:
When life's o'ershadowed by a cloud   85
        The only way's to *blow it*!
It has been my cure, if other folk
        Would only deign to try it,
The cares of life would end in smoke,
        Let him, who can, deny it.   90
Of pain they'd take a *bird's eye* view,
        Of grief feel no returns, sirs,
For care not care a single *screw*,
        And disappointment spurn, sirs!
With every ill the effect is the same,   95
        Whatever cause may rack ye—
The widower might his *weeds* disclaim,
        And sing out 'I O Backy'!
        Then on all hands, &c.
Some with the juicy grape their cares bid go forth,   100
And sing "Fill up the sparkling bowl," and so forth—
"Fill up the meerschaum bowl"'s my only cry;
I eye my pipe, and then I pipe my eye:

For e'en that fails to chase my fears away,
The die is cast, and I must die to day! 105
I can't pretend—and he's a fool who would—
Bear death at forty-two with fortitu-de;
Yet I am in for it, I must confess,
With no great chance of getting out, unless
Some friend were here to serve me with his wit. 110

Enter ORCUS *L.*

ORCUS

I as your friend can serve you—with this writ;
Nay, don't be frightened—It is only I—
Your little bill, sir, of mortality (*presenting it*)

ADMETUS

Oh curse it!

ORCUS Spare your curses, my young spark,

ADMETUS

I merely made a cursory remark. 115

(*He takes the Bill and looks at it.*)

ORCUS

Ah! look at it. I fancy e'en your skill
Can't find a flaw there.

ADMETUS To your little bill
I am no stranger, though I never *meet* it.

ORCUS

It has been long standing.

82.3 SD Comic song written by John Martin, printed by Bebbington Printer, Manchester and sold by J. Beaumont, Leeds, ca. 1855–1858 (Labern, *Comic*, p. 160).

98 **Backy** tobacco (*OED*, *n.*³), pun with 'weeds' (l.87) as tobacco and clothes of mourning. Also 'ἰὼ Βάκχε' vocative innovation to Bacchus, here Backy.

101 "**Fill … bowl**" from William Hazlitt's *Table Talk* (1821), a collection of essays on various topics such as art, literature and philosophy.

102 **meerschaum** a mineral resembling clay (*OED*, *n.* 1). The 'meerschaum pipe' was a tobacco pipe 'having a bowl made of meerschaum' (*OED*, *n.* 2).

ADMETUS   Standing? pray *re-seat* it;
    Or if you think such proposition strange,   120
    We'll let it *run* a little for a change.

ORCUS
    It's very well to talk, but these facetiae,
    However specious, won't supply the specie—
    I'm no great talker, so with me to sup
    You must stump down, sir, if you can't *stump up*.   125
    (*Admetus kneels to Orcus who repulses him. Orcus sings.*)

Woodman spare that Tree.

    My good man, spare thy knee,
    Make not one single bow,
    Thy youth won't shelter thee,
    I mean to have you now!
    I've a conveyance here at hand   130
    To take you from this spot—
    My good man, you'd better stand,
    Your *axe-ings* touch me not!

Enter ALCESTIS, *from the house, she advances*
majestically down the stage, and stands between them.

ALCESTIS
    Hey! Hoity-toity, what on earth's the matter,
    That in the public street you make a clatter?   135
    (*to Admetus*) Explain, what means this? how the ninny quakes;
    Till now I always thought him "no great shakes."

ADMETUS
    Why I've discovered in our empty till
    A disability to pay his bill;
    Can't settle the account: and so you see   140
    Must go to the account which settles me.

ORCUS

    (*aside*) To curb my rising love I idly tries,

    I eyes the idol that I idolize!

ALCESTIS

    (*to Orcus*) Good Mr. Death, find something else to do,

    Than suing one who is not worth a sou.   145

ADMETUS

    At least a moment suffer me to lag,

    To cram a few things in a carpet bag.

    (*Orcus signifies in the negative.*)

    A hair and tooth brush in a sac-de nuit.

ORCUS

    I'm very sorry, but it cannot be;

    Such things you'll find no use for, though you may, sir,   150

    When *sunk so low*, be glad p'rhaps of a *raiser*.

ADMETUS

    My plaintive tears your hands bedew, you see.

ORCUS

    You may be *dew*, indeed are *due* to me,

    And so *a-dieu* to life.

ADMETUS   Yet hear me.

ORCUS   Nay:

    I want no prayers, I only claim my prey.   155

    You've but one chance—a poor one—can you find

    A greater fool than you are, who's inclined

    To take your place, and in your stead to go?

    I'll wait for you another year or so.

---

122 **facetiae** 'Humorous sayings or writings' (*OED*, *n.*).

123 **specious** plausible arguments yet fallacious (*OED*, *adj.* 3b).

125 ***stump up*** pay down (*OED*, *v.*¹, 17b).

125.2 SD Well-known poem by the American editor and songwriter George Pope Morris (1802–1864). Initially published in the New York *Mirror* as 'The Oak' in 1837.

145 **sou** French coin that designated the five-centime piece (*OED*, *n.*).

148 **sac-de nuit** a night-bag, a travelling bag (*OED*, *n.*).

152 **bedew** 'to wet or moisten gently or by drops' (*OED*, *v.* 2).

ADMETUS
>You're very good—I've tried it on, but most of 160
>My friends don't seem disposed to be disposed of
>At such a sacrifice: my father e'en,
>Though in a green old age, was not so green,
>But instantly the proposition flouted,
>And mother didn't seem to care about it. 165
>How true, that when misfortune overtake us,
>The whole 'Society of Friends' are *Quakers*.

ORCUS
>Yet, why thus the inevitable step shun?
>I'll promise you below a warm reception.

ADMETUS
>Yes, but your warmth I fear 's all of the wrong sort. 170
>(*to Alcestis*) Have you no *voice*, dear, for your *mourning* consort?

ALCESTIS
>What can I urge? yet stay, I've half a mind
>To do the heroine I (*to Orcus*) suppose I were inclined
>To close with you.

ORCUS
>   I've time for supposing,
>I am an advocate for *'early closing'*. 175

ALCESTIS
>Well, since he hasn't pluck then to go through it,
>My mind's made up—never say die—I'll do it!

ORCUS
>You'll take his place; that's odd.

ALCESTIS
>   'Tis *even* so

ADMETUS
>I'm stupefied!

ALCESTIS
>   You hadn't far to go.

ORCUS
>Well, I embrace your offer.

ADMETUS (*to Alcestis*)   And I you, 180
>My tears resolve themselves into *a-dieu*.
>Alcestis, love, I cannot find the heart
>With one so captivating e'er to part!

ALCESTIS
>I may be captivating, but Death stronger
>Will not be *kept-a-vaiting* any longer. 185

ADMETUS
>Go, then; and, better to indulge my grief,
>I'll fetch another pocket handkerchief. *Exit into the house.*

ORCUS
>(*to Alcestis*) You're ready?

ALCESTIS
>How are we to go, old chap?

ORCUS
>Oh! never fear, I drive you in my *trap*.

ALCESTIS
>I must go packing down your trap, and so 190
>You'll let me pack up my traps ere I go?
>And grant me a few minutes, I beseech,
>For the delivery of my maiden speech.
>'Tis usual.

ORCUS
>I'll give you in that case,
>If it is meet, say half-an-hour's *grace*. *Exit. L. H.* 195

ALCESTIS
>'Tis done, the very ferry boat I see,
>And Charon, who's to take such care on me.

---

163 **green old age** 'an old age that is full of vitality' (*OED*, *adj.* and *n.*[1], P2)

167 **'Society ... Quakers**. The Society of Friends is the formal title of the Quaker movement, a religious group which began in England in the seventeenth century.

175 **'early closing'** The 'Early Closing Movement' sought to free clerks from late evening hours. In 1871 the Early Closing Movement and Bank Holidays Act established restrictions to working hours.

176 **pluck** explicit allusion to Admetus' cowardice. See pp. 33-36 for an analysis of strong-minded women.

189 **trap** both 'small carriage on springs' (*OED*, *n.*[1], 7), trap door on stage (*OED*, *n.*[3]), and belongings (*OED*, *n.*[7]). See lines 190, 191, 412 and 422. See p. 32.

193 **maiden speech** 'the first speech delivered in the House of Commons or the House of Lords by a new member, or to any such assembly by a new member of that assembly' (*OED*, 'maiden', *n.* and *adj.*) Furthermore, as a classical heroine, and also following in the line of the she-tragedies of the seventeenth and eighteenth centuries, Alcestis here alludes to the expectations of the audience for the speech of the heroine. Such metatheatrical references abound in Victorian burlesque.

193-221 and also 248-407 adapt some well-known passages in Euripides such as allusions to Charon (l.252-256), Hades and her offspring (l.260-263) in the lyrical dialogue with Admetus, and Alcestis' own *rhesis* (l.280-325).

197 **Charon** he ferries the souls of the deceased across the Styx in Hades.

E'en now in fancy I'm across the Styx,
And now I'm nothing, literally *Nick's*.

(*Sings.*)

AIR

The Waterman.

For, of course you have heard of that jolly old waterman, 200
    Who o'er Styx is accustomed to ply—
He feathers his oars with much skill and dexterity,
    Rowing the parties who're going to die.
    He looks out so sharp, and he reckons so steadily,
        That none can escape, go they ne'er so unreadily: 205
    And he eyes all us gals with so greedy an air,
    That this waterman ne'er gives a chance to a fair.

AIR

Nix my dolly.

In the boat of that old muff' I am borne,
There a premature widow I sit forlorn,
    (*to orchestra*) Scrape away! 210
    My noble husband, now, I dare say,
Thinks he's nothing to do but cut capers gay,
While Nick my body will take away,
    Nick my body will take away.
But I don't so much care, for some fine day 215
Folks will dub me a heroine, I dare say
        In a play,
And I as a martyr shall chronicled be,
As the heroine great of some trage-dee;
    So Nick my body may take away, 220
        Nick my body may take away! *Exit into the house.*

(*Polax is heard outside. L.H.*)

POLAX

    Move on, there! don't stand blocking up the street.

Enter, (L. H.) he is habited in a classic dress, with the exception of his hat,
    cape, and staff, which are those of a modern policeman.

    I've ventured a few yards beyond my beat;
    The fact is that I can't withstand the looks
    Of Phoedra, handsomest of all *plain* cooks.   225
    Romeo's soliloquy to slightly vary,
    I do remember an approximate arey,
    And thereabouts she dwells, a thrifty elf,
    On seven pounds a year, and finds herself
    In tea and sugar, from which fact I'm led   230
    To fear my Phoedra is n't over-fed.
    In her small kitchen dries a reindeer's tongue
    Suspended from a book, and by it hung
    Are other ill-made dishes; on the drawers, sirs,
    A beggarly account of cups and saucers,   235
    With earthen pots and pans; while in the dresser
    She keeps the love-letters I write her—bless her!
    Remnants of finery—a half-knitted cuff,

---

198   **Styx** river that links the earth with the underworld in Greek mythology.

199   **And ... nothing,** reference to l.391 in Euripides' *Alcestis*. Part of the last words of the heroine before going to Hades.
    Nick's 'the devil' (*OED, n.*²). Also pun with 'nix', 'nothing, nobody' (*OED*, B. *n.*¹, a).

199.2   SD Song from the homonymous ballad opera by Charles Dibdin (1745–1814) first performed at the Haymarket in 1774.

207.2   SD Song in *Jack Sheppard*, a drama by John Baldwin Buckstone, first performed at the Adelphi in 1839 (Nicoll, *History*, IV, p. 275).

210   **Scrape away!** 'Used disparagingly for "to play a fiddle"' (*OED, v.* 6).

218–19   Alluding to the establishment of a ritual in Athens and Sparta, the chorus in Euripides claims that Alcestis will inspire hymns by the servants of the Muses in lines 446–454 of the tragedy.

222   SD Costume was a major device to build the anachronistic contrasts that fill the burlesque stage.

226   **Romeo** Romeo's soliloquy must have been easily recognisable by the audience (see Norwood 2012 for a list of performances of Shakespeare's plays in the period). Furthermore, refigurations of the tragedy were widely performed during the nineteenth century including Hector Berlioz's dramatic symphony *Romeo and Juliet* in 1827, the comic *Romeo and Juliet Travestie* by Andrew Halliday (Strand, 1859) and Maurice Dowling's *Romeo and Juliet: 'As the Law Directs'* (1837). (Marshall, *Shakespeare*; Schoch, *Not Shakespeare*; Young, *Punch*).

227   **arey** array, order (*OED, n.*).

And that peculiar substance, kitchen stuff,
Composed of candle ends—indeed whate'er 240
The family inconveniently can't spare.
Her Sunday bonnet too, although I doubt
She doesn't often get a Sunday out!

SONG— AIR

Rumpti Bumpti.

I'm monarch of all I survey,
    My will there is none dare dispute, 245
From street organ and image boy's tray,
    To the bag-pipes and cracked German Flute.
If apple-woman dare me to annoy,
    Vending oranges, apples, or pears
There is nothing I so much enjoy, 250
    As to pop on her wares—unawares!
Although I object to street fights,
    And vote burglary rather a bore,
On a boy hall my size I delights
    To exert the strong arm of the law— 255
        For I'm monarch, &c.

And, if I don't mistake, the house is here;
At any rate, I'll try it (*Calls.*) Phoedra, dear!

(*Phoedra appears at the area gate, opens it, and comes down.*)

PHOEDRA
    Who calls so loud?
POLAX
              One who's allowed to call.
PHOEDRA
    Why make a *rout*, then, when you give a *bawl*? 260
POLAX
    Phoedra, I have observed of late, with pain,
    Your constant swaying from your constant swain,
    And, though I do not wish to be censorious—

PHOEDRA

    What? You are jealous, are you? This is glorious!

POLAX

    I don't half like those Sunday evening walks—   265

PHOEDRA

    But you can't think how prettily he talks!

POLAX

    Flattery's his profession—I see through it—
    He's bred to butter, and of course he'll do it.
    A cook should be a cook, not a coquette.

PHOEDRA

    I don't intend to give it up though yet.   270

SONG —AIR

I'm afloat.

    I'm a flirt, I'm a flirt, yet on thirty's bright side,
    And numbers have offered to make me their bride;
    Yet though suitors don't flag in attention to me,
    I'm a flirt, I'm a flirt, and my hand is yet free!
    I turn up my nose at the gent and young lord,   275

243.2   SD 'rumty iddity' refers to a meaningless refrain (*OED*, *int.* and *n.*). 'Rumpti Bumpti' was a popular song of the period and was also sung by Gratiano in Talfourd's *The Merchant of Venice Travestie: A Burlesque in One Act* (1849).

244–56   Lyrics adapted from the poem 'Verses supposed to be written by Alexander Selkirk, during his solitary abode in the Island of Juan Fernánez' (1782) by William Cowper. Cowper's poem made the phrase 'monarch of all I survey' famous. Selkirk (1676–1721) was a Scottish sailor who lived as a castaway on a remote island in the South Pacific Ocean.

247   **German Flute** 'A musical instrument, consisting of a hollow cylinder or pipe, with holes along its length, stopped by the fingers, or keys which are opened by the fingers. The flute of the ancients, whether single or double, was blown through a mouthpiece at the end. About the middle of the eighteenth century this was entirely superseded by the *transverse flute* or *German flute*, which is blown through an orifice at the side' (*OED*, 'flute', $n.^1$, a).

248   **apple-woman** 'now rare and hist. A woman or girl who sells apples especially from a stall.' (*OED*, 'apple', *n.*)

248–407   See 193–221n.

259   **Who ... loud?** after William Shakespeare's *Romeo and Juliet* V.i.

266   **he** unclear. There is no other known second suitor to Phoedra in the play.

270.2   SD Adapted from 'I'm Afloat! I'm Afloat', song by Henry Russell with lyrics by Eliza Cook published in the 1840s. The original song follows in the line of sailor and marine warfare songs that fill the play.

> Though by their attentions I'm constantly bored;
> And ne'er as a wife at the altar I'll kneel,
> While my eyes carry fire, and my heart remains steel!
> In all that I do, I consult my own mind,
> And I warrant I leave all the slow girls behind; 280
> For, though puppies don't flag, no, nor waver, you see
> I'm a flirt, I'm a flirt and my hand yet is free!
>
> But since you take to schooling others, pray sir,
> What has detained you such a time away, sir?
> I haven't seen you for a week.

POLAX   So long?   285

> Come—not a week—that's coming it too strong, —
> But by you—anything you please—I vow—

PHOEDRA

> Your vows are not the slightest matter now;
> A pretty state your pretty protestations
> Have brought me to—with such acts I've no patience. 290
> The fire you kindled in my breast forsaking,
> You've put out now, sir, by your constant *raking*.

POLAX

> Nay, you mistake, nought can my ardour change.

PHOEDRA

> Such fire comes not within my kitchen range
> Of intellect, so best at once we part. 295

POLAX

> Nay, let me follow suit dear to your *heart*.

PHOEDRA

> But I prefer another, therefore, sir,
> I must *discard* the suit which you *prefer*,
> Who are a shuffler and a double dealer.

POLAX

> (*kneeling*) Hear the appeal of an appealing 'Peeler.' 300

PHOEDRA

> Nonsense! your useless courtship better cease, man.

POLAX

    Be not a 'crusher' to your fond policeman!
    See, here I kneel, the picture of despair!

PHOEDRA

    Picture by *Constable*, extremely rare!

POLAX

    Nay, cruel Phoedra, hear me, do you choose   305
    My head should illustrate some Grecian *noose*?
    Yes, yes, since you of pity know no sense,
    Better at once be hanged than in *suspense*:
    A cord will sweetly end my mind's distraction.

PHOEDRA

    In legal phrase, '*a-cord* and satisfaction.'   310

POLAX

    But hearken, my death at your door I'll lay.

PHOEDRA

    Then in the morning 'twill be swept away.

POLAX

    And can you laugh? I'll stab myself, and go
    A groaning ghost down to the shades below!

PHOEDRA

    Poor ghost! you'll stab yourself, and be, of course,   315
    In-spectre of the *stab-you-lary* force.

296–9 In these lines Phoedra plays with lexicon related both to love plots and to card games. For example, 'suit' is both 'wooing or courting a woman' (*OED*, *n*. II.12) and 'any of the four sets of which a pack of playing-cards consists' (*OED*, *n*. V, 20a). Also, a 'shuffler' is both 'one who acts in a shifty or evasive manner; a slippery, shifty person' (*OED*, *n*. 2) and 'one who shuffles cards' (*OED*, *n*. 4).

300 **'Peeler'** 'Originally: a member of the Irish constabulary. Later: a police officer, spec. a member of the original London Metropolitan force' (*OED*, *n*.³). Sir Robert Peel (1788–1850) helped to develop the body of the police force while Home Secretary.

302 **'crusher'** slang: policeman (*OED*, *n*.⁴).

304 **Constable** John Constable (1776–1837), English Romantic painter known for his landscape scenes.

310 **'a-cord and satisfaction.'** Law. An agreement to accept something in exchange for giving up the right of action (*OED*, 'accord', *n*.). Also pun with a cord, a rope.

314 **ghost** ghosts were recurring characters in nineteenth-century theatre as they allowed the display of various scenic effects. See, for example, *Ruddigore; or the Witches Curse* by W. S. Gilbert (1887).

316 **stab-you-lary** pun with 'stab' and also with 'constabulary', 'belonging to the official organization for the preservation of public peace and order' (*OED*, *adj*.).

POLAX

    Look kindly on me—I'll be evermore
    Your constant swain.

PHOEDRA   You'd be a constant bore.

POLAX

    But to be plain with you—

PHOEDRA   That's no great feat,
    You must be *plain* with everyone you meet.   320

POLAX

    Oh! I look not on my form with too much rigour,
    I'm real good *stuff* although at a low *figure*;
    Nar, hear my suit.

PHOEDRA   Each word your chance, sir, lessens,
    What? try *a suit on* in a lady's presence!

POLAX

    Why this rough treatment at your hands?

PHOEDRA   Oh—stuff—   325
    'Tis the *chaps* like you on them that makes them rough!

POLAX

    Why, Phoedra, because once I chance to fail,
    Jump at conclusions, *take o—ffence* and *rail*!

PHOEDRA

    (*giving her hand*) Well, there! that I was hasty, I confess.

POLAX

    And you will yet be Mrs. Polax?

PHOEDRA   Yes.   330

POLAX

    O happiness! alas! my duty tears
    Me from thee to my rounds upon the Squares;
    Yet, one kiss on that cheek before I quit.

PHOEDRA

    I wonder you've the cheek to ask for it!

POLAX

    'Tis but to sign our bargain.

PHOEDRA	Sign it? Pooh!	335

      I'll *put my hand* to it, if that will do.

      (*Offers to slap his face.*)

POLAX

      You'll make your mark, you mean? No; when you write,

      The down strokes of your round hand are not light.

PHOEDRA

      There then (*He kisses her.*)

POLAX   If e'er were day of rapture this is!

      So now I'm off.

PHOEDRA	Oh! goodness gracious, missis!	340

(*Alcestis appears at the top of the door steps, with two children in either hand, and comes down.*)

                                                    Exit Polax L.H.

ALCESTIS

      Phoedra, inform me truly, if you can,

      Who is that very free and rude young man?

PHOEDRA

      (*hesitating*) Why, if you please, that's—

ALCESTIS   No prevarication!

PHOEDRA

      My cousin.

ALCESTIS   That's a very old *relation*.

Don't think with cousins though to cozen me.	345

PHOEDRA

      Then, he's my husband, please, as is to be,

      A young policeman.

ALCESTIS   Then my scoldings cease,

      All *petticoats* are caught by the *Pellise*.

---

345 **cozen** 'to beguile' (*OED*, *v.* 2a). Also obsolete form of cousin (*OED*, *n.*).

348 **petticoats** undergarment and also, 'by metonymy; the wearer of a petticoat' (*OED*, *n.* 3 fig. b).

Pellise pun with 'police'. 'Pellice' is 'a woman's long cloak' (*OED*, *n.* 3a).

   Now go in-doors. I'm going to speak, you see,
   The regular classical soliloquy. *Exit Phoedra into the house.* 350
(*Alcestis advances with the two children.*)
   Oh! sun, and moon, and stars! oh day and night!
   Oh every thing above an inch in height!
   Oh Day! as black as black of Day and Martin,
   To what infernal realms must I be starting!
   Oh bed I-beg pardon-nuptial couch, I mean, 355
   'Twere green though to regret now Gretna Green,
   Else might I ask, were not the question idle,
   Why was I ever saddled with this bridal?
   Or why —but these, alas, are *whys* too late—
   Did I with such a milksop link my fate? 360
   Why at the altar did we join our hands?
   Why Hymen e'er unite us in his bands,
   Those *bands* which ne'er have played the *heavy waits*,
   A-*merry-key* in our *united states*?
   Why was my heart to be with such a spoony un, 365
   A wretched picture of a poor *heart* union?
   For life with him was nothing but a curse,
   And though I took him 'for better or for worse,'
   The world can't surely wonder I forsook him, for
   I found him such a deal worse than I took him for. 370
   Oh parent hearth! oh earth, air, fire, and water!
   Oh son in petticoats and unmarried daughter!
   What's to become of you when my sun sets,
   Props of my house—I may say, *par-a-pets*?
   They say that beauty's but a snare, if true, 375
   They'll be *caught* in it who are *courting* you;
   But rather may your grace, bewitching *naiveté*,
   And noble *carriage* be a *handsome's safety*.
   My Eumelus, too, who is to insert
   The missing button in his baby shirt 380
   When I am gone? or who supply the stitches
   That may be wanting in his infant trousers?

And when in youth his jacket he outwears,
And sows his wild oats, who's to *sow* his *tares*?
And is't for this I've led the virtuous life   385
Of tender mother and affectionate wife?
And I should add, obedient daughter too,
But that I might, in a strict point of view,
Account myself an *orphan*, for so *seldom*
My parents were apparent till hell held 'em,   390
(Forgive the monosyllable, sweet ladies,
I meant but Tartarus, or the classic Hades)
That I'd no time to aggravate Mama,
Or make my Pa my foe by *a faux pas*!
I might on this sad theme expatiate,   395
But dying so soon I've no time to *di-late*:
So I have done —another observation
Would be entire supererogation.

349–50 **I'm ... soliloquy** see 193n. References to topical issues abound in this soliloquy with a cursory reference to the Woman Question. Alcestis' words are not as piquant as Medea's in Brough's burlesque yet she still draws some interesting questions on marriage and the role of wives and daughters.

351 Alcestis' first words on stage in Euripides (l. 244–245).

353 **Day and Martin** boot blacking factory. Also slang word for 'negro' between 1840 and 1910 (Partridge, *Dictionary*, p. 245).

356 **Gretna Green** famous Scottish destination just across the border for eloping couples since 1754, when Lord Hardwicke's Marriage Act came into force in England and Wales but not in Scotland.

358 **saddled** 'provided with a saddle' (*OED, adj.*) and also 'to load with a burden, to encumber with something as a burden or responsibility' (*OED, v.* 5a).
bridal a wedding feast (*n.* and *adj.*). Pun with 'bridle', 'the head-gear of the harness of a horse or other beast of burden' (*OED*, 'bridle', *n.*).

360 **milksop** see 176n. Alcestis would be another strong-minded woman. See pp. 33–36.

362 **Hymen** god of marriage ceremonies, usually addressed in wedding songs.

365 **spoony** 'A simple, silly, or foolish person' (*OED, n.*). Also, colloquially, from 'spoon' (*OED, v.* 2, II.6a), to make love, especially in a sentimental or silly fashion.

372–84 In Euripides Alcestis sacrifices for her own children and urges Admetus not to marry again so that her children will not have a stepmother (l.299; l.304). Talfourd modernizes the elements that identify mothers in the tragedy and uses 'petticoats' instead.

378 The base text includes the following note which probably alludes to lines inserted in the soliloquy: 'Other ideas for mine I scorn to grab, / But "handsome's safety" must be owned —a cab.' A 'hansom cab' is a 'low-hung two-wheeled cabriolet holding two persons inside, the driver being mounted on a dickey or elevated seat behind, and the reins going over the roof' (*OED, n.* a) The earliest record in the *OED*, dates from 1852.

379 **Eumelus** son of Admetus and Alcestis. He succeeded Admetus as King of Pherae.

385–6 Reference to lines 323–325 in Euripides where Alcestis speaks of herself as a model for women.

391–2 Address to the audience. Tartarus and Hades both refer to Hell and the underworld.

398 **supererogation** 'that which is more than duty or circumstances require' (*OED, n.* 1b).

My life, 'tis clear, no words of mine can save,
And I must pass at once from 'gay to *grave*!'   400
That bourne from which each traveller born soon learns
T' expect 'small profits and no quick returns.'
I must descend; egad, I can't help thinking
E'en now I'gin to feel a son of sinking;
I'll show them though how well real good stuff dies,   405
No woman tears shall dim my closing eyes,
I'll not e'en *hit* off 'one of my own *sighs*.'

Enter ORCUS, *L.H.*

ORCUS
    Be quick and die.

ALCESTIS   Why, don't you know, you dunce,
    Nobody can be *quick* and *dead* at once?

ORCUS
    You're humming me, or must excuse my humming   410
    The popular words, 'You are a good time coming.'

(*Sings.*)

AIR

My skiff is on the shore.

    My trap is in the floor,
    And waiting for thee:
    I can't allow no more,
    You must travel with me;   415
    And as we're sinking down my song shall be
    My dearest Alcestis I love but thee!

ALCESTIS (*Sings.*).   Yes I fear you're got me now
    You're got me now—you're got me now,
        So I don't intend to make a row,   420

But must reconciled be.

BOTH Your ⎫ trap is in the floor
      My ⎭

      And waiting for ⎰ me,
                      ⎱ thee,

      You won't ⎫ allow no more
      I can't   ⎭

      I   ⎫ must travel with ⎰ thee   425
      You ⎭   ⎱ me

      And as we're sinking down ⎰ your ⎱ song shall be
                                ⎱ my   ⎰

ALCESTIS Whatever you please for it's nothing to me!

ORCUS   My dearest Alcestis I love but thee!

(They have been standing upon trap C during the above, and gradually descending—they sink.)

Enter ADMETUS *from the house.*

ADMETUS

Woe! woe! in vain I weep, my tears will flow,
And I can't stop these *coursers* with my *woe*.   430
She was a pattern to her sex, I doubt
Ere this the Styx has washed the pattern out!
Her laugh, so merry in the days of yore,
Will never echo through the building more;
That airy footfall hushed will plainly tell   435
How Death from me has *wrung my airy belle*!
And, dull as is a rainy Vauxhall fete,

---

400   **'gay to *grave!*'** 'From grave to gay, from lively to severe'. Famous line in Alexander Pope's *Essay on Man* (Ep. IV, l.380).
401   **bourne** 'boundary' (*OED, n.*², 1).
402   **small ... returns** rephrasal of 'Small profits, quick returns'.
403   **egad** used as a softened oath (*OED, int.*).
411   **'You ... coming.'** 'There's a good time coming', song by Charles Mackay with music by Henry Russell popularized in the 1840s.
411.3 SD Song popularized by the Ethiopian Minstrels in the United States (ca. 1848).
412   **trap** see 189n.

426   **sinking** see 189n.
431   **pattern** on several occasions Alcestis is referred to as the model of perfect woman in Euripides; by the Choriphaeus in l.150-151; by the servant before Alcestis comes on stage in l.152-156; and by Alcestis in her own *rhesis* in l.323-325.
437   **rainy Vauxhall fete** Vauxhall Gardens was a popular pleasure resort between the seventeenth and the mid-nineteenth centuries. George Cruikshank immortalized the Vauxhall fete that celebrated the achievements of the Duke of Wellington in a homonymous satirical print in 1813.

My fate will now become, I calculate;
But I'm prepared, do with me as you will, Fate,
Vauxhall is nothing to my *Rush-of-ill-fate*! 440
Ah! who comes here? not Hercules sure, is it?

Enter HERCULES, *L.H.*

HERCULES

I've just dropped in to pay a flying visit:
My leave of absence lasts but a few days,
And I've no time for any *waste* in *stays*.
In fact, I'm going to astound the neighbours, 445
By the recital of *my* dozen labours.

SONG—AIR

Paddy Miles.

I am Hercules, famed for my deeds and my labours,
    With honours a trump turning up at a rub,
For slaying my foes and assisting my neighbours
    By the aid of this 'Juvenile Travellers' *Club*'! 450
Although I'm apprenticed to one called Eurystheus,
    And bound to perform whatever he sets;
Yet he finds all his dodges are not of the least use,
    For his driest of tasks but my appetite whets!

When first in my cradle and counted a suckling, 455
    Two snakes tied around me their '*Knotting em Twist*,'
But I twisted their necks like a pair of young ducklings,
    And arrested their strength by the strength of my wrist.
A friend had a nice little property formerly,
    But a *lion upon it* there happened to be: 460
Straight I followed my *bent*—though that seems an anomaly,
    And hided the lion whose hide now hides me!
The stag of Diana I hunted a long while,
    O'er mountains, hills, valleys, plains, rivers, and rocks:

His long running account I soon balanced in strong style,   465
    For I staggered the stag, and unsettled his stocks!
For Augeas that *stable* improvement I wrought too,
    That to modernized Smithfield I fain would apply,
But—the rest of my labours old Ovid has taught you,
    And Lempriere's Classical Dictiona-ry!   470

ADMETUS

(*aside*) I must dissemble. (*aloud*) Sir, you haven't dined.

HERCULES

I'll pick a bit with you, you're very kind.
But how is this, Admetus, my frivolity
You don't receive with your accustomed jollity.

ADMETUS

Well, since you must know all, this day my wife   475
Was by a rough artist taken from the life;
'Twas Death, and the original is his.

HERCULES

I see the *illustration* by your *phiz*;
But since I know of this, my friend, for grub
I'll not annoy you, but dine at my *club*.   480

---

442   **flying visit** in Euripides' *Alcestis* Herakles visits Pherae in his way to fulfil the eighth labour imposed by Eurystheus.

446   The twelve labours of Herakles are a penance imposed by the Delphic oracle. Even though the story of the labours is recounted in various sources, many of them are already depicted in primitive Greek art.

446.2   SD ***Paddy Miles*** popular song. Also made famous in New York by J. L. Poole.

450   **'Juvenile Travellers' Club'** probably *The Juvenile Travellers: Containing the Remarks of A Family During a Tour Through the Principal States and Kingdoms of Europe* (1801), a book by Priscilla Wakefield (1751–1832), a Quaker and English educational writer.

451   **Eurystheus** Herakles was enslaved to him while he performed the twelve labours.

455–70   Hercules relates here some well-known episodes in his life (i.e. the death of the serpents) together with the first labour (the Nemean lion).

456   **'Knotting em Twist'** Nottingham is well known for its lace industry. The machine-made flat lace originally produced in Nottingham, for example, is known as 'Nottingham lace' (*OED*, 'Nottingham', n. 1c).

468   **Smithfield** probably Smithfield livestock market. After heated debates on the hygiene of the site, the Smithfield Market Removal Act was passed in 1852 and the market relocated to another area. The debates on the market were recalled in the press of the time (i.e. *Hereford Journal*, 19 June 1850, p. 2; *Morning Chronicle*, 5 July 1852, p. 5).

469   **Ovid** Ovid's *Metamorphoses* recount episodes of the life of Hercules in books VII, IX, XII, XIII and XV.

470   **Lempriere's ... Dictiona-ry Classical** education in Latin and Greek was restricted to a small highbrow elite during the nineteenth century. Therefore, other more popular books such as Lemprière's dictionary were the major sources of classical knowledge.

480   **club** the nineteenth century was the age of the formation of urban men's clubs. An account of the entertainments in such clubs may be found for example in Marsh (1828) and Timbs (1866).

ADMETUS
>Excuse me, I won't bear of your departure,
>To friendship I prefer to be a martyr;
>So you shall stay, we'll make you up a bed.

HERCULES
>You're very good; and is she really dead?

ADMETUS
>Extremely so.

HERCULES
>　　　　　Since such, then, is the fact, 485
>Tell us, Admetus, how d'ye mean to act?

ADMETUS
>I'm at my wits' ends.

HERCULES
>　　　　　　　I dare say you are.
>(*aside*) That little territory don't go far.
>(*aloud*) But don't be shut up, what is to be done, man?

ADMETUS
>I'll be *shut* up, and in my *man-sion shun* man? 490
>Yes, live on bread-and-water for a year,
>Discourse with no one, nobody shall dare
>To offer the most trivial observation,
>Or volunteer a word of consolation;
>I'll taste no wine till on my bier I'm stretched, 495
>And every one about me shall be wretched!

HERCULES
>Amiable mourner! it is quite appalling
>To see a rising chap like you so chap-fallen,
>So I'll appease my hunger with a snack,
>As you proposed, then start off in a crack, 500
>And do my best to bring Alcestis back!

SONG—AIR

Cavalier.

>Like a dutiful knight,
>I'll set off honour bright,

> When my hunger and thirst I have stayed,
>> And this gay devil here, 505
>> Very small shall appear,
> As the lady I seek, sir, and aid!
>> For I'll soon let him know
>> 'Tis a word and a blow,
> Or two blows and no words with me; 510
>> And I ne'er will give o'er,
>> Till old Orcus I floor,
> And have made Alcestis free!
>> If he entertain thought
>> Which he didn't to ought, 515
> And not at all becoming his age,
>> I'll engage, never fear,
>> He'll give up such idea,
> And his *passion* will yield to my *rage*!
>> So, wiser by far, 520
>> You'll light up a cigar
> And go home—leave the matter to me.
>> To the lady I slopes,
>> Soon to lead her, I hopes,
> And restore her ere long to thee! 525

ADMETUS

> You're very kind, but the attempt is vain,
> She is a *loss* I ne'er shall see *a-gain*.

HERCULES

> Don't be too sure of that, I yet may save her;
> I first shall put it to him as a favour,
> Should he refuse her restoration hither, 530
> I must oblige him to oblige me with her.'

---

495 **bier** sepulchre (*OED*, *n.* 3); pun with beer as alcoholic drink (*OED*, *n.*¹).
498 **chap-fallen** crestfallen (*OED*, *adj*, 2).
501.2 SD **Cavalier** song popularized in the United States by Miss Agatha Mandeville.
523 **slopes** depart (*OED*, *v.*²). Humorous use of 'slopes', third person singular of the present indicative for first person.

ADMETUS
>You cannot mean—

HERCULES   That I must Orcus drub,
>And from my strong hand play my winning *club*;
>I'll polish him, I warrant.

ADMETUS   What? in fight?

HERCULES
>In fight? how else? d'ye think those noodles right,   535
>Who with a sanctimonious visage go forth
>To preach the polished arts of Peace, and so forth?
>To me such notions are entirely foreign;
>Polish of Peace! for *polish* I try '*Warring*',
>So now I'm off, I'll not be long away,   540
>'My soul's in arms,' et cetera, good day!   *Exit Hercules into the house.*

ADMETUS (*Sings.*)

AIR

Jolly Nose.

>Goodness knows what I suff'er to think of the grip
>>That old Orcus has laid on my deary:
>
>Though for doing as she did and missing my lip,
>>I'm, I calculate, rather too leary!   545
>
>Goodness knows when I look at myself in the glass
>>I am struck with the sad recollection
>
>Of how plump I was once—now, sir, brought to a pass
>>Of thinness which won't bear *reflection*!
>
>When I think of my lass I all comfort refuse,   550
>>And repudiate all consolation,—
>
>I'm a prey to the most undeniable blues,
>>And the wretchedest dog in creation!
>
>Some say she was easy put out, but I'm quite
>>Sure the blockheads knew nothing about her;   555
>
>Now, she's *put out*, and with her is put out *de-light*,
>>For I live but in darkness without her!

Within the house I must bewail my bride,
 For such deep sighs as mine can't be *out-sighed*.

 Enter PHOEDRA *angrily from the house.*

 How dare you, Phoedra, rudely thus intrude 560
 Upon the widowed mourner's solitude?
 Peace and begone!

PHOEDRA

    No peace, sir, you will find,
Until you've heard a small piece of my mind:
I've lived with you, when Monday next appears,
As maid of all work and no play, three years; 565
And, though my saying it may p'rhaps seem funny,
You wouldn't find a better at the money;
I've served in many families, but must say
Never was served as I have been to-day;
And if it is repeated, some fine morning 570
Give you fair warning, I shall give you warning!

ADMETUS

 This everlasting rattle, prythee, cease,
 And tell us calmly what's the matter, please.

PHOEDRA

 Oh! it's that friend of yours, that Hercules,
 That warrior in *undress* uniform, 575
 Since he came in has done nothing else but storm,

---

539 '*Warring*' polish and to fight (*OED*, v.¹). Probably also referring to 'Warren's Blacking', a famous blacking factory. Charles Dickens worked in Warren's at the age of twelve.

541 '**My …arms**' famous quote from Colley Cibber's version of Shakespeare's *Richard III*, V, iii (Anson, *Shakespearean*, p. 62).

541.4 SD The topic of the 'jolly nose' for a song dates back as early as 1607 in *The Knight of the Burning Pestle* by Francis Beaumont. It is also one of the King's Mirth or Fremen's Song in *Deuteromelia* (1609) (Mackay, *Songs*, p. 120).

545 **leary** eye rhyme with 'deary' and alternative spelling of 'leery', 'suspicious' (*OED*, *adj.* 2, 1b).

565 **three years** there is no time evidence for the work of the servant in Euripides.

572–4 a long parenthesis straddles these lines in the right margin in *1850*.

575 **undress uniform** humorous reference to Hercules' eclectic attire in marked contrast to formal military full dress uniform.

>   Not only walks into our house and stops,
>   But also walks into our mutton chops,
>   With such a *twist* as gave me quite a *turn*.

ADMETUS
>   But what's your special grievance?

PHOEDRA
>   You shall learn: 580
>   First, he informs me that the meat is spoiled,
>   Then finds the vegetables overboiled;
>   'Service is no inheritance,' then where's
>   The use of giving us poor servants *airs*?

ADMETUS
>   He seems to make no bones.

PHOEDRA
>   No bones? The glutton 585
>   Has nothing made but bones of our cold mutton!
>   If he comes here for supper, I'll grow bolder
>   And show him—

ADMETUS
>   That's right—show him the *cold shoulder*.

PHOEDRA
>   And I must add, after a loss so recent
>   Such conduct is especially indecent. 590

ADMETUS
>   Nay, he's our friend at bottom.

PHOEDRA
>   Then, would he
>   Were our friend at the bottom of the sea.
>   However, he is gone, and there's an end on't,
>   But if he comes again, I go, depend on't.
>   (*Sings.*)

AIR

>   That I'm a menial I'm aware, sir. 595
>   And with such term must e'en live branded,
>   But, if you go too far, prepare, sir,
>   For a blow up, for I won't stand it.

ADMETUS

        Phoedra now—don't make a row,
  Why put yourself out of humour?   600
           Don't dear, now!

PHOEDRA

  It's little I get in shape of wages,
      And with such as it is, I'm quite contented;
  But whoever puts upon me I engage
      Great or small he shall repent it!   605

ADMETUS

        Phoedra now—don't make a row,
  Why put yourself out of humour?
           Don't dear, now!

Voices are heard outside in altercation, then enter HERCULES *with* ALCESTIS *veiled,* ORCUS *following, L.H.*

ORCUS

  Well there, I give her up then, since it seems
    You must be thwarting all my little schemes.   610

HERCULES

  Admetus, do you know this lady veiled?

581–4 Herakles' gluttony provides the contrast between comedy and tragedy in Euripides for which some critics consider *Alcestis* a predecessor of tragicomedy. Gluttony is a common attribute of Herakles both in Greek tragedy and comedy, for example in Aristophanes' *Frogs*.

583 '**Service ... inheritance**' from Jonathan Swift's *Directions to Servants* (1731).

589-90 These are the claims of the servant in Euripides' *Alcestis*, l.747–772.

602 **wages** low wages were a major concern for domestic female workers during the nineteenth century. The problem is made evident in various literary works of the period, for example in *Esther Waters* (1894) by George Moore. See Field (2013) for further analysis on the topic.

608.2 SD **veiled** the visual effect of unveiling a woman or a statue was commonplace in the Victorian arts and culture. In the English literary tradition, for example, unveiling or uncovering a woman is recurring in Shakespeare, where Hermione is discovered by Paulina from behind a curtain (*The Winter's Tale*, V, iii) and Hero is unmasked before Claudio (*Much Ado*, V, iv). It is also noticeable that Admetus' refusal of a new wife, keeping his word to Alcestis, is completely removed from the scene (see *Alcestis*, l.1037–1122).

ADMETUS
>With hope and fear at once I am assailed:
>It must be she, and yet I own it's puzzling
>Her features to distinguish through the muslin;
>Pluck off that envious veil, nay, wherefore pause? 615
>'It is the *gauze*, my soul, it is the gauze'
>Must plead excuse for me, the only test is,
>Thus to remove it—yes, it is Alcestis!
>(*He removes the veil Alcestis faints.*)
>With sudden joy her senses have gone from her,
>Who'll put a *full stop* to this fearful *coma*? 620
>Is it a swoon, or nothing but a feint?
>Alas! I fear she's dead!
>(*Alcestis recovering*). You're wrong, I ain't.

ADMETUS
>Ah! she revives! (*to Hercules*) and did you win her?

ALCESTIS   Pooh!
>Of course I'm won, and now I'm coming *to*.
>(*Phoedra has fetched the children from the house; Alcestis embraces her and them.*)
>My own dear Phoedra! and my blessed children! 625
>This sudden happiness is quite bewildering!

ORCUS
>It's very well for you, but I've been treated
>Most shamefully indeed, I may say cheated.

HERCULES
>Well, if you feel agrieved at this my action,
>I'll give you every sort of satisfaction— 630
>Pistol, sword, single stick-though there are few
>Who'd like to cross the single Styx with you.

ORCUS
>No! No! of kicks and cuffs I've had my fill!
>You are a knight—'*knocks et praeterea nil,*'
>Indeed they are as terrible, an error 635
>'Twere scarce to call you son of *Nox* and *Terra*.

Besides, I know in spite of all that's passed,
They're pretty sure to come to me at last!

Enter APOLLO, *R.H.*

APOLLO

I've just looked in in time to wish you joy.
Why, Orcus, you don't look as well, old boy,   640
As when we parted, scarce an hour ago!
But, not to further snub a fallen foe,
There is my hand, you'll take it in good part,
And let our quarrel drop?

ORCUS   With all my heart.
And now you must excuse me if I go,   645
I've urgent business in the shades below.

APOLLO

Well, if you must, farewell! and for myself, I
Am going to my own *shades*, those *at-Delphi*.

Enter POLAX, *L.H.*

616	Famous quote from Othello's soliloquy in William Shakespeare's homonymous play (V, ii).
618	SD *faints* fainting heroines were a recurring trope in Victorian melodrama. Yet in this scene fainting is not coherent with the character of Alcestis, who takes the place of her husband before death and reproaches him for his weakness. Talfourd is here satirizing the drama of the time as he does in the various metatheatrical references in the play.
623	**win** in Euripides, Herakles claims to Admetus that Alcestis has been won in a contest (l.1010–1040).
624	Note that Alcestis does not speak here in Euripides and she is identified according to a rite.
630-2	The origins of duelling can be set up in the Italy of the late fifteen and mid-sixteenth centuries; in England, the practice lasted until the 1850s (see Banks, *Polite* for an in-depth analysis on the topic).
634	**knight** pun 'a military servant' and 'night'.
	knocks pun 'sounding blows' and 'nox' (l.636), which is often used as the personification of 'night' (*OED, n.*[1]).
634	**et . . . nil** and beyond that nothing.
636	**Nox and Terra** 'Nox' is the Latin translation of Nyx, the Greek goddess of the night; 'Tellus' or 'Terra' is a goddess of the earth in Roman mythology.
	Terra pun with 'terror'.
638	SD Apollo leaves the scene at the beginning of the play in Euripides. There is a wide discussion on the role of Apollo and on the fact that it is Herakles and not him, probably under the influence of Orphism, the one who saves Alcestis from Hades.
641	**scarce . . . ago** allusion to the time of the performance.
648	**at-Delphi** both the Oracle at Delphi and the Adelphi Theatre in London.

POLAX
>   I fear to enter or to interfere
>   In so much happiness, but, Phoedra, dear, 650
>   You'll pardon me in venturing to express,
>   With due apology for suddenness,
>   A hope, since things are in this happy state,
>   You'll not with me *decline* to *conjugate*.
>   Phoedra, do but consent to be my wife, 655
>   And hear my plan of happiness through life,
>   So we'll to all a pair of patterns jog!

PHOEDRA
>   A *pair of patterns*? What? When one's a *clog*?

ALCESTIS
>   A truce to *badinage*, for, to say sooth,
>   Whatever's bad-in-age is worse in youth. 660

PHOEDRA
>   I must take time to think on't, I don't know—
>   But a proposal does come *apropos*.
>   Tomorrow you I'll with an answer favour,
>   Till then must waive reply.

POLAX
>   Nay, it were safer
>   To seal it with a kiss, and not a *waiver*. 665

ALCESTIS
>   Come, kiss him, Phoedra, why a grievance make it?
>   You know you like it.

PHOEDRA
>   Well then he may take it.

POLAX
>   That's better. (*Kisses her—she gently boxes his ears.*)

PHOEDRA
>   Mind, sir, I said 'take,' not 'snatch!'

POLAX
>   Your *tinder-box*: assures me we're a *match*.

ALCESTIS
>   That's settled then, and as delays I hate, 670
>   The marriage contract shall be drawn up straight.

ADMETUS
>Yes, that's all very well, but you'll admit
>We must get these kind friends to *witness* it;
>The document is valueless, of course
>Unless it bear the seal of their applause. 675

ALCESTIS
>(*to audience*) Our story's finished, and our trouble ends here;
>But should the approbation of our friends here
>Nerve us to re-enact our fancied sorrow,
>We'll but adjourn it till this time to-morrow!

ADMETUS (*Sings.*)

AIR

Trab Trab.

>So now our story's told, sirs, 680
>   And you'll not fail to see
>With our author we've made bold, sirs,
>   Less welcome pr'aps than free!
>Yet, as we're evanescent,
>   And Euripides will stay, 685
>Let our insect life be pleasant—
>   We but ask to live a day. —So
>   Clap, clap, clap, clap, lustily,
>   Clap, clap, clap, clap away!

ORCUS (*Sings.*)

---

669 **tinder-box** allusion to commodities of the nineteenth century which manifests the anachronistic character of Victorian classical burlesque.

673 **kind friends** address to the audience.

679.3 SD Popular German song. Melody by Friedrich Wilhelm Kücken.

682–5 Allusion to the prevalence of classical literature over the trifles of burlesque.

AIR

Rosin the Beau.

  I have been most disgustingly cheated.   690
     Most shamelessly shamelessly used,
  But I'm ready to have it repeated
     If by it you'll say you're amused!
       If by it, &c.

APOLLO (*Sings.*)

AIR

Non piu Mesta.

  Some few misters can't abide to laugh   695
    At what's correct and classical,
  Or give to what's too sad by half
    A termination farcical.
  To such a critic I would say,
    As those who work most best can play,   700
  So, I'd invite them to reflect
    That, after all there may be
  Such thing as gravity incorrect,
    And *meet* without the *grave-y.*
  Then why your feelings throw away   705
    On a fictitious sorrow?
  Nor weep for others' woes to-day,
    You may have cause to-morrow!

Row Polka.

ALL
  Then let the curtain fall,

ALCESTIS
  A fair good night to all!   710

ALL

    Our troubles are over, sufferings all ended,
        Frown not, nor turn our pleasures into pain;
    More than once ere this your kindness has *befriended*
        Him who asks that indulgence again!

ALL

    Then let the curtain fall, &c.   715

THE CURTAIN FALLS.

689.3 SD Also 'Old Roisin the Bow', popular song probably of an Irish origin. The song can be traced back to the seventeenth century and became a great hit in America where it was sung by black and white singers, and street performers (Lhamon, *Jump*, p. 447).

694.3 SD From *La Cenerentolla, ossia La bontà in trionfo* operatic *dramma giocoso* in two acts by Rossini (1817). The libretto was written by Jacopo Ferretti and based on the fairy tale *Cendrillon* by Charles Perrault. The air is sung by Apollo, interpreted by Miss Adams (see Lacy's edition paratext, 18n.).

Textual notes

0.1 SD (*L.H.*) *Practicable*] *not in LC*
and] *not in LC*
0.2-3 SD (*R.H.*) ... βελλ.?] *not in LC*
0.4 SD *L*] *not in LC*
2 *frankly own it*] LC must confeſs
11 altars!] LC altars—! ah!
15 *much less*] LC much ˡᵉˢˢless
26 SD *L.U.*] *not in LC*
42 *lightish*] LC lighted
51 *propriâ personâ*] LC (propria persona)
54 *natur*] LC (nature)
68 SD–76 SD] *not in LC*
68 SD SONG] *this edn*; 1859 SONG.—Orcus
81–99] *not in LC*
107 *fortitu-de*] LC (fortitude-e-)
110 SD *Enter* ORCUS *L.*] *not in LC*
111 *this*] LC my
113 SD] *not in LC*
115 SD] *not in LC*
117 *flaw*] LC (flow)
122 *these*] *not in LC*
123 *won't*] LC don't
125.1 SD–133] *not in LC*
133 SD] LC Enter Alcestis from house
135 *street*] LC (streets)
136 SD] *not in LC*
141–143] LC Sylph-like in form—a goddeſs too in feature
    To sum all—a most stupendous creature!
    To curb my rising love I idly tries,
    I eyes the idol that I idolize!
144 SD] *not in LC*
147 SD] *not in LC*
154 *a-dieu*] LC (adieu)
160 *of*] LC of my
166–167] *not in LC*
171 SD] *not in LC*
173 SD] *not in LC*

inclined] *LC* inclined ~~To close/with you/~~ To close with you
175 *closing*] *LC* c<u>losein</u>g ~~closing?~~
180 SD] *not in LC*
187 SD] *this edn; 1850* | Exit Admetus into the House; *LC* <u>Exit</u>
188 SD] *not in LC*
195 SD] *this edn; LC* Ex<u>it</u>; *1850* | *Exit* (L. H.)
199 SD (*Sings.*)] *this edn; LC* Ex<u>it</u>; *1850* ALCESTIS *sings*
200–221 SD] *not in LC*
221 SD *Exit into*] *this edn; 1850* | *Exit Alcestis into*
222 SD] *LC* E<u>nter</u> P<u>olax</u>
228 *thereabouts*] *LC (*there a bouts*)*
232 *reindeer's*] *LC (*rein deer's*)*
234 *made*] *LC* shaped
237 *keeps*] *not in LC*
240 *Composed*] *LC* Compound
243 SD–256] *not in LC*
243 SD SONG] *this edn; 1850* SONG—POLAX
257 *is*] *not in LC*
258.1 SD] *not in LC*
258.2 SD] *LC* <u>Phoedra comes to area gate</u>
260 *bawl*] *LC (*ball*)*
261–283] *LC* <u>Pol</u> Im sorry if my noise annoys you
                                P<u>hea</u> Pray sir.
270.1 SD SONG] *this edn; 1850* SONG—PHOEDRA
288 *matter*] *LC* weight, sir
292 *now … raking*] *LC* P<u>ol</u> How?
                                  P<u>hoe</u> Like others fires—by—raking
293 *can my ardour*] *LC* ^{my ardour} can
299 *dealer*] *LC* dealer
                So shuffle off and cut
                Pol   My h<u>earts</u>' dear stealer
300 SP] *not in LC*
SD] *not in LC*
317–326] *not in LC*
328 *o—ffence*] *LC (*off<u>ence</u>)*
329 SD] *not in LC*
331 *duty*] *LC* harsh duty
336 SD] *not in LC*
339 *then*] *LC* there

SD] *not in LC*
340 SD] *LC* Enter Alcestis with her two children
342 free and rude young] *LC* free young^{& rude}
343 SD] *not in LC*
349 go in-doors] *LC* then retire
350 SD] *LC* Exit Pho
357–364] *not in LC*
375–378] *not in LC*
387–398] *not in LC*
407 SD *L.H.*] *not in LC*
411 SD *Sings*] *LC; 1850* | *Orcus sings*
412 in] *LC* on
418–428 SD] *LC* Orcus descends trap with Alcestis
441 SD *L.H.*] *not in LC*
442 a] *LC* you a
446 SD–470] *not in LC*
446 SD SONG] *this edn; 1850* SONG HERCULES
471 SD (*aside*)] *not in LC*
SD (*aloud*)] *not in LC*
474 receive] *LC* seem receive
476 the] *not in LC*
488 SD] *not in LC*
489 SD] *not in LC*
491–494] *not in LC*
495 my] *not in LC*
500 proposed] *LC* (*propose*)
501 best] *not in LC*
501–525 SD] *not in LC*
501.1 SD SONG] *this edn; 1850* SONG HERCULES
541 SD] *not in LC*
544 Though] *LC* But
lip] *LC* tip
545 leary!] *LC* leary—/sighs/
546–557] *not in LC*
559 SD] *LC* Enter Phoedra
561 widowed mourner's] *LC* widower's mourning
562 begone] *LC* (*be gone*)
564–567] *not in LC*
571 Give] *LC* I give

fair] *not in LC*
574 Oh! it's that] *LC* That precious
576 in has] *LC* in's
580–590] *not in LC*
594 comes] *LC* comes comes
594.2 SD AIR] *not in LC*
595] *LC; 1850* SP PHOEDRA
596 e'en live] *LC* ee'r lie
602–608] *not in LC*
608 SD] *LC*/Voices heard outside/Enter Hercules/with Alcestis veiled, Orcus following
615–617 nay … is] *LC* for me—the only test is
618 SD *Alcestis*] *LC* she
623 Ah!] *LC* Oh
624 SD] *LC* Enter Phoedra with Children
625] *LC; 1850* SP *Alc.*
631 Pistol] *LC* (pistols)
sword] *LC* (swords)
stick] *LC* (sticks)
635 as] *LC* so
638 SD *R.H.*] *not in LC*
640 as] *LC* so
643 in] *not in LC*
648 SD *L.H.*] *not in LC*
655–660] *not in LC*
676 SD] *not in LC*
679 this time] *LC* this time
679 SD–710] *not in LC*
711 SP ALL] *not in LC*
713 has *befriended*] *LC* for
714 Him] *LC* One
asks] *LC* now asks
715 &c.] *not in LC*
715 SD THE CURTAIN FALLS.] *LC* The End

4

Medea; or, the Best of Mothers, with a Brute of a Husband

Robert Brough

(1856)

Medea; or, the Best of Mothers, with a Brute of a Husband was first staged at the Olympic Theatre in London on 14 July 1856. The text is based on the 1856 printed copy published at Lacy's, collated with the LC unbound manuscript, BL Add MS 52960, K, held at the Lord Chamberlain's Plays Collection at the British Library.

Robert Brough

Robert Barnabas Brough (1828–1860) was born in London, son of Barnabas Brough, a brewer and wine merchant, and the poet Frances Whiteside. He was educated at a private school in Newport and started his working career in Manchester as a clerk. Robert's literary career included translations, prose and a complete dedication to journalism, where he displayed his talent for satire even more than on stage. He founded *The Liverpool Lion* in 1847 and also wrote for *The Man in the Moon*, *Diogenes*, *Comic Times*, *The Train*, and *Household Words*. In 1859 he published *Songs of the Governing Classes*, a set of radical poems which illustrated the political implications of some of his burlesques. Robert worked together with his brother William, also a playwright, on various burlesques which included *The Enchanted Isle; or, Raising the Wind* (Amphitheatre, Liverpool, 1848), *Frankenstein; or, the Model Man* (Adelphi, 1849), and *The Sphinx* (Haymarket, 1849), which recounted the story of

Oedipus. Other classical burlesques written by Robert Brough were *The Twelve Labours of Hercules* (Strand, 1851) and *The Siege of Troy* (Lyceum, 1859). Robert Brough died in Manchester only a year later, in 1860, but his brother continued writing burlesques while Lionel Brough, the other sibling, took up a career in acting. William Brough wrote *Endymion, or the Naughty Boy who cried for the Moon* (St James's, 1860), *Perseus and Andromeda; or, the Maid and the Monster* (St James's, 1861), *Hercules and Omphale; or, the Power of Love* (St James's, 1864) and *Pygmalion, or the Statue Fair* (Strand, 1867).

Manuscript paratext

f. 1

9/7/56.

12/7/56.

Royal Olympic Theatre

July 1856

Medea

or

The Best of Mothers

with

a Brute of a Husband

(A Burlesque

in one act)

Mr. R. Brough

June 1856

Lacy's edition paratext

MEDEA; THE BEST OF MOTHERS WITH A BRUTE OF A HUSBAND
A Burlesque, IN ONE ACT, BY ROBERT B. BROUGH, Author Of
Twelve Labours of Hercules—Lord Bateman's Overland Journey—
The Moustache Movement—Kensington Gardens— AND JOINTLY OF
The Enchanted Isle—Mephistopheles—Sphinx—Ivanhoe, &c. &

MEDEA.

Originally produced at the Royal Olympic Theatre,
On Monday, July 14th, 1856.

CHARACTERS.

CREON, *King of Corinth, a tyrant of the old school, a genuine Greek, but nevertheless a terrible Turk,* MR. EMERY.

JASON, *a hero of antiquity, of fabulous courage, about to marry the second time without the slightest hesitation,* MISS JULIA ST. GEORGE.

ORPHEUS, *his intolerably good-natured friend, first fiddle at the ancient concerts, Corinth,* MISS FANNY TERNAN.

A CORINTHIAN, *of excitable temperament,* MR. E. CLIFTON.

LYCAON, MELANTHE, *two miniature souvenirs of Jason, left for Medea to keep,* MISS ROSINA RANOE, MISS CONWAY.

MEDEA, *a conjugal lesson, surpassing in intensity anything of a similar description attempted even at this establishment, an awful warning to every single individual,* MR. F. ROBSON.

CREUSA, *a more agreeable prospect from the same point of view*, MISS BROMLEY.

SAIRÉE, *Creusa's nurse, combining the antique virtues of the good old body and the jolly old soul*, MISS STEVENS. 25

SCENE I. A PALACE NEAR CORINTH.
(*At all events near enough for Burlesque purposes.*) Enthusiastic Reception of a Popular Performer on his Return from the Provinces—Factious Opposition to a Proposed Measure for 30
Legalising MARRIAGE WITH A NON-DECEASED WIFE'S RIVAL ARRIVAL OF MEDEA, A RIVAL OF CREUSA
Mutual Explanations of the most Unsatisfactory Description.
Serious Disturbance, Violent Outbreak
TREMENDOUS AGITATION!! 35

SCENE II. CLASSIC INTERIOR WITH SEVERAL COLUMNS OF THE TIMES. DESPERATE BROAD-SWORD COMBAT! (N.B. ONLY ALLUDED TO) Between Miss Julia St. George, and a Giant Eighteen Feet Seven Inches in height—a Native of Greece, weighing 35 Stone, and never having had a day's illness in 40
his life—who has been engaged expressly for the occasion!
— (the Engagement resulting in his Total Defeat).
The Long-Lost Found—Melancholy Occurrence—"J" is

Notes to the Lacy's edition paratext

10 **Corinth** the action is set in Corinth, where Jason arrives with Medea escaping from Iolcos.
11 **Turk** 'applied to any one having qualities historically attributed to Turks; a cruel, rigorous, or tyrannical person; any one behaving barbarically or savagely. Also: a bad-tempered or unmanageable person; a man who treats his wife harshly'. Often collocated with 'terrible'. (*OED*, *n.*¹, 4a). As 'barbarians', usually opposed to the Greek in classical literature.
15 **first fiddle** first violin, in allusion to Orpheus as the quintessential singer. He is usually associated with a Lyre.
17 **A CORINTHIAN** the character is designated as CITIZEN throughout.
25 **Sairée** see the List of Roles, 7n.
27–8 **NEAR ... purposes** note the anachronistic nature of burlesque where a classicizing atmosphere was combined with topical allusions for the purposes of humour.
36–7 **CLASSIC ... TIMES** reference to the classicizing setting of the burlesque.
37 **COMBAT** stage combats were common in Victorian entertainment, particularly in circuses (Stewart, *Acrobat*, pp. 34, 57, 70). Actors were trained for the purpose (Jackson, *Victorian*, p. 108).

advertised that, if he will Return to his disconsolate Wife
and Family, he will hear of Something to his Advantage—
but he doesn't see it!!!

SCENE III. BANQUETING HALL IN PALACE OF CREON.
Preparations for Wedding Festivities, Illuminated by a
Brilliant Effect of PHOTOGRAPHY, or SUN-WRITING, never
before attempted on the Stage—An Unwelcome Guest, who
will not be ejected, though everybody else is put out. Medea
Goes to Work with a Vengeance Very Critical Situation—
The Sorceress pours out her Vial of Wrath, and has a stopper
put to it! BARBAROUS MURDER OF TWO UNOFFENDING
BEINGS, (Euripides and Legouvé.) Allegorical Groupe of
Sculpture, DESIGNED AND EXECUTED BY SIGNOR MONTI.

COSTUME.
CREON.—Long red shirt and robe, red sandals, wig and
beard, crown.
JASON.—White merino tunic, trimmed with red, red toga,
fleshings, red boots, fillet of white ribbon for head.
ORPHEUS.—White merino tunic and toga, fleshings, buff
sandals, laurel wreath.
CITIZENS.—Red and white shirts, fleshings, sandals.
COURTIERS.—Red and white shirts, togas, fleshings, sandals.
LYCAON AND MELANTHE. First dress—Brown shirts,
fleshings, and sandals. Second dress—White merino shirts,
trimmed with silver, fleshings, sandals.
CREUSA.—White merino train dress, trimmed with silver,
white wreath.
NURSE.—Blue dress, brown long cloak, green veil.
BRIDESMAIDS.—White petticoats, blue and yellow short robes.
MEDEA.—Yellow skirt and body, trimmed with cabalistic

characters in black, large brown cloak or robe, ringlet wig, ribbons in hair, sandals.

75

Time of Representation—One Hour.

MEDEA

---

49 **PHOTOGRAPHY ... WRITING** the Victorians consumed a very pictorial culture. The development of photography and its predecessors, heliography and the daguerreotype were part of the science and entertainment of the period. Sun-writing, or heliography, was introduced by Nicéphore Niépce, an amateur French inventor who devised a method by which light could draw the pictures he needed in the 1820s. (Curley, *Britannica*, p. 48). Also note that Medea was the granddaughter of Helios, the sun.

53 **Sorceress** representations of Medea as a sorceress in connection to Hecate abound in Victorian arts and literature. See, for example, *Medea* (1868) by Frederick Sandys and *Jason and Medea* (1907) by John William Waterhouse.

55–6 **Allegorical ... Sculpture** according to the reviews, the sculpture was designed in honour of Ristori and included a colossal bust of the actress on a pedestal with the names of the characters she had performed, a descending ray of gold with her names on the centre and the figures of Tragedy and Comedy (see *London Standard*, Tuesday 15 July 1856, p. 1; *Morning Post*, Tuesday 15 July 1856, p. 5).

57 **COSTUME** details on costume provide evidence of the classicizing tone of the performance. The cabalistic characters in Medea's robe should be highlighted as they allude to the magical powers of the heroine, to her portrayal as a barbarian, and to the orientalized description of the character throughout the nineteenth century. Note also that gipsy women characters were dressed up with cabalistic signs in their robes. Robson's ringlet wig imitated Ristori's hair and her use of it for her impersonation of Medea (see *London Standard*, 5 June 1856, p. 1).

List of Roles

CREON	*King of Corinth*
CITIZEN	
CROWD	
ORPHEUS	*fiddler and singer*
JASON	*husband of Medea* 5
CREUSA	*daughter of Creon and Jason's fiancé*
NURSE	*nurse of Creusa*
MEDEA	*wife of Jason*
LYCAON	⎫
MELANTHE	⎬ *sons of Jason and Medea*

Attendands, Bridesmaids, Courtiers, Guests and Populace.   11

---

1 CREON King of Corinth. Jason and Medea flee to Corinth from Iolcos. Both in Euripides and Seneca Medea kills Creon by magic.

4 ORPHEUS Son of Apollo and a Muse and mythical singer par excellence; as such, he saves the Argonauts from the Sirens with his song. As narrated by Virgil and Ovid he is in love with Eurydice, whom he cannot save from death. Legouvé includes Orpheus as a character in his tragedy *Medea* yet he appears neither in Euripides nor in Seneca. Brough uses the character to increase the comic effects of the burlesque. At the beginning of 1.2, he also performs the role of the Coryphaeus.

5 JASON Son of Aeson and leader of the Argonauts in their quest for the Golden Fleece. He is loved by Medea, who aided him in his deeds and gave him descendants.

6 CREUSA Daughter of Creon and princess of Corinth.

7 NURSE The character is designated as NURSE throughout in SPs and SDs and in the dialogue except for 1.284 where she is 'Sarah!'. Usually, both in the classical texts and the classical tradition she is either referred to as Nurse or Oenone. The 'Character List' in the Lacy's paratext refers to her as 'Sairée' and in Legouvé she is 'Ianthe'.

8 MEDEA Granddaughter of Helios, daughter of Aiētēs, King of Colchis and priestess of Hecate. She is associated with Jason's quest of the Golden Fleece. Medea fell in love with Jason and helped him in his deeds by, among other things, killing her brother Apsyrtus. She fled with Jason to Corinth where Jason abandoned her for Creusa. Wretched and infuriated, Medea killed Creusa, Creon and the children she had with Jason in revenge. Medea is also known for her powers and cunning sometimes related to magic.

9 LYCAON Son of Jason and Medea and brother to Melanthe. The two children take their names from Legouvé (Lycaon and Melanthus). Even though they are nameless characters in Greek and Roman drama they are variously named in classical literature; for example, Hyginus gives them the names Mermeros and Pheres (*Fabula* 25) as in the scholia to Lykophron; Apollodoros gives them the same names in book 1 of his *Library* (1.9.28), as also does Pausanias (2.3.6-9). In Diodorus Siculus's *Library History* Jason and Medea have three children: Thessalos and Alkimenes, who are twins, and Tisandros, the youngest (Pache, *Child Heroes*, pp. 18–22).

10 MELANTHE See 9n. In *1856* the character only speaks in 3.148 and therefore gives more prominence to the character of Lycaon, who speaks Melanthe's lines in *LC*.

Medea; or, the Best of Mothers   143

1.1 *A public place outside the gates of Corinth. A wood of olive trees, R. H. A statue of Diana, supposed to be on the threshold of that Goddess' temple, up stage, R. C.; steps to temple, R. U. E.; at back, L. H., a hill descending in direction of the town. Flourish at the rise of curtain.*
CREON *on steps of temple, R., attended with* CITIZENS *of Corinth in the act of welcoming* ORPHEUS, *C., who is attended by a small tiger, carrying a violin in bag, &c.* JASON *standing moodily apart, L. H.*

CREON

    (*R.*) Wandering minstrel, welcome home once more!
    We trust engagements upon foreign shore
    And in provincial town, melodious cousin,
    Have brought your active bow abundant 'Rosin.'
    We fear'd our city you had given the slip,   5
    Meanly abandoning your leader-ship
    Of Corinth's orchestras; 'Yes, sure enough,'
    We said, 'he's cut his baton in a huff,
    'And spurning penalties of pound or dollar,
    'Thrown off his *op'ra tie* through *warmth of choler.*'   10
    But, minstrel, since you've calmed our fears *to-day* so
    We're glad to see you, and have come to *say* so.

A CITIZEN

    (*enthusiastically*) Cheers for the fiddler! Hip!

CROWD (*vociferously*)   Hooray!

ORPHEUS (*C. checking them with a gesture*)   My friends,

---

0 SD Brough keeps Legouvé's setting.
0.2 SD **Diana** Roman goddess associated with chastity, named Artemis in Greek.
0.6 SD **tiger** Orpheus charmed the beasts with his music, therefore he is usually represented surrounded with wild animals such as lions, serpents and tigers. See, for example, the Imperial Roman mosaic 'Orpheus' (third century AD) at the Antkaya Museum, Turkey; and the painting *Orpheus* (1896) by John Macallan Swan.

1 **Wandering minstrel** common collocation for prophets and charlatans in nineteenth-century England. For example, in John Symmons' translation of Aeschylus' *Agamemnon* in 1824, Cassandra is pejoratively depicted as a 'wandering minstrel' (Symmons, pp. xvii–xix).
2 **foreign shore** in Legouvé Orpheus is expected to join the celebration of the nuptials of Creusa and silence the fatal omens presaged for the ceremony.
4 **Rosin** pun. 'Rosin' is both an alcoholic drink, originally a refreshment for fiddle players (*OED*, *n.* 2a) and the resin rubbed on the bow hair of violins and similar stringed instruments (*OED*, *n.* 1a).

	These violin delights—have violent ends.
	(*to Creon, modestly.*) Great Creon, why these honours thrust on me, 15
	Whose services are—pshaw! Fiddle-de-dee!
CREON	
	(*R.*) Orpheus, you give your work too mean a place,
	Make for your instrument a better case.
	Why, man, all classes—soldier and civilian,
	Own thou hast music for at least a million. 20
	Have we not seen thy strains their magic proving,
	By num'rous instances of table moving?
	Sofas—clocks—bedsteads—capering away—
	(Highly convenient on quarter day.)
	Nor rests thy fame on tables' legs, or chairs! 25
	Go ask the dancing dogs—and dancing bears.
	Do we not know thy matchless reels and jigs
	Can soothe the porcupines, and please the pigs?
	Could hats of coppers full e'er pay the piper,
	Who from our hedge-row steals away each viper. 30
	Whose witching melody, so softly deep
	Catches the artful weasel while asleep,
	Till fascinated by the cadence drop,
	The interesting animal goes 'pop!'
	Cats, rats, bats, gnats, sprats, periwinkles, salmon— 35
	All join the chorus of thy praises—
JASON	(*L.*) Gammon!
CREON	
	(*R.*) Jason, that's rude.
JASON	Is it? I'm very sorry!
	Talk common sense, then! What a pretty story!
	A wretched squalling, cat-gut scraping sinner
	Who sings for lunch, and whistles for his dinner— 40
CREON	
	(*interrupting mildly*) Jason, the services to you we owe, (*Crosses to C.*)
	We quite admit. No gentleman we know
	Of savage tribes, or pirates so defiant,

You've not your match in tackling—say—a giant.
Or when an awkward dragon's in the way 45
I don't care whom it's to I always say,
(Feeling, in fact, I ought to, as a friend,)
'Jason's the party I can recommend;'
But still the crown of Orpheus wouldn't fit
Your head! you're no musician you'll admit. 50
There's not a single instrument you play—
Save your own trumpet—which *you'll crack some day*.
    (*Crosses to R.*)

JASON

(*laughing scornfully*) 'Twas ever thus—in trumpet times of war,
Us fighting men alone you've honours for;
But piping times come round—our claims get mouldier, 55
You *pay the piper*—and *halfpay the soldier*!
(*changing his tone*) Come, Orpheus! here's a challenge!
    what d'ye say?
A giant landed on these shores to day.

CREON

(*alarmed*) No! (*general consternation*)

JASON   And will soon his foot this city place on

CREON

(*eagerly, crossing to C.*) Orpheus, stand back! My lion-hearted
    Jason! 60
(*Embraces Jason, who thrusts him aside.*)

21-36 Allusion to the power of Orpheus' music to appease the beasts interspersed here with nineteenth-century séances, usually associated with phenomena related to physical mediumship.

24   **quarter day** 'each of the four days fixed by custom as marking off the quarters of the year, on which some tenancies begin and end, the payment of rent and other quarterly charges fall due, and on which quarterly meetings were formerly often held' (*OED, n.*).

27   **reels** the music for a traditional Scottish dance typically involving four or more dancers characterized by repeated passages of rapid quavers (*OED, n.*³, 1).

27   **jigs** the music for lively, rapid dance (*OED, n.*¹, 2).

34   **pop** allusion to the nursery rhyme 'Pop, goes the Weasel', 'a country dance popular in the mid 19th cent.; the tune or song of the same name to which this dance is performed' (*OED, adv.* 2).

36   **Gammon** 'rubbish, nonsense' (*OED, n.*⁴ and *int.* 3). Here begins the confrontation between Jason and Orpheus in Legouvé which also opposes war to arts.

52   *trumpet* 'To blow one's own trumpet', to sound one's own praises (*OED, n.* 3).

52   *crack some day* one day Jason will be unable to live up to his reputation; his trumpet will break.

56   *pay ... soldier* pun. 'To pay the piper' to pay the price of something; to answer for one's actions (*OED, n.*¹, P1).

JASON
>   (*to Orpheus*) The grim Antestor! Does the title strike you?
>   (*Orpheus looks alarmed.*)
>   I meant to settle him myself.

CREON (*rapturously*)   Just like you.

JASON
>   (*to Orpheus*) Perhaps you'll quell him with your arts enlighten'd,

ORPHEUS
>   (R.) I could, if—

JASON (*L.*)   What?

ORPHEUS (*laughing*)   Well! if I wasn't frighten'd.
>   Come, Jason, let's not quarrel, you and I— 65
>   My share of work commences by and bye.
>   *You* crush the foe with heart and muscle strong,
>   I'll sing your deeds in an undying song,
>   But I'm in fiddling time, it seems—that's hearty!
>   Creusa going to marry? who's the party? 70

CREON
>   (*pointing to Jason*) The favour'd individual you perceive.

ORPHEUS
>   (*starting*) Jason!

CREON   Precisely! (*aside*) With the giant's leave.

ORPHEUS
>   He wed your daughter?

JASON (*proudly*)   Ay, sir! why not?

ORPHEUS   You?

CREON
>   You've the king's word for it

ORPHEUS   It can't be true!

CREON
>   Fiddler!

ORPHEUS (*agitated*) A whirl of mystery and doubt 75
>   Maddens my brain. (*to Creon and others*) Here—all of you—Get out!
>   Leave us together.

CREON (*indignant*)   Minstrel!

ORPHEUS (*impatiently*) Will you fly?
    You won't? The pow'r of music then I'll try.

Seizes his violin from his attendant, who has got to R. 1 E. and plays it above the bridge— Creon, and all but Jason, run off R., U. E. and L. U. E., holding their ears in agony. Orpheus then gives back violin to attendant, who exits, R. 1 E.

ORPHEUS
    (*laughing*) I thought that little scheme would not miscarry.
    (*Comes down confronting Jason.*)
    So, my young person that's about to marry—   80
    Where is thy wife, Medea?
JASON (*L.*) (*nervously*) Hush! don't name her—
    'Twasn't a happy match—I couldn't tame her,
    She left me in a tantrum of impatience—
    I think she's gone to stay with some relations.
ORPHEUS
    'Tis false!
JASON How now?
ORPHEUS I know the woman's heart.   85
JASON
    (*rubbing his head*) I know her hand!
ORPHEUS From you—Medea part?
    Why, man, that matchless woman from your side
    You couldn't drive away.
JASON (*aside*) No! for I've tried.
ORPHEUS
    Or, if you had attempted it, I know
    The more you drove—the more she wouldn't go.   90
    She'd stay—if but to prove herself a martyr—

---

61 **Antestor** allusion to the giant Antestor in Legouvé's *Medea*.

JASON
    Orpheus, you must admit—she *was* a *Tartar*?
ORPHEUS
    (*coldly*) Sir, as the ladies' champion, I've some fame
    When wives are bad, the husbands are to blame.
JASON
    (*mildly*) Cases exceptional you must admit?   95
ORPHEUS
    None.
JASON   Three legg'd stools for instance?
ORPHEUS   Not a bit.
JASON
    (*Makes action of throwing.*) Projected bootjacks?
ORPHEUS (*shaking his head*)   Can't allow the plea.
JASON
    Candlesticks!
ORPHEUS   Burning lights till half-past three.
JASON
    At least, you'll own, no weight of female wrongs
    Can justify the use of kitchen tongs?   100
ORPHEUS
    In vain your plan, as innocent you'd figure me.
    Mon petit ami, your intention's *big-amy*!
JASON
    I own it. Fate a girl has pleased to find me—
    Better than her—(*looking round nervously*) I hope—
        I've left behind me.

SONG—AIR

The girl I left behind me.

    I made a slight mistake in youth,   105
        Experience plain has shown it;
    I was to blame, and that's the truth,
        I'm not ashamed to own it.

                A dame strong-minded I espoused,
                    Who round her thumb entwined me;   110
                One night in secret I 'vamoused,'
                    And the old girl left behind me.
                Her vixen ways of all my days
                    Contrived the peace to toss awry.
                She magic spelt, and largely dealt   115
                    In poison, cup, and sorcery.
                A wand'rer since, renown'd in war,
                    All martial feelings bind me,
                Except the soldier's weakness for
                    The girl I left behind me.   120

Harp music, distant.—Creusa appears ascending the hill, L. U. E., with her Nurse and Bridesmaids, bearing garlands and offerings—they disappear.

ORPHEUS

   (*going up R.*) What strains are those?

JASON   My love, with Nurse and Bridesmaids,
   A path has down the mountain's flow'ry sides made.
   She comes to ask forgiveness of Diana,
   For her desertion of that virgin's banner.

ORPHEUS

   I'll to the king at once, and let him know   125

92	**Tartar** 'a native inhabitant of the region of central Asia extending eastward from the Caspian Sea' (*OED*, A. *n.*², 1). In a figurative sense 'a person supposed to resemble a Tartar in disposition; a rough and violent or irritable and intractable person' (*OED*, *adj.* 3a). In the seventeenth century, also 'an old cant name for a strolling vagabond, a thief, a beggar' (*OED*, A. *n.*², 2b). It refers to Medea both as an enraged woman and as a barbarian.		
102	**big-amy** see pp. 26–29.		
104.2	SD popular song from ca. 1758–1759 in England. Also known as *Brighton Camp* or *Blyth Camps*. It accompanied English country dances and travelled to the colonies. Thomas Osborne Davis (1814–1845), an Irish politician and journalist, adopted the theme for one of his poems written between 1842 and 1845.		
109	**strong-minded** see p. XXX.		
115–16	Medea shares with her aunt Circe the mastery of salves and potions. This has resulted in numberless refigurations of Medea as a witch and a sorceress in art and literature. Examples in the Victorian period abound: i.e. Frederick Sandys, *Medea* (1868); Valentine Cameron Prinsep, *Medea the Sorceress* (1880); John William Waterhouse, *Jason and Medea* (1907).		
120	SD follows Legouvé's stage direction.		
123	**Diana** see 0.2 SD.		

That you're a benedict already.

JASON   Go!
Spread discord, minstrel, 'stead of harmony;
Say that the marrriage tie's no noose to me.
What then? Let Creon find a champion better—
Though he give fifty brides he'd be my debtor.   130

DUET

Sul campo della gloria—(Belisario).

JASON

Decamp I will to glory, ah!
   To slay the giant, start oh!
      To Creon I am far too
Important to let go.
      No mortal hint or story, ah!   135
      Can make him me overthrow—
      You'll see, see, see, &c.

ORPHEUS

In scampishness you glory, ah!
   To Creon I will start, oh!
      Your secret to impart, ah!   140
He really ought to know—
      The mention of your story, oh!
      Will soon your schemes o'erthrow.
      You'll see, see, see, &c.

Exeunt— Orpheus, R., and Jason, L.

Harp music.—Enter CREUSA, *with* NURSE, *down platform L. U. E., preceded by Bridesmaids, who cross stage and exit into temple, R. U. E.*

CREUSA

Dear Nurse, whose thoughtful care ne'er slept a nod,   145
Or spared the child in fear to spoil the rod;

> Whose views on discipline and education,
> Fully developed, would whip all creation—
> Deck with these offerings Diana's shrine,
> To-morrow frees me from her rule and thine. 150
> Pout not! 'Tis no great fall from honour's top;
> You know you always liked a *little* drop.
> Possets of comfort you shall never lack,
> The sherry—or, if needful, mind—the sack! *Exit into temple, R. U. E.*

NURSE

> (*solus*) Dear, happy soul! what tenderness she merits! 155
> I'm fond of anything that's full of *sperrits*.
> Her taste in dress so perfectly complete—
> How I do like a little something *neat*.
> Always so ready with her purse or needle
> To help poor people—(*looking off, L.U.E., sees Medea*)
>   Beggars! Where's the beadle? 160
>   *Exit hastily, R. 1 E.*

---

126   **benedict** 'a newly married man; *esp.* an apparently confirmed bachelor who marries' (*OED*, B. *n.* 1)

127   **minstrel** see 1n.

130.2 SD Flavius Belisarius was a well-known general of the Byzantine Empire whose heroic deeds were immortalized by numerous plays and novels. Here it recalls a passage from Gaetano Donizetti's opera *Belisario* (1836) after Luigi Machionni's adaptation of Eduard von Schenk's play.

138   **scampishness** with the characteristics of a scamp, a rascal. See 'scampish' (*OED*, *adj.* DERIVATIVES 'scampishness' *n.*)

145–54 **Dear … sack!** child education was a major concern much debated in Victorian England which prompted the passing of various laws such as the Education Act of 1870.

152   **drop** drunkenness was a serious problem during the Victorian period. The temperance movement advocated for reducing and forbidding the use of alcoholic beverages. The problem was mirrored on the stage with the temperance melodrama inaugurated by Douglas Jerrold with *Fifteen Years in a Drunkard's Life* (1828) (Booth, *Theatre*, p. 132).

154   **sack** 'Sherry sack', a class of wine (*OED*, *n.*^{3}).

156   **sperrits** alternative spelling of 'spirits' (to rhyme with merits); both 'Liveliness, vivacity, or animation in persons, their actions, discourse, etc' (*OED*, *n.* III.14b) and 'strong alcoholic liquor for drinking, obtained from various substances by distillation' (*OED*, *n.* V.21c). See 152n.

160   **Beggars!** a coeval example of refigurations of Medea as an ethnic outsider is Franz Grillparzer's *Das goldene Vlies* (1821); subsequent examples such as *Médée* by Jean Anouilh (1946), *Medea la encantadora* by José Bergamín (1954), and *Lunga note di Medea: tragedia en dos actos* by Corrado Alvaro (1949) who also reinterprets Medea as a beggar.

160   **beadle** related to the parish officer appointed to keep order in church, punish petty offenders and act as the servitor or messenger of the parish in general (*OED*, *n.* 4a). A well-known beadle in Victorian literature is Mr. Bumble in Charles Dickens' *Oliver Twist* (1838).

Slow Music.— 'The Beggar's Petition.' *Enter* MEDEA *with her two* CHILDREN, *one in her arms, the other by her side, down platform, L. U. E. They come down C.— She then puts the child down, and they stand like street beggars; the smallest child having a placard on its neck, inscribed—(*Φα θερλεσσ, ORPHELINS, ORFANI, FATHERLESS*)The other has a little tin begging-box and wallet.*

MEDEA

>My Grecian friends, with deep humiliation
>I stand in this disgraceful situation.
>Though unaccustom'd publicly to speak,
>I have not tasted food since Tuesday week.
>Three sets of grinders out of work you see,   165
>Through the invention of machinery.
>A landlord, as inclement as the weather,
>Has seiz'd our flock bed—we were out of feather.
>Shoeless and footsore, I've through many lands
>Walked, with this pair of kids upon my hands.   170
>The tear of infancy requests you'll stop it—
>(*looking round*) Bother! there's no one looking at
> us—drop it! (*The Children go up R. C.*)

Re-enter NURSE, *R. 1 E.*

NURSE

>I wonder where that beadle is?

MEDEA (*seeing Nurse for the first time—snappishly*) Here, you—
>Is this Epirus?

NURSE   Yes.

MEDEA   Oh! that'll do.

NURSE

>(*aside*) She must be some of the better sort,   175
>To take a common person up so short.

MEDEA

>(*seeing the Nurse occupied*) What are you at?

NURSE (*curtseying*)   Your ladyship, I'm threading
>Garlands, and so forth, for my nurse child's wedding.

MEDEA

    A wedding?

NURSE   Truly! though she's scarce left school.

    The sweetest chicken breathing—

MEDEA   Name the fool!   180

NURSE

    The gentleman?

MEDEA   No, idiot! the other,

    Who robb'd an ass, by suckling from his mother.

NURSE

    (*aside*) She's some great queen disguised, beyond all doubts.

    You don't belong, I think, to hereabouts?

MEDEA

    (*turning upon her fiercely*) I don't belong to hereabouts or

        thereabouts,   185

    Woman! For months I haven't had a whereabouts.

    I lodge at number nothing—nowhere.

NURSE (*shrinking terrified*)   Spare me!

MEDEA

    (*with increasing mildness*) Nobody'll have me—nobody can bear me!

    Nobody will keep me, with my woes import'nate ;

    Or if they do a week, they won't a fortnight.   190

    To overseers, if I make application

    To join the Union, there's a conflagration:

    To model lodgings I'm not endurable—

160.2   SD popular poem by Thomas Moss published in 1769. Referred to in Jane Austen's *Northanger Abbey* (1817).

160.4   SD Φα θερλεσσ fatherless in Greek characters.

160.5   **begging-box** 'begging' used *attrib.* and *comb.* in compounds (*OED, n.* C1).

162–291   The whole passage illustrates the wretched condition of abandoned wives by the 1850s. The stage directions which refer to the progressive enraging of Medea are well worth noting as they point to Robson's masterful imitation of Ristori's pathos.

173 SD   Stage directions throughout the play mark Medea's fits of rage and changing emotions. Reviews account for Frederick Robson's masterful impersonation of such changes.

174   **Epirus** region in southeast Europe between Greece and Albania. The geographical reference is directly transposed from Legouvé.

191   **overseers** overseer of the poor. 'In England and Wales: a parish officer responsible for organizing relief and employment for the poor' (*OED, n.* 1c). Among the general duties of the overseers were organizing the work for the paupers and apprenticing poor children.

192   **join the Union** for the relief and employment of the poor, parishes joined in Unions which were under the direction of the Poor Law Guardians after the Poor Law Amendment Act in 1834.

	Hospitals kick me out, as past incurable!	

　　　　　　Hospitals kick me out, as past incurable!
　　　　　　Soup kitchens don't consider me the ticket—　　　　195
　　　　　　I'm even bowl'd out at the gaoler's wicket.

NURSE

　　　　　　(R.) Unhappy being! whence this fate pernicious?

MEDEA

　　　　　　(L.) Well, do you know, I fear I'm rather vicious.
　　　　　　I kick a little—when things don't go right.
　　　　　　'Tis also rumoured that I sometimes bite.　　　　　　200
　　　　　　The fact is, I'm the daughter of a nation
　　　　　　A little backward in civilization.

NURSE

　　　　　　Lor'!

MEDEA　　　　　　Yes. For instance, captive foes—you treat 'em
　　　　　　With leniency?

NURSE　　　　　　　　Decidedly.

MEDEA　　　　　　　　　　　　We eat 'em!
　　　　　　Parents again, who thwart your schemes and spoil 'em—　　205
　　　　　　You talk them over?

NURSE　　　　　　　　To be sure.

MEDEA　　　　　　　　　　　　We boil 'em!
　　　　　　And husbands, who should stay at home, but won't—
　　　　　　How treat you them?

NURSE　　　　　　　　Forget the brutes!

MEDEA (*in a shriek*)　　　　　　　　　　*We don't!*
　　　　　　Woman, my breast is charged with vengeful thunder!
　　　　　　I had a husband—

NURSE (*cowering before her*)　　And he died? No wonder!　　　210

MEDEA

　　　　　　I said not that. French leave of me he took it.'

NURSE

　　　　　　(*tumbling on her knees*) So, you're a widow?

MEDEA　　　　　　　　　　　　Yes, bewitch'd!

NURSE　　　　　　　　　　　　　　You look it.

Harp music.— Medea turns away from the Nurse, to the latter's great relief. The Children come down C.

MEDEA

(*through music*) The bride, no doubt. Boys, in her pathway stop her,
And supplicate her for the lowly copper.
Look sentimental—if a grin you're trying, 215
Remember what you got just now for crying.

Goes up L. H.—the Children stand in front, R. C., begging. Re-enter CREUSA, *from temple, R. U. E., and comes down R.*

CREUSA

My happiness on all the world I'd visit;
Let all who want Creusa's aid solicit.
Till of her worldly goods they drain and dreg her.

LYCAON

Give me a kiss.

CREUSA   You saucy little beggar! 220
(*Takes him up and kisses him, laughing.*) Who bade thee ask?

LYCAON   My mother—there she is.
(*pointing to L. H.*) She bade me beg —I thought I'd beg a kiss.

MEDEA

(*aside, L*) How like his father!

CREUSA   Well, my champion bold,
Here's something better worth accepting—gold!

LYCAON

Give that to mother.

MEDEA (*Taking gold, and crossing to L. C. to Creusa, offers her a veil from the basket she has previously taken from the child.*)
From our slender store, 225

201–2 Referring to Colchis.
219 **drain** figuratively, 'to deprive a person or thing of possessions, properties, resources, strength, etc. by their gradual withdrawal; to exhaust' (*OED*, *v.* 8).

219 **dreg** obsolete 'to make dreggy, to render turbid as with dregs', used figuratively (*OED*, *v.*).
225.1 SD **veil** πέπλους (l.1159) in Euripides; *uestes* (l.817), 'robes' in Seneca.

    Lady, this gift—I see she's got plenty more. (*aside*)
    If you'd accept—
CREUSA   Nay—keep your gift.
MEDEA (*shutting up box*)   I will.
    (*Gives box to Child, and the two Children go up and stand R. C.*)
CREUSA
    But what's the matter? You look worn and ill.
    That face proclaims a mind distress'd and harried.
MEDEA
    It couldn't well be otherwise—I'm married.   230
CREUSA
    Ha!
MEDEA   To a hero—also to my sorrow!
CREUSA
    Please don't—I'm going to marry one tomorrow.
MEDEA
    I'm sorry for you.
CREUSA   Why *my* prospects damp,
    Because your own choice may have been—
MEDEA   A scamp!
    I sacrificed my duty as a daughter;   235
    Betray'd my native town to fire and slaughter;
    Robb'd my fond father, killed my aged mother;
    Also (but that's not much) my little brother.
    I stuck at nothing criminal or awful
    To serve the wretch! And now, his consort lawful 240
    He leaves—in search of some vile minx to match him.
    (*with sudden calm*) You can't conceive how I should like to catch him.
CREUSA
    You'd punish him?
MEDEA   Him? Well, not him alone.
    With him, of course, I'd have to pick a bone.
    But *as* to bones, if free to choose and nib,   245
    The one I'd pick would be *his second rib*.

CREUSA

>(*aside*) My heart within my bosom pit-*a-pat* jumps!
>In what way would'st thou act?

MEDEA

>   The way the cat jumps
>Upon a tender, unsuspecting mouse,
>Loose in a pantry, no one in the house,   250
>Nibbling away, with confidence unshaken,
>Eating his cheese up first, to save his bacon.
>She's in no hurry; with dilating eyes,
>And undulating tail, she crouching lies—
>Till his enjoyment's crisis he is at,   255
>Then pounce!—she makes a spring and has him 'pat!'
>(*using the action of a cat tossing a mouse about*)
>To a short game of pitch and toss she treats him—
>Tears him to pieces slowly, then—sc-runch !—*eats* him!

CREUSA

>(*terrified*) From injured ladies, all the gods deliver us!
>With tastes so cruel—not to say carnivorous.   260
>But let me have your history in full.

MEDEA

>There's been much cry about a little wool—
>The Golden Fleece.—You've heard of it?

CREUSA (*agitated*)   Proceed!

MEDEA

>Of Orpheus and of Jason?

CREUSA (*eagerly*)   Yes—I heed.

---

229   **harried** 'worried, tormented'. See 'harry' (*OED*, v. 4).
230   **married** see pp. 14, 26, 28.
235–42   According to the classical sources Medea helped Jason to retrieve the Golden Fleece by betraying her father and killing her brother Apsyrtus (see Appolonius, *Argonautica*).
246   According to the Christian tradition, God created a woman out of one of Adam's ribs (Gen 2.21). Here Medea refers to Creusa.
247   **pit-*a-pat*** 'a series of alternating or repeated light sounds; the action producing these sounds; palpitation, pattering' (*OED*, B. *n*. 1).
263   **Golden Fleece** King Pelias of Iolcos sent Jason to recover the golden fleece of a ram in Colchis. When Jason and the Argonauts arrived in Colchis, King Aiētēs set him tasks to accomplish his deed, which he achieved with the help of Medea.

MEDEA
  Know, then, I owe this form and features haggard—   265
            Enter ORPHEUS, *R. 1 E.*

ORPHEUS
  (*not seeing Medea*) Creusa!

MEDEA   Orpheus here!
  (*Crosses hastily and seizes him by the wrist.*)
           Now, where's that blackguard?
  Vive? Is he alive, and—speak, my chicken!
  Say that he's but alive—I'll do the kicking.

      QUARTETT.

     The Blue Bells of Scotland.

MEDEA
  Oh where, and oh where, is those children's daddy gone?

ORPHEUS
    Oh, he's gone to fight a giant for King Creon on his throne. 270
    And it's oh, in my heart I wish you'd stay'd at home.

CREUSA
    What name, oh, what name does your children's daddy bear?

MEDEA
  Oh, his name when he's at home is Jason—but he's seldom there.
  (*Creusa faints.*)
    And it's oh, in my heart I can see the whole affair.

  (*Changes to Air from Norma.*)

MEDEA
       Guerra! guerra!   275
    Let me rend and tear her.
   She in sev'ral pieces for my benefit shall act.

NURSE
        Where are—
        Where are

ORPHEUS

    The police?   280

    Oh, spare her!
    Don't you see she's fainting?

MEDEA

    I observe the pleasing fact.

CREUSA

    Sarah! Sarah!
    Please of me take care, ah!   285
    Save me from her—

MEDEA

    If she does I'll own that it's my fault.

ALL

    Scold her!
    Hold her!
    Clap her on the shoulder,   290
    Take her into custody on charge of an assault.

(*During this they struggle up the stage, and are closed in.*)

1.2 *Hall in the Palace of Creon, an opening, C, first and second grooves. Enter* ORPHEUS, *R. C.*

ORPHEUS

    The stars are in a fog, I can't see through it!
    What's to be done—and who is there to do it?

---

267 **Vive?** taken from the Italian version of Legouvé's *Medea* 'Is he alive?'.

268 **alive … kicking** 'alive and kicking', lively and active (*OED*, 'kicking', *adj.* a).

268.2 SD popular Scottish Air probably written by Anne Grant [neé McVicar] in 1799 and published in 1803 in a collection of her verses.

273 SD Typical attitude of melodramatic heroines.

274 SD ***Norma*** Alexandre Soumet wrote the play *Norma; ou, L'Infanticide*, upon which the opera *Norma* by Vinzenzo Bellini and Felice Romani, first staged in Milan in 1831, was based. One of the sources for *Norma* was Medea. (See Willier,

Bellini, pp. 76, 147). The success of the opera was such that it was translated into English by James Robinson Planché, one of the masters of burlesque.

275 **Guerra! guerra!** famous chorus from *Norma* II.vii.

280 Example of the anachronistic nature of Victorian classical burlesque.

284 **Sarah! Sarah!** Creusa's nurse. See List of Roles, 7n.

1–4 Cancelled in *LC* with blue ink. Note cue with 'See opposite' referring to f. 21b.

1–22 Orpheus plays the role of the classical chorus by summarizing the plot.

To set things right, I fear I've come a *bit* too late.
Let me the state of matters recapitulate, (*Considers.*)
Medea rages like a fiery dragon— 5
A female cup of wrath—a full Moll Flaggon,
Cauldron and witch combined—she boils and bubbles,
Catching all comers in her toils and troubles.
Jason has gone to kill the giant—good!
His wild oats he has not yet sown—he should; 10
His wife, though, soon will bring him to a dead-lock,
And bruise them for him—a la Mary Wedlock.
Creon's alarm'd—Creusa much enraged—
She holds herself to Jason still engaged.
To check the woes Medea's wrath foretells, 15
Creusa ought to marry some one else.
Could I Eurydice's sweet mem'ry shelf,
To save the plot, I'd sacrifice myself!
I'd do it, too, could I a fair apology
Offer to Constancy—and to Mythology. 20
(*looking off, L. 1 E.*)
She comes in tears—and really tears become her!
How very much she has improv'd this summer!

        Enter CREUSA *weeping, L. 1 E.*

CREUSA
 (L.) Oh, Orpheus! (*falling on his shoulder*)
ORPHEUS (*R.*)   Creusa!
CREUSA   I shall die.
ORPHEUS
 Not yet, Creusa—make it by and bye!
CREUSA
 You've always been so kind.
ORPHEUS   Yes, have I not? (*aside*) 25
 I will if necessary to the plot!
CREUSA
 She is his wife—that sorceress accurst.

ORPHEUS

    We'd better be prepared to meet the worst—

    I fear she is—

CREUSA   Then what's to come of me

    Without a husband?

ORPHEUS (*aside*)   Ah! I'm book'd I see!   30

    Let no vain scruples with my duty mingle.

    (*magnanimously*) Creusa, if the worst should come, I'm single!

    Or stay—to know what course is best to follow—

    I'll go and ask the poet's friend, Apollo.

DUET— AIR

Polly won't you try me, oh?

ORPHEUS

    I'll go and ask Apollo's aid,   35

---

5 Various similes are used throughout the play to illustrate Medea's passionate character. On some occasions this is equated with nineteenth-century strong-mindedness.

6 **Moll Flaggon** also 'Mol Flagon'. Female character from *The Lord of the Manor* (1780) by Lieutenant General John Burgoyne. Interpreted with success by Mr Suett in Drury Lane between 1780 and 1781 (Genest, *Account*, p. 179). The character was so popular that it became a recurring reference in the press of the nineteenth century (e.g. 'Photographic caricatures at Rome.' *Punch*, 21 December 1861, p. 251). Charles Dibdin wrote a homonymous version of the opera which was first staged at Covent Garden in 1812 (Nicoll, *History*, p. 293).

7 see 1.1.115–116n.

10 **wild oats** 'to commit youthful excesses or follies; to spend early life in dissipation or dissolute courses (usually implying subsequent reform)' (*OED*, 'wild oat', *n.*).

12 **Mary Wedlock** pun 'merry wedlock'. Ironic reference to what happens in 'merry wedlock' – the wife puts an end to her husband's gallivanting around with other women.

17 **Eurydice** Orpheus' tragic love for Eurydice is narrated by Virgil and Ovid. In Virgil, the newly-wed Eurydice dies of a snakebite. Orpheus descends to Hades to rescue her with his music. This he is allowed to do, provided he does not look back at her when returning from the underworld. When he does she dies.

18 **plot** metatheatrical allusions are common in Victorian burlesque. In this sense, Orpheus also alludes to the variations of the plot in 1.2.26.

20 **Constancy** fidelity (*OED*, *n.* 2).

26 see 18n.

27 **sorceress** see 53n to Lacy's edition paratext.

34 **Apollo** son of Zeus and Leto. Among his diverse functions prophecy and care for poetry are renowned.

34.2 SD *Keemo Kimo, or Polly, Won't You Try Me, Oh?* is a folk song from the Catskills, in the United States, and composed by Charles White. It was published as *Musical Bouquet* in 1855 (see Cazden, *Folk*, p. 527). As a caricature of American people, it soon spread in Victorian entertainment (Ritchi, *Night Side*, p. 94; Mayhew, *London Labour*, p. 184).

CREUSA
        Sing song Apollo won't deny you, oh!

ORPHEUS
                To learn what cards had best be play'd,

CREUSA
        Sing song Apollo won't deny you, oh!

ORPHEUS
      But to tunes like this, don't you think he will?

CREUSA
        Sing, song, Apollo they must try you, oh!   40

ORPHEUS
      Could we the muses treat more ill?

CREUSA
        Sing song Apollo would defy you, oh!

ORPHEUS
             Kemo!

CREUSA
                   Kimo!

ORPHEUS
                         When?

CREUSA
                              Yes—when?

ORPHEUS
              My high—my low—
              This style of Yankee singing!   45

(*spoken to Audience*) Excuse a brief parenthesis of 'spoken,'
    If with America peace should be broken,
    Defence on Europe's side must surely well lie.
    This song alone would form a *casus belli*.
        (*sung together*) Sometimes medley winkum, lingtum nip cat,   50
        Sing song, Apollo, don't it try you, oh?

ORPHEUS
    What's this breaks off our duo in the middle?
                            Enter CREON, *L. C, agitated*.

CREON
    (C.) Orpheus, be good enough to get your fiddle,

Go out and try to calm the people common—
They're pitching into that unhappy woman. 55

CREUSA

(*L.*) Medea!

CREON (*C.*) Just so! they say—(and p'raps it's true.)
Their champion will have work enough to do
To thrash the giant—and if spared with life,
Will need repose—therefore they'd kill his wife.

ORPHEUS

I'll calm them down with measures strong and quick too.
(*Crosses to C.*) 60
Cheer up, Creusa, what I said, I'll stick to. *Exit L. C.*

CREUSA

(*L.*) Papa!

CREON (*R.*) My angel child!

CREUSA (*timidly*) After the turn
Affairs have taken, I should like to learn
What are your views in reference to me?
My match with Jason broken off must be— 65
At least, I should suppose so.

CREON You suppose it?
My angel child, not if your father knows it;
You know our way—so don't look cross or nettled,
This married lady must be somehow settled;
We'll set her up in bus'ness—when she's cool, 70

43–5 see 34.2n.
46–9 Probably referring to the tense Anglo-American relations of the mid-nineteenth century dominated by the British anxiety about possible American expansion in Central America and the problems arising from the Crimean War.
49 **casus belli** act or reason for war (*OED, n.*).
51 The original song reads 'Sing song Polly won't you try me, oh'.
52 Footnote cue at the bottom of f. 24 with the words 'Opposite' referring to f. 23b.
53 **fiddle** Orpheus is usually linked to the lyre rather than to a fiddle.
54 Allusion to Orpheus' power to appease the beasts.
55 Thanks to the debates on divorce laws and the situation of married women, the focus of the burlesque plays of the nineteenth century is not so much on Medea the infanticide as on Medea the wronged wife (see Macintosh, *Medea*, p. 82).
70 A major problem for abandoned wives in Victorian England was how to provide for themselves and their children. See pp. 14, 29, 30, 36.

> Or get her boys into the Blue Coat School.
> But let's ascend to watch from yonder height—
> 'Tis time they telegraphed about the fight.
> I've bet on Jason rather heavily,
> And so feel nervous—(*Shouts outside, C.*)
> Shouts of victory! 75
> It must be—we can scarcely keep our wig on
> For tremor.

Enter an excited CITIZEN, *hastily, L. C. and down C.*

CITIZEN (*delighted*) All's right! Jason's wopp'd the big 'un!   *Exit, L. C.*
CREON
> Ring all the bells—light up no end of candle!
> Grind ev'ry organ box that's worth a handle!
> With rare device of colour'd lamp and gilding 80
> We'll decorate the front of ev'ry building.
> And hit on some new plan, by which, at night,
> Some of them shall at least, be seen alight.
> Haste, daughter! dress in gorgeous array.
> Stint not yourself in washing bills—we'll pay!   *Exit Creusa, L, 1 E.* 85
> Not ev'ry day we a fine giant slaughter—
> And so—what, ho! Who waits without?

Enter an Attendant, R. 1 E.

Hot water!
Exit Creon, preceded by Attendant R. 1 E.

Shouts very loud, L. C.—Enter JASON, *with sword and shield, followed by the Populace, cheering, the mob remains in opening, C.*

JASON
> (*C.*) Thanks, thanks, my friends—enough! Although the winner,
> I've wounds to see to, and I've had no dinner.
> Here are two shillings—get them changed for copper. 90

(*The Populace retire, L. C., cheering as they go.*)
That giant was, and yet was not—a wopper.
His head's outside—I hope they may be able
To get it in the wash-house—or the stable.
Whew! Giant killing's really no light work.
Fighting's a duty, though, I never shirk. 95
The honest homages of friend and stranger,
On your return, make up for all the the danger.

SONG

The British Grenadiers.

They talk of queer provisions,
    Of trench work in the cold,
Of tents in bad conditions, 100
    And huts that water hold.
But with such to check a warrior's zeal,
    The task as vain appears
As to cow, or to row, or to bow wow wow
    The British Grenadiers. 105

---

71 **Blue Coat School** charity school. 'a charity school at which pupils wear blue coats; *spec*. Christ's Hospital, originally situated in Newgate, London, now in Horsham, West Sussex; (later more generally) any charity school; now also in the names of conventional schools, some of which were originally charity schools, (*OED*, 'blue coat', *n*.). Victorian school for poor children in London and Liverpool (see Elmes, *Dictionary*, p. 69; Mann, *School*, pp. 322-25).

73 see 1.1.280n. The use of commercial telegraphy was extended in Britain in the 1830s and the Electric and International Telegraph Company was founded in 1855.

77 **wopp'd** 'to strike with heavy blows' (*OED*, 'whop', *v*. 2a).
big'un big one.

79 **organ box** 'organ-grinder', an itinerant street musician who produces music by turning the handle of a barrel organ' (*OED*, *n*. 1). 'barrel organ' is a musical instrument of the organ type, the keys of which are mechanically acted on by a revolving barrel or cylinder studded with metal pins. Also extended to similar instruments' (*OED*, 'barrel organ', *n*.).

85 **washing bills** 'a statement of laundry-charges' (*OED*, 'washing', *n*.).

90 **copper** copper money; a copper coin; a penny or halfpenny. (*OED*, *n*.¹, 2a).

91 **wopper** 'whopper', something enormous (*OED*, *n*. 1a).

97.2 SD Anonymous war song dated ca. 1780 (see Butler, *War*, pp. 162-163). The song became popular and was referred to in numerous literary works of the time, for example, Charles Dickens' *Bleak House* (1853).

    In leathern stocks half strangled,
      We scarce could shut our eyes,
    In broadcloth strangely mangled,
      We've shown you warlike guys.
    If you ask me why we bear so much,   110
      An answer meets your ears,
    You'll allow in the row, you are making now,
      To the British Grenadiers.
  Now at the fair Creusa's feet to lay
  Antestor's spoils to grace our wedding-day,   115
  To fresh deeds fired, as in her smiles I revel
  Bold, aye! and strong enough to face—

Going, L. 1 E. is confronted by Medea, who has entered with her garments slightly disordered, she stands rigidly looking at him, L.

    The devil! (*Returns to R. H.*)

  Would I could make my boast good to the letter.

MEDEA

  (*L., aside*) The brute! I never saw him looking better. (*a pause*)
  I'm in no hurry, (*Stands calmly.*) sir, I wait your leisure.   120

JASON

  (*faltering—his back to Medea*) Really—this—very—unexpected—
    pleasure—

MEDEA

  (*with continued calmness*) You do not recognize me, I perceive,
  I'm altered, I can readily believe;
  Through suffering, a little worn and livid.
  Besides, (*referring to the state of her dress*) as you
          have heard, I've just been 'chevied,'   125
  (*with bitter irony*) Giason io son Medea—

JASON (*aside*)   'Tis most bewild'rin'!
  I don't know what to say—how are the children?

MEDEA

  Thank you, they're bobbish.

JASON (*a little bolder*)   So, good news you bring—
  Are they in want of boots, or anything?
  Or are the school bills due? Because, if so,   130
  Draw on me for what sums you like—and go!

MEDEA
  (*preserving her forced calm throughout*)
  Go?

JASON   Y—es.

MEDEA   Where to?

JASON   Wherever 'tis you stay.
  Let me no obstacle be in your way;
  We both are free—

MEDEA   *Free*, am I?

JASON   Yes. (*aside*) Much more
  Than welcome, any day. Our ties are o'er.   135

MEDEA
  O—oh! I was not aware.

JASON   Why, yes, of course;
  Our separation equals a divorce.

MEDEA
  A—ah!

JASON   You can marry any one you please.
  (*aside*) If any one you *can* please. And to ease
  You of a load that heavily must press—   140
  I meant, when I could meet with your address,
  To write to you. (with money, I should state,)
  To send the boys to me to educate.

106	**leathern** made of leather (*OED, adj.* 1).	126	*Giason . . . Medea* allusion to a famous line from Ernest Legouvé's *Medea* in II.iv 'Giasone io son Medea' and popular after Adelaide Ristori's performance.
108	**broadcloth** 'fine, plain-wove, dressed, double width, black cloth, used chiefly for men's garments' (*OED, n.*).		
115	**Antestor's** see 1.1.61n.	128	**bobbish** 'well; in good health and spirits' (*OED, adj.*).
117.2-3	SD Disordered garments were a sign of madness and frenzy in Victorian literature and arts.	128-31	see pp. 14, 29, 30, 36.
		137	**divorce** see pp. 28-31.
125	**chevied** derivative of 'chevy ? chivy', chased (*OED, v.*).	142-43	see 128-131n.

MEDEA

    (*suppressing her emotion*) The boys to come to you, and part from me?

JASON

    You understand what's reas'nable, I see.   145
    Of course 'twould never do for boys like those
    Within whose veins the blood of princes flows,
    To be brought up by (no offence) a vagrant,
    Given to sorcery and crimes as flagrant.
    You understand me?

MEDEA   Quite.

JASON   I'm glad to find   150
    For once, at any rate, we're of one mind.
    So, you've forestalled my wishes—brought the boys?
    For velvets they shall change their corduroys.
    Crack tutors they shall have, and guardians fond—
    Don't be alarmed—I'll let you correspond.   155
    Nay, more, for shewing such praiseworthy animus,
    Towards yourself—I'll do the thing magnanimous.

MEDEA

    You overwhelm me!

JASON   Pray don't mention it!
    A treasure-ship to-morrow out I'll fit,
    Laden with spoils, won by my arm victorious,   160
    To sail where'er you please—won't that be glorious?

MEDEA

    De—licious! and yourself—

JASON (*awkwardly*)   Why, I remain.
    A rumour you have heard—no doubt with pain—
    I'm going—I mean—you follow me?

MEDEA   I do, sir!

JASON

    (*slowly*) I'm—going—to marry—the Princess—Creusa.   165

MEDEA

    Cre—u—sa?

JASON   Yes! (*eagerly*) A state alliance!

MEDEA   Oh?
    I see!
JASON   A mother's love, the boys, she'll show
    Equal to yours—with pow'r to help them stronger.
MEDEA

    (*giving sudden vent to her suppressed passion*)
    Now drop it! I can't stand it any longer!
    Oh, gods celestial and gods infernal!   170
    Oh, pow'rs of mischief—dark and sempiternal!
    Demons above, and deities below,
    I ask ye sternly—isn't this a go?

                DUET—AIR

              Robinson Crusoe.

MEDEA

        I have done for this man,
        All that tenderness can,   175
  I have followed him half the world through, sir,
        I've not seen him this year,
        And the first thing I hear,
    Is, 'he's going to marry Creusa,'
      Going to marry Creusa,   180
      Going to marry Creusa,
          Ting a ting ting!
          Ting a ting ting!
      All I can say, sir, is, *do* sir.

---

147   **princes** for being the offspring of Medea according to the classical sources.
148–9 Pejorative allusions to Medea prevail here instead of her royal lineage.
166   **state alliance** emphasis on the political reasons for abandoning Medea.
167–8 see 128–131n.
173.2 SD **'Robinson Crusoe'** besides Defoe's novel, in 1847 the burlesque *Crusoe the Second, or the Shipwrecked Milliners* by Stocqueler was first staged at the Lyceum. With Alfred Wigan in the title role, Mr and Mrs Keeley were also part of the cast in that production. In 1860 Henry James Byron's *Robinson Crusoe* was first staged at the Princess's Theatre and in 1867, Byron, W. S. Gilbert, T. Hood junior, H. S. Leigh, W. J. Prowse and Arthur Sketchley wrote another burlesque version of the novel. In 1876, H. B. Farnie's *Robinson Crusoe* was performed at the Folly (Adams, *Book*, pp. 193–194; See O'Malley, Sullivan).

JASON

If you'll take my advice, 185
You'll pack up in a trice,
Nor of time to pack off be a loser,
For the popular wrath
Might be likely to froth
'Gainst a foe to myself or Creusa. 190
I'm going to marry Creusa.
And believe me the best thing for *you's* a
Fast ship to bespeak,
And some desert isle seek,
Like a sort of she Robinson Cruiser. 195

Exit, R. 1 E.

MEDEA

(*solus*) *Sangue! sangue! Straziar spezzar suo cuore,*
Which means, translated, something red and gory.
Unche di spavento's atroce strano—
Murder in Irish! No—Italiano!
Ai! Ai! Dia mow Kephalas flox owrania, 200
By-ee tiddy moi zeen èté Kurdos—
Stop, that's Euripides! *Du sang! du sang!*
Briser torturer son coeur—oui! That's wrong!
I've got confused with all these versions jinglish—
Thunder and turf!—And even that's not English. 205
To rend that fellow's heart, now—claw and grip it—
But, psha! a chisel even wouldn't chip it.
To pulverize it—I my rank forget—
I haven't come down to stone breaking yet.
Stone! Ha! a dreadful thought itself suggests. 210
His gallivanting taste that never rests
Has led him to make eyes e'en at—Medusa.
(*reflecting on the rhyme*) 'Dusa!' The deuce, ah! You, sir!
    (*Shrieks.*) Ha, Creusa!
Yes, there my path of vengeance lies; to-morrow,

> To change their festive merriment to sorrow. 215
> It's very seldom I mince matters—(*Draws knife.*) yet—
> Jason in search of his new wedded pet,
> Fresh from the bridal toast and sparkling cup,
> I fear will find her very much cut up.
> I've thought—I've plann'd—resolv'd—and I'll go through it. 220
> Hooray! hooray! hoooray! I'll do it. (*Shout of pursuit, L.*)

Enter CREUSA, *L. 1 E.* MEDEA *conceals her knife.*

CREUSA
> Fly, wretched individual?

MEDEA
> What's the matter?

CREUSA
> Dost thou not hear that direful noise and clatter?

MEDEA
> What of it?

CREUSA
> 'Gainst thee still the people's ireworks—
> They're going to have a grand display of fireworks. 225

MEDEA
> What then?

---

196 Allusion to a famous line in Legouvé's *Medea* II.v. Footnote cue in *LC* f. 31 referring to a fragment rewritten in f. 30b.
198 Allusion to a famous line in Legouvé's *Medea* II, v.
199 **Irish** pejorative reference to the Irish accent. **Italiano** Ristori's famous performance at Théâtre Italien, Paris on 18 April 1856 and at the Lyceum Theatre in June the same year were in Italian.
200–1 The lines correspond to line 144 ff in Euripides' *Medea*.
201 1856 includes the following footnote 'To be pronounced exactly as spelt'.
202–3 Translation of line 196 into French.
204 **jinglish** 'jingle' 'to play with words for the sake of sound; (depreciatively) to rhyme' (*OED, v.* 3b) burlesquing the mixture of languages of the production in Italian, from a French text derived from an Ancient Greek hypotext to an English audience.
208 **I . . . forget** Medea was granddaughter of Helios and daughter of Aiëtēs.
212 **Medusa** Medusa was a gorgon, a female monster in Greek mythology. Her dreadful gaze turned to stone anyone who looked at her.
223 **direful** 'dreadful' (*OED, adj.*).
224 **ireworks** pun 'ire works' to keep the rhyme with fireworks (l.225).

CREUSA   Fly!
MEDEA   Why?
CREUSA   And she can ask me why?
    Canst thou not guess? (*Leads her forward.*) They seek thee for a guy!
    This way—they come! (*trying to force her off, R. H.*)
MEDEA   Let go—I won't be lugged!
CREUSA
    Stay then, misguided woman, and be smugged!
       (*footsteps and murmurs, L. C.*)

MEDEA
    (*aside*) This unforeseen pursuit my vengeance baulks.   230
    Guys, eh? I'll show them knives instead of Fawkes!

   Attempts to stab Creusa —Orpheus runs in R. 1 E., and wards off the blow.
   CREON *enters, L. C., keeping back the crowd.* JASON *enters, L. 1 E.*

CREON
    (*C.*) Woman, that guilty look and striking attitude,
    Betrays the very pitch of black ingratitude.
    Since thus our kind protection is requited,
    Let the avenging lucifer be lighted.   235
       (*Crowd rush forward.*)

ORPHEUS
    (*R.*) Nay—back! The woman's griefs her rage excuse.

JASON
    (*L.—conceitedly*) That's true. A husband like myself to lose
    Is no light trial. Creon, let her go—
    The creature's to be pitied.

CREON   Be it so.
    'Gainst her, of banishment, we'll strike a docket.   240
    So, with to-morrow's tide—

      Enter, L. C., the usually excited CITIZEN.

CITIZEN (*in opening C.*)   There's the first rocket.
    (*All are running out C.*)

CREON

    Hold! (*They stop.*) This unseemly haste our court disgraces.

    Form a procession—and start fair for places.

    (*The Citizen all rush out hastily, C.*)

DUET AND CHORUS

AIR

The Young May Moon.

JASON

    (*to Creusa*) The bright maroon is beaming, love,

        And the Roman light is gleaming, love,   245

           Let's seek some alcove,

           Or sequestered grove,

        To be safe from the rocket-sticks streaming, love.

CREON

    Look awake! the Heavens are bright, my dear,

(*to Medea, ironically*)   I'm sorry you can't see the sight, Medea.   250

           But I think the best way

           To make sure you don't stray,

    Is to keep you locked in for the night, Medea.

CHORUS

    Look awake! the Heavens are bright, my dear,

    I'm sorry, &c.   255

    Exeunt all but Medea, C.—the opening is then closed upon her.

---

227 **guy** with reference to the effigy of 'Guy Fawkes' (1570–1606), conspirator known for the Gunpowder Plot. The effigy is traditionally burnt on 5 November on the anniversary of the plot. 'The figure is habited in grotesquely ragged and ill-assorted garments [...] and was formerly accompanied by other similar effigies (representing unpopular persons), to which the name of "guys" is often given by extension' (*OED, n.²*, 1a). See 231n.

229 **smugged** 'smug', 'to smarten up (oneself or another, one's appearance, etc.)' (*OED, v.*1, 1).

231 **Fawkes** see 227n.

231.1 SD ***Attempts ... Creusa*** note that in Euripides Medea murders Creusa with a poisoned veil.

243.4 SD poem by Thomas Moore (1779–1852). Brough's air reproduces the rhyme of the poem: 'The young May moon is beaming, love, / The glow-worm's lamps is gleaming, love; / How sweet to rove / Through Morna's grove [...]'.

248 **rocket-sticks** 'a conductor's baton' (*OED*, 'stick', *n.*¹ 4h).

SOLO

West Country air.

MEDEA   Procrastination's the thief of time, they say
Don't leave till to-morrow things that might be done to-day.
I've lots of time, now, for every preparation,
And to decide on my plan of operation.
        Something very brutal it'll   260
        Be, I'll either shoot a little
        Poison'd dart, or *two* too little
            For the purpose deem.
Drop some stuff in port a little
Ever such a mortal little,   265
Quite a little vital it'll
        Prove towards my scheme.
        Ri tle itle, &c. (*dances off, R. 1 E.*)

1.3 *Banquetting Hall in the Palace overlooking gardens. A gigantic statue of Saturn with altar steps, C. A banquetting table going up the stage, R., splendidly dressed—seats, R. H.* CREON, JASON, CREUSA, *Guests, Courtiers, &c., assembled to celebrate the nuptials of Jason and Creusa.* ORPHEUS *standing C. with a goblet in his hand, bowing as if he had just completed a song. Chorus as the scene opens.*

[ALL]
        A jolly good song—and jolly well sung,
        But none of us feel very sorry it's done.

Creon and all the Guests rise and come forward, and Attendants clear off table, &c.

CREON
        (*R. C.*) Thanks, minstrel, for thy song; the air was grand;
        The words we didn't clearly understand.
        But that's an indispensable condition,   5
        From all I hear, in modern composition.

I hope this licence won't be long. I say,
Jason, what's needful on a wedding day
You should have known — you've done the thing before.

JASON

(R.—*looking at Creusa*) Please, I don't mean to do so any more.   10

CREON

Now where's that messenger? He took a cab.

JASON

A dark thought seizes me!

CREON   Out with it—blab!

JASON

Some adverse pow'r of vengeance with a nice sense,
Has stopp'd his cab, and ta'en away his licence.

CREON

Step out and look. (*Jason runs out, L. 1 E.*)

ORPHEUS   (*aside*) No licence, cab or curricle   15
Will bring, till I've my answer from the Oracle.
(*A Messenger entering L. U. E, gives Orpheus a scroll.*)

ORPHEUS

(*reading*) *Sun Office*. Phoebus's own hand, I see.
Glorious Apollo! God of Harmony!
(*Tears open letter and reads.*)
Dear Orpheus,—We have just received your letter.
The spots on our face are rather better.   20

0.1–2 SD **gigantic ... Saturn** god in ancient Roman mythology with multiple associations. Related to the rites of the Saturnalia, where various inversion rituals take place. For example, the statue of Saturn, bound for the whole year, was freed for this day. Saturn was identified with the Greek Cronos. From Cronos' marriage with his sister Rhea the race of the Olympian gods was born. Cronos, fearing to be overcome by one of them ate his children on birth. Legouvé alludes to this interpretation of Saturn to prefigure Medea's murder on various occasions. Also in Legouvé, both Medea and her children take refuge at the foot of the statue of Saturn when they are followed by the crowd. In Brough's Legouvé it allows the common display of sculptures in grand and transformation scenes so common in the popular theatre of the time.

3   **minstrel** see 1.1.1n.
9–10 Allusion to second marriages and bigamy. See pp. 26, 28, 29.
11   **cab** illustrating the anachronistic nature of Victorian classical burlesque.
15   **curricle** 'a light two-wheeled carriage, usually drawn by two horses abreast' (*OED, n.* 2).
16   **Oracle** see *Antigone*, 288n.
16   SD **scroll** note the classicizing intention of the use of this prop.
17   **Sun office** Apollo, also known as Phoebus, was among others the god of the sun.

In ref'rence to the matter that you mention—
It shall receive our very best attention.
We'll see all right.' So then, no risk we run.
Dear Orpheus, always your paternal son.'
A postscript, though—*We would have written sooner,*   25
But have been bother'd by our sister Luna.
In anger, some astronomer she taxes
With saying that she hasn't got an axis.

Re-enter JASON, *eagerly, with a scroll, L. 1 E.*

JASON

(*Crosses to R. C.*) Dearest, behold the document at last—
The roads were heavy and the horse stuck fast.   30
Come, let us haste, our tender vows to chronicle,
Or we shall really miss the hours canonical.
What feeling's this? I should be glad and merry.
  (*Offers his arm to Creusa, suddenly changing his tone.*)
Yet grim forebodings seize me.

CREON (*coming down on Jason's L.*)   Take some sherry? (*offering goblet*)

JASON

(*C.*) I couldn't look at it. (*Creon goes up.*) My feelings savour.   35
No whit of golden hue, or nutty flavour.

CREUSA

(*huffed*) Well, if the gentleman repents—

CREON   (*harshly on her R.*)   You hush!

JASON

Methinks, impending on my head to rush,
A torrent hangs of woe and misery.

CREUSA

(*L. C.*) What a delightful compliment to me!   40

JASON

Dearest, I meant not that—come, let us go!
Though Fate, cold water on our bliss to throw
All the earth's cataracts be gathering

In one huge shower bath—I'd pull the string;
Hence! idle fears! our sacred ties concluding.   45
What shall prevent—

Enter MEDEA, *L. 1 E., turning to go, he sees her standing at his elbow.*

MEDEA (*meekly*)   I hope I'm not intruding.
   (*Curtsies. General consternation.*)
JASON
   (*C.*) Medea, by all that's villainous!
MEDEA (*L. C.*)   Just so!
ORPHEUS
   (*aside, R.*) I see there's going to be a row—I'll go!   *Exit, R.*
JASON
   (*C. to Creon, R. C.*) Speak to her! I'm not well! (*Goes up a little, and down, R. H.*)
CREON   (*crossing to L. C.*) Woman!
MEDEA (*L.*)   Your ludship!
CREON
   How comes it that you are not, in fact, aboard ship?   50
   And bring, forgetful of our usage lenient,
   Your presence where it's not at all convenient?
MEDEA
   Forgive a poor lone woman's schemings, pray,
   I really couldn't keep myself away.
   You've been so thoughtful of my wants and ailings,   55
   So very lenient to my little failings.
   My grateful impulses too weak to stem,
   'Something,' I said, 'I'll go and do for them,

---

26 **Luna** Artemis, sister of Apollo, was equated with Selene, goddess of the moon.

42 **Fate** the common Greek words for fate mean 'share', 'portion' (Chantraine, *Dictionnaire*). One's share is appointed or falls to one at birth. 'The most important share is man's universal fate of death from which not even the gods can protect him' (Roberts, *Dictionary*, pp. 283-284). Here Jason anthropomorphises the term and juxtaposes it with a modern meaning for destiny.

53-6 Cancelled in *LC* with pencil and black ink. Footnote cue referring to *LC* f. 41b.

       'If it's to bestow my blessing.' (*aside*) Drat 'em!
       'And throw an old shoe after them.' (*aside*) Or at 'em!   60
         (*Shows a highlow she has got concealed under her robe.*)
       (*to Creusa, and going to C.*) How well you look, my love—excuse me, pray,
       Taking the liberty—And Mr. J.—
       Like one of his own sons, I vow,—but then,
       The wedding costume so sets off the men;
       It makes a difference when they've thrown it by;   65
       It's odd—but so it is—I wonder why?
       But I detain you, and delay's unpleasant—
       I wished to make the bride a trifling present. (*producing veil*)
       When this you see her wearing at the kirk,
       You'll own I've made *a pretty piece of work*.   70

CREUSA
       (*pleased*) The veil you showed me yesterday?

MEDEA   Precisely!
       But then you'll find I've done it up so *nicely*!

CREUSA
       (*admiring the veil*) Oh! give it me!

MEDEA   Expressly for your marriage!
       (*Creusa is about to put it on—Medea stops her quickly.*)
       Not yet!

JASON (*impatiently*)   Your maid can fix it in the carriage.

MEDEA
       Say at the altar! it would be a shame   75
       To scrunch it!

JASON   True! thank—Mrs.—what's-her name!

MEDEA
       (*sharply*) Got none!

JASON (*confused*)   Ahem! the carriage waits!
       (*Crosses to C.*)

MEDEA   One word!
       I know the weakness will appear absurd,
       But might I be allowed farewell to say
       To the two boys that were mine yesterday?   80

JASON

    (*R. C.*) You ask too much!

CREUSA (*R.*)   Oh! grant her that for charity!

JASON

    My life! The woman's coarseness and vulgarity—
    Well, I consent!

MEDEA   Ah!

JASON   Dearest! there's the bell—come!

    (*to Medea*) Don't thank me! For I cannot say you're welcome!

        The bridal procession moves out at back, R., all exeunt but Medea.

MEDEA

    (*calling after them and taking out her shoe*)

    May ev'ry blessing of earth, sea and skies   85

    That walks, or jumps, or creeps, or swims, or flies,

    Conveying bliss through all the solar system

    Follow—and never overtake you.

        (*Throws shoe after them savagely.*)   Missed 'em!

    Their mirth, as soon as she puts on that veil

    Will change to something very like a wail.   90

    I've charmed the web, it's action instantaneous

    Will cause combustion equal to spontaneous.

    That pretty piece of flesh that *he* admires

    But once submitted to it's deadly fires

    Will leave no trace, but just a smoking cinder   95

    And a few crinkey, twinkey flakes of tinder.

    And now, to kill the boys! it must be done!

    I must forget I ever had a son!

60.2 SD **highlow** see *Antigone* 177n.

77 **Got none!** alluding to her marital state.

84.3 SD–88 Shoe-throwing in weddings for good luck and for transferring the authority over the bride from the father to the husband was a custom in England (Crombie). Medea plays on the tradition to increase the comic effect of the scene.

96 **crinkey** emitting a 'sharp, thin sound' (*OED*, 'crink', *v.*).

Twinkey 'to make a light clear abrupt ringing sound; to clink, chink' (*OED*, 'twink', *v.*²).

> They are his sons—of bride and children 'reft,
> With not a soul to care for, he'll be left, 100
> Doomed in his own society to pine,
> I do believe he'd just as soon have mine.
> Those well-known steps—but feeling I must smother.

Enter LYCAON *and* MELANTHE, *R. 1 E. spendidly dressed.*

LYCAON
> Somebody want us? Why—it's only mother!

MEDEA
> I'll try them! Dears! I've come to say *good bye*. 105

LYCAON
> Please don't be long!—We've got a kite to fly.

MEDEA
> Wretched young ingrates! I no longer own ye!

LYCAON
> Wretched! oh, that we're not! I've got a pony;
> He's just been getting shod!

MEDEA
>   Affecting proof!
> Shod is he! it's for me to pad the hoof! 110
> And is that all to me you have to say?

LYCAON
> Oh, no! we've pies for dinner ev'ry day!

MEDEA
> They talk of dinner!

LYCAON
>   *Now*, we do,—But steady—
> As we are talking of it—(*Looks at his watch.*)

MEDEA
>   Well?

LYCAON
>   It's ready!

(*Both are running out R. H. 1 E., Medea pulls them back by the skirts.*)

MEDEA
> (*getting them on each side of her*)
> So—she has poison'd then my children's hearts 115
> With pies and puddings, or with pizen'd tarts!

One last appeal—(*with little hope*) I'll proffer
Boys— have ye nothing your mamma to offer?

LYCAON
Yes, look! here's this!
(*Gives her a scroll from his pocket.*)

MEDEA (*tearing it open*) How? from Creusa? (*Reads.*)
What?

I sympathize with your unhappy lot, 120
Though forced by my papa, your spouse to marry,
I would not, needlessly, your feelings harry,
Your children I restore. Should wants distress you,
I enclose money—may the Heaven's bless you.

Medea at first astonished, then wholly overcome by this sympathy, stands trembling—crushing the letter in her hand; then she falls sobbing on her knees, embracing her two children, who have knelt on each side.

LYCAON
(*tenderly*) Mamma! what is the matter? Tell us, pray? 125
Have we been naughty?

MEDEA (*starting up wildly*) From my sides, away!
Touch not my hands, there's blood upon them seething,
For I have slain the sweetest lady breathing.
I've killed Creusa—the divinest she—(*suddenly*)
No! 'Twasn't I that murder'd her—'twas he. 130
(*murmurs without—gradually increasing*)
Those sounds! the spell has work'd! 'Tis past time!
He comes to urge me to another crime—

107–16 Lines cancelled in *LC* f. 45 with black ink with a footnote cue that refers to f. 44b, where the lines are rewritten.

114.2–3 SD In imitation of the famous scene interpreted by Ristori.

116 **pizen'd** pun; referring to 'pies and tarts' and also 'poisoned tarts'.

124 The following footnote is included in *1856* p. 33: 'From the reading of Creusa's note to the final denouement, the action must be conducted by all the characters as in tragedy.'

126 SD **starting up** detailed stage directions on the attitudes of Medea manifest the relevance of the performance by Ristori and Robson's imitation of the actress.

This way, my babes!
(*Crouches down, R., sheltering her two children with her robe.*)
In vain my robes I gather
Round ye—I cannot save ye from your father.
(*Murmurs approach.*)
He comes! his vengeance swells like gath'ring thunder! 135

She rushes with the two children, first to L. U. E. then to R., and round back of statue, when she is encountered by Creon, L. And Populace, who rush in.

CREON
Quick! Tear the she-wolf and her cubs asunder.
MEDEA
(*grasping the children*) Approach one step!
CITIZEN   The murd'rous witch to death.
CREON
Secure the children!
MEDEA   Not while they have breath!

The Crowd have concealed her from the Audience —two plaintive cries are heard—Creon and the Crowd start back with a shriek of horror—Medea is seen standing alone, on steps, C. quivering with emotion—a reeking knife in her hand—the Children lying on the steps, apparently dead. Jason appears R. U. E. with drawn sword, but is witheld by the Populace.

JASON
(*struggling*) Back for your life—her life to me is due.

He breaks away R. to rush at Medea —stops horrified seeing the bodies of his two Children.

My boys both murder'd! Who has slain them?
MEDEA (*with one foot on steps, darting towards him*)   You!   140

The dagger she has hitherto grasped is discovered at this moment to have been changed into a jester's bauble, with cap and bells—Medea very much astonished, comes forward C. inspecting it.

Holloa! what's this? I thought it was a knife
With which I'd robb'd my blessed babes of life!
Who's been employing magic and cajolery
To change my serious business to tom-foolery—
Making a bauble of Medea's blade? 145

ORPHEUS *enters L. U. E., with Creusa on his arm.*

ORPHEUS

(*L. C.*) Some of us comic poets, I'm afraid—

MEDEA

Creusa! and alive! without a scar?
Then—p'raps the blessed infants—

LYCAON, MELANTHE (*starting up from steps and running to her*)

Here we are!

MEDEA

(*leading them forward C.*) What can a poor, lone, helpless woman do—

---

133 SD Ristori's attitudes with her two children sheltering them with her robes were widely known thanks to the photographs by André-Adolphe-Eugène Disdéri. See, for example, 'Mme Adélaïde Ristori et ses enfants en huit poses'. Collection Maurice Levert, Musée d'Orsay, Paris.

134 Following the tradition of throwing responsibility for the death of the children on Jason.

136 After the SP, there is a footnote cue in LC which refers to the following lines written at the bottom of the same folio: 'Note From the Reading of Crëusa's letter up to the final denouement—the action must be conducted by all the characters—as in real tragedy.. : Creon on his exit entrance must desist himself of any mannerism —not in accordance with the feelings of a father whose child has just been murdered'.

138 SD Legouvé also follows the classical precept of not showing blood murders on stage.

140 SD following the comic spirit of burlesque Brough transforms the deaths of Lycaon, Melanthe and Creusa into a trick. For a similar approach to the burlesque of tragic plots see Francis Talfourd's *Macbeth Travestie* (1850).

144 **tom-foolery** 'silly trifling' (*OED*, 'tom-foolery', *n.* 1a).

Baffled on all sides—but appeal to you? (*to Audience*) 150
My plot destroyed—my damages made good,
They'd change my very nature if they could.
Don't let them—rather aid me to pursue
My murd'rous career the season through;
Repentance is a thought that I abhor, 155
What I have done don't make me sorry for.
Even for my least pardonable crime—
Which I'll explain in a familiar rhyme.

FINALE

[ALL]

One horse Shay.

  There was a little man,
   And he made a little fun 160
Of a very great woman 'bove his head, head, head,
  And he got some other bucks
  And a lot of little ducks
To assist him in the project that he led, led, led.
  And he trusts you'll carry hence 165
  Of his harmless impudence
No impression to your supper or your bed, bed, bed,
  Save the merry chirping sound,
  Of a gadfly buzzing round
The wreath upon a noble statue's head, head, head. 170

The statue of Saturn disappears, discovering an allegorical groupe.

CHORUS

  And he trusts you'll carry hence
  Of his harmless impudence
No impression to your supper or your bed, bed, bed,
  Save the merry chirping sound

Of a gadfly buzzing round 175
The wreath upon a noble statue's head, head, head.

CURTAIN

CITIZENS. JASON. STATUE. CITIZENS.

CREON

CREUSA

ORPHEUS

MEDEA & CHILDREN

150–8 For a discussion of these lines within the context of Victorian marriages see Macintosh, 'Medea', pp. 97–98)
158.1 SD In 1858, Oliver Wendell Holmes first published the poem 'The Deacon's Masterpiece, or, The Wonderful "One-Hoss Shay"' in *The Atlantic Monthly*, which immortalized the chaise. A satiric version of the poem was published in *Punch*, 23 March 1867, p. 117.
159 **little man** referring to Jason.
161 **very great woman** Medea.
166 Footnote cue in *LC* f. 47b referring to a fragment in f. 48 which at the same time refers back to f. 47 for the ending of the play.
170 SD **allegorical groupe** see Lacy's paratext 55–6n.

Textual notes

1.1

0.1 SD *R. H.*] LC ~~R. (?)H.~~ Opposite

0.2–3 SD *up … E.*] *not in LC*

0.4 SD *Flourish … curtain*] LC (N.B. In set a close copy of the same scene at Lyceum *********

0.5 SD *on … R.,*] *not in LC*

0.6 SD *in … c.*] LC case and portmanteau

0.7 SD *L.H.*] *not in LC*

1 SD *(R.)*] *not in LC*

13.3 SD *C*] *not in LC*

14–15 ends / (*to*)] LC ends

~~With wear and tear like that of lungs and throat~~
~~Your bankrupt voices won't by worth a note~~
(/to

36 SD *L*] *not in LC*

38 What] LC *(What?)*

41 SD *(Crosses … C.)*] *not in LC*

50 head!] LC *(head)*

52 crack] LC burst

SD] *not in LC*

59 No!] LC *(No?)*

60 SD *crossing … C.)*] *not in LC*

back!] LC *(back)*

64.1 SD *R*] *not in LC*

64.2 SD *L*] *not in LC*

69 that's hearty] LC it's true

70 who's … party?] LC Creon. Quite

         Orpheus   Whom to?

71 SD] *not in LC*

perceive] LC perceive —/pointing

72 Precisely!] LC *(Precisely)*

73 sir!] LC *(sir)*

You?] LC you!

78.1 SD *who … E*] *not in LC*

78.2 SD *Creon*] LC ~~Jason~~ Creon

SD *off*] LC out

R . . . E] *not in LC*
78.3–4 SD *Orpheus . . . E.*] *not in LC*
86 you] *LC (you!)*
96 bit] *LC* bit!
97 (*Makes . . . bootjacks?*] *LC* Projected bootjacks—? /makes action of throwing
104.1 SD SONG] *this edn; not in LC; 1856* SONG.— JASON | AIR
106 plain] *LC* sad
113 Her] *LC* The
114 Contrived . . . peace] *LC* The Peace contrived
115 She] *LC* The
120. 1 SD *Harp . . . distant*] *LC* Distant music
SD *L . . . E*] *not in LC*
121 SD] *not in LC*
124–125 banner. . . . I'll] *LC* You ^know^ that goddeſs from her cloudy moon attics
                Protects old maids and other sorts of lunatics.
                    ~~Orph. Creon, to look her up I'll * importune~~
                    ~~You shan't persuade the girl to shoot the moon~~
                          ~~Duet~~
                            X
                      ~~Exeunt Orpheus and Jason~~
                                ~~severally~~
                    ~~Bridal music resound. Creusa, Nurse~~
                    ~~and Bridesmaids enter.~~
                    ~~Creusa lays a garland at the foot of~~
                    ~~Diana's statue~~
                    ~~Song/Creusa)~~
                  sorts of lunatics.
130.1 SD DUET] *this edn; not in LC; 1856* DUET.— ORPHEUS AND JASON
130 SD–144 SD.1] *LC*
                Duett
            ~~Song~~/air Bobbing around)
       Jason.   Of whats my due he ne'er can pay
            A bob in the pound the pound the pound
       Orpheus. Mischief to you is as ***** as hay
            To a donkey or cob in the hound.
                =
       Jason. *I'm for the Giant —with ****
                      └ first rate
            To wop in a round a round a round

Orpheus.ˬ ⁽ᶜᵃˡˡⁱⁿᵍ ᵃᶠᵗᵉʳ ʰⁱᵐ⁾) I'll call on the **** your.****/exit

to ******

To sign a robin that's round

~~exeunt ******~~

f.11

Orpheus solus / or growing duett ******* harmonized

~~English **** poetry'll going-ᵍᵒ** round~~

~~And running aground~~

~~Running, aground, aground, aground~~

English Poetry's going to wreck

Running aground aground aground,

Thoughts by Yankees about the necks

With skeins of Bobbin around

∟ Exit

X X X X X X X X

Creusa ———— all creation

**** ****

~~Deck with these offerings • Diana's shrine~~

~~While I go in my fealty to resign~~

~~To the chaste Goddeſs —"Chaste" though~~

Moves my laughter

~~I never heard that she was ******~~

~~∟ runs after~~

~~***~~

~~***~~

f.11b

Both- /? concerted)

(or *****Orpheus alarm)

~~English~~

English poetry is ~~I'm afraid~~ ᵍᵒⁱⁿᵍ ᵗᵒ ʷʳᵉᶜᵏ

* ~~dropping~~ ᵃⁿᵈ ʳᵘⁿⁿⁱⁿᵍˬ aground, aground, aground

144.2 SD *Harp music*] not in LC

SD *with*] not in LC

144.2-3 SD *down . . . by*] not in LC

149 shrine] LC; 1856 shrin

154 SD *Temple . . . E.*] LC <u>Temple followed by bridesmaids</u>
<u>Medea and Children see</u>

                    descending the hill
                                    ~~Lycaon and Melanthe~~
                    ~~Enter Medea and her two children~~
                    ~~whom she leads one by each hand~~
                    ~~She walks slowly:~~ ^her bearing is stern and^ *** majestic ********

~~Medea My babes! If you have any strength left, stretch it~~
        ~~Shelter's at hand —/ Lycaon mind! You'll catch it).~~
155 SD *solus*] LC S<u>o</u>la
158–159 *neat. / Always*] LC neat!—
                    ** ~~So healthy too! I'd kiss her all day long—~~
                    ~~No one's lips cling to anything that's strong!~~
                    Always
160 SD *sees Medea*] not in LC
160–161 *beadle? / My*] LC
                    ~~Who's **** a crying beggar ****—what brought her~~
                    ~~I ha* the way ***ght of wh*** and w***~~
                                        (disappears
                                        into the temple)
                    Enter Medea & children
                    /they stand like s**nd cadgers ^ ****
                    ** ~~boys~~ **** she hangs a placard
                    on ***** the neck of one child inscribed
                    "Fatherleſs" —!? Grecian characters) To the
                    Other she gives a little tin begging box—
165–168] not in LC
172 (*looking . . . there's*] LC Bother! there's /*looking round*/
SD (*The . . . E.*)] LC
                    ~~In yonder town, kind hearts will soften at~~
                    ~~The tear by sufferring childhood shed—~~
                        /~~Boxing the ears of Melanthe, who has began~~
                        ~~to whisper.)~~
                        ——— ~~Drop that!~~
                        ——— ~~(C)~~
                    ~~She stands motionleſs~~ ********
                    ****
173 I] LC ✝^aside)• /~~A likely looking woman f****~~Why, I
188 SD *mildness*] LC wildeneſs

189 Nobody] *LC* No one
198 SD] *not in LC*
199 little—when] *LC* I kick a little—~~sleeping at night~~ ^when things don't go right^
208 SD *in*] *LC* ~~with~~ ^in^
210 SD *before her*] *LC* ~~in fear~~
wonder!] *LC (wonder)*
211] *LC* ~~Scarce had he caught my heart when he **** took it~~ ^i said not that. French leave of me he took it.^
212.1 SD *Harp*] *not in LC*
212.1-2 SD *The . . . C.*] *not in LC*
213 SD] *not in LC*
The bride] *LC* ~~Who's this?~~
              ****
              The bride
216.1 SD *L.H.*] *not in LC*
in . . . C,] *LC* before the temple
Re enter] *not in LC*
216.1-2 *from . . . R*] and Bridesmaids come out).
222 SD] *not in LC*
223 SD *L*] *not in LC*
225.1-2 SD *crossing . . . child.*] *LC* offering Creusa a veil from a casket she has brought with her)
226] *LC* This humble offering/a<u>side</u>) she's got lots more—
227.1 SD] *LC* (shutting it up in box)
227.2 SD] *not in LC*
229–230 harried / It] *LC* harried
        ~~Creusa.~~   **************
        ~~What ** up ****** ***** face with owe~~
        ~~By what perplexity thy soul is harmed?~~
        Medea. ~~Maiden ****** the things as clear up mind I'm married.~~ It
233 prospects] *LC; 1856* prospests
234 A scamp!] *LC* ~~****** ^fiercely^)~~ /A ~~An infernal~~ ^scamp!^
237 fond] *LC* ~~old~~ ^fond^
246-247 *rib* | CREUSA] *LC* rib
        ~~Creüsa./alarmed) What wouldn't ***** do the her?~~
        ~~Medea/intensely) Do? Eh! What does the Leopard~~
        ~~When—the bold, watching,—like a sly Jack Shepperd,~~
        ~~He sees/ the guardian having turn'd his back?~~
        ~~An opportunity the crib to crack—?~~
        ~~With one fell bound, he leaks the hurdle-girdle:—~~

<the life -streams of the sheepish inmates curdle>
          Creusa
248 act] *LC* acts
256 SD] *LC* /acting of a cat toʃsing a mouse about
257–259 SD To . . . (terrified)] *LC*
          <Palls him to pieces as a ******> To a short game of pitch and toss she treats him
          <Gets hungry with the sport and> Tears him to pieces slowly,
                    └ then Sc-runch!—eats him!
          <She'll bound, thy shake, in piteous and perverse stead,>
          <Their wooly **** sides, /so shortly to be worsted).>
          <Each leg of mutton, fix'd by Terror's force,>
          <Cut off—from its accustom'd caper source:—>
          <The burglar crouches low to make one spring—>
          <But first looks round to do his marketing.>
          <He fixes on a tender leg of lamb—>
          </not caring for one single ram—or dam)>
          <A dainty morsel—which as new sacrified lint>
          <And worthy ah no treasures of the mint!—>
          <S-c-runch! Through thou flesh, his friendish teeth go>
                    <***** └ ******   └ "wobbling">
          </I call them friendish for he is a =gobblin')>
          <One spring I think I said? The hungry comer>
          <One swallow gives, enough to make a summer!>
          <L***, Neck, trotters, fry, chops, down his throat, sends>
                              └ slicking—
          /with int*** ^gusto).
          <Then gives his own chops such a folly licking!—>
                    /******************)
          Creusa. */ (terrified)
260–261 carnivorous / But] *LC* carnivorous
          <But here I nip your story in its boûtons>
          <You spoke of sheep—revenons à nos moutons.>
          <W*ll to pr*end which of the sub**t full>
          <Medea.> But
261 full] *LC* (full?)
264 Orpheus] *LC* <Jas> Orpheus
265 SD R . . . E] *not in LC*
266 Creusa!] *LC* Creüsa!
266.1 SD *Crosses hastily*] *LC* runs

268.1 SD QUARTETT] *this edn; not in LC;1856. . . .* QUARTETT. | MEDEA, ORPHEUS, CREUSA, AND NURSE.; *LC* Trio
268.2 SD *The*] *not in LC*
270 Oh,] *LC* /co<u>n</u>***d)
271 heart I] *LC* heart that I
stay'd] *LC* stopp'd
272 SP CREUSA] *LC* Cre<u>us</u>a./ a<u>la</u>rmed)
273 SD] *LC* Creusa faints with Norma's arms.~~)~~

　　　　　　　　　=

　　　　/Medea suddenly *********)
274 heart I can] *LC* heart but I
274 SD–291] *LC* ?~~A Chrorus~~ <u>N</u>orma—?
　　Guerra ?

1.2
0.SD *Hall*] *LC* /<u>front</u>)—~~Hall~~
0.SD *an . . . C.*] *LC* ~~unfurnished.~~

~~Music to which Grecian ******* vases &~~
~~ri** slowly~~
　　　　Enter <u>Orpheus</u>***** * ~~fiddle (*************which~~
~~***~~
~~*****　As soon as the furniture has risen he stops.~~
1–4] *LC* <u>Orpheus</u>. ~~/throwing violin out)~~
　　　　~~Thou! Creon ow<u>es</u> she something I'd ******~~
　　　　_{~~The stars are in a fog! I can't see through it~~}
　　　　~~For furnishing his halls and ******bare~~
　　　　_{~~What's to be done and who is then to do it.~~}
　　　　~~*********************************~~
　　　　~~*** as~~ ^{~~On me~~} ~~the only part in the play~~
　　　　~~Such little *****~~ _{~~the task of **** devolves *~~} ~~do an**********~~ ~~Clear away~~
　　　　~~I must~~ ^{~~E'ry obstruction~~} ~~****** thoroughout the various scenes~~
　　　　~~To bring about~~ ^{~~bring round~~} ~~an and to crown****~~ _^ ~~the means.~~
　　　　~~I'm with poetic justice quite consistent~~
　　　　~~—————— /*****)~~
　　　　~~Yet such an end at present's reather distant~~
　　　　~~The stars look black!~~^{~~I wish I knew~~}~~— what c***** ought * to follow?~~
　　　　~~I think I'll go and ask my friend Apollo~~
　　　　~~He as the sun some light ca surely throw—~~

> ~~Medea rages like a fiery dragon—~~
> ~~A female cup of wrath—a full Moll Flaggon,~~
> ~~Cauldron and witch combined~~
> ~~Upon the matter—yet I ******* hardly know—~~
> ~~Poets invent so!—when one truth requires~~
> ~~Is't best to ask the God of Precious Lyres?~~
> (considers)

12 a] *LC* (à)

15 foretells] *this edn; LC* (fortels)*; 1856* (fortels)

20 SD] *not in LC*

22 How] *LC* ~~She~~ How

SD *L . . . E*] *not in LC*

23.1 SD (*L.*)] *not in LC*

SD *falling*] *LC* <u>falls</u>

23.2 SD] *not in LC*

24 bye!] (bye)

30 see!] *LC* (see)

33 Or stay] *LC* ~~At any~~ Or stay

34 SD.1 DUET] *this edn not in LC; 1856* DUET.— ORPHEUS AND CREUSA; *not in LC*

36 Apollo] ~~Ap'~~Pollo

37 learn] *LC* know

40 Sing] *LC* /~~***~~(a<u>s</u>ide)^Sing

42–43 oh! | Kemo!] *LC* oh!

> Chorus
>
> <u>Orph.</u>   ~~Kemo!~~ Kemo!

44 high] *LC* (high!)

45 singing!] *LC* (singing—)

47 If with] *LC* ***If, with

51–52 oh? | What's] *LC* oh? / /<u>Tumult outside</u>) / <u>Orpheus.</u> What's

52 SD] *LC* (L) <u>Enter Creon</u> <u>agitated.</u>

53 SD] *not in LC*

56.1 SD] *not in LC*

56.2 SD] *not in LC*

they. . .true.)] *LC* Just so! with her ~~they'v cut up rough~~ ^{they say—/and p'raps it's true}

57 Their champion] *LC* ~~They say~~ Their champion

58] *LC* To thrash the giant;~~—and return from strife~~ ^{if spared with life}

60 SD] *not in LC*

61 SD *this edn*] *LC* <u>exit</u>)*; 1856 Exit* ORPHEUS, L. C.

62.1 SD] *not in LC*
62.2 SD] *not in LC*
71 Or] *LC* ~~And~~ ₍Or₎
72] *LC* But let's ** ~~look out from the gall'ry's~~ ᵃˢᶜᵉⁿᵈ ᵗᵒ ʷᵃᵗᶜʰ ᶠʳᵒᵐ ʸᵒⁿᵈᵉʳ; height—
75 SD C.] *not in LC*
77 For] ~~With~~ ᶠᵒʳ
77.1 SD *hastily . . . C.*] *LC /c.*)
All's] *LC* All
77.2 SD *Exit. . .C.*] *LC /exit*)
77SD–78 C / Ring] *LC* ~~Creon./ embracing Creusa).~~
        ~~My angel child—this is a joyous day~~
        ~~G*****************************~~
        ~~With honour to receive your ********~~
        ~~W********************************~~
        ~~Ring all the bells in ****** ****** church ****rey.~~
78 candle!] *LC (candle)*
79 handle!] *LC (handle)*
81] *LC* ~~We'll barely decórate each public building~~
    ********** We'll decorate the front of ev'ry building
85] *LC* Stint not, yourself in washing bills—we'll pay!
~~************************************~~
~~************************************~~
~~***********************************~~
~~************************************~~
~~**********************************~~
    <u>/exit Creusa R</u>
87.1 SD *Attendant, . . . E*] *LC* <u>attendant</u>
87.2 SD *preceded*] *LC (preceeded); 1856 (preceedeed)*
87.2–3 . . . C] *LC* <u>Exit preceedeed by attendant,</u>
    <u>shouts Enter Jason C.</u>
    <u>followed by the Populace cheering</u>
88 SD] *not in LC*
90–91 copper / That] *LC* copper.
*****^{shuts} <u>doors on populace. Cheers</u>
    <u>heard receding)</u> Jason ~~********~~ <u>shows</u>
    ~~different trophies he has brought with~~
    ~~him. All of preposterous size~~
    ~~Antestors to ******* ring tobacco stopper.~~
    That

92 may] LC ~~will~~ ^may^
95 I] LC I'd
shirk] LC (shirk)
97.1 SD song] *this edn; not in LC; 1856* song.— jason; *LC*
115] LC ~~From trophies proud~~ ^Antestor's spoils^ to grace our wedding-day
117 Bold, aye!] LC (Bold aye)
117.1-2 SD *Going . . . disordered,*] LC <u>Going, is confronted by Medea who has entered with her garments torn —and marks of violence—mud on her face &c—</u>
117.3 SD] LC /<u>falls on to a crouch overcome</u>)
118 letter.] LC (letter!)
119 SD L] *not in LC*
brute!] LC ~~beast~~ ^brute^
119–120 *a pause*) | I'm] LC <u>Jason.</u> ~~Oh! here's a sell! (aside)~~.
121 SD *his. . . Medea.*] *not in LC*
122 SD *calmness.*)] LC <u>calmn</u>
124 Through] LC ~~By~~ ^Through^
125 have heard] LC perceive—
126 *Giason . . . Medea*] LC ~~Jason I am Medea~~ 'Giason io son Medea—'
bewild'rin!] LC (bewild'rin)
139 please. And] LC (please and)
143] LC educate
    ~~Med.   Where to?~~
    ~~Jason   Wherever 'tis you stay.~~
    ~~Let me no obstacle be *** in your way.~~
    ~~We both are free—~~
    ~~Med~~   ~~Free am I?~~
    ~~Jason.~~   ~~Yes—(aside) Much more~~
    ~~Than welcome, any day— Our ties is~~ ^are^ ~~o'er=~~
    ~~Yet charge me not with ingrate selfishneſs~~
    ~~I meant— when I could meet with your addreſs=~~
    ~~To write= (enclose~~ ^to you with^ ~~money I should state.)~~
    ~~To send the boys to me to educate.~~
    ~~Medea. To send the boys~~
    ~~Medea. (with*************~~) /suppreſsing
144 SD *emotion*)] LC <u>emotions</u>
147 princes] *this edn;* LC ~~monarchs~~ ^prince's^; *1856* prince's
162 yourself—] LC (yourself?)
164 I'm . . . mean] LC To *******—mongst their numerous disasters
        Is this—We're never wholly over masters—

In love affairs—
166 Oh?] *LC (Oh!)*
167 mother's] *LC (mothers)*
170 infernal!] *LC (infernal)*
171 Oh, pow'rs] *LC* ~~Pow~~ Oh Pow'rs
dark] *LC* ~~darkneſs~~ dark
173 sternly—isn't this a go] *LC* Isn't this ~~ag~~ a go?
173 go?] *LC* go?/ ~~The throats I cut for him without repentance~~
~~Cut—why I've nearly cut my whole acquaintance~~
~~. And then when~~
~~He's going to marry the Princeſs Creusa.~~
173 SD.1] *this edn; not in LC; 1856* DUET. —MEDEA AND JASON
179 Creusa,] *LC (Creusa!)*
186 up] *LC* ~~off~~^{up}
195 SD] *LC (Exit) LC* <u>Duet</u>
        (<u>The saucy Arethusa</u>)
        <u>Medea.</u> Of all the folly scoundrels bold.
        With faces cast in ~~***~~ brazen mould.
        The biggest's he who just has told
            He's going to wed Crëusa
        She is a princeſs • rich and brave.
        A cast off wife is a cast off slave
            ~~*********************~~
            The cake is mix'd
            And the wedding fixed
        But Bridegrooms Bridesmaids friends and Sirs
        *n it take plan, shall all expire
            With the saucy jade Crëusa
        <u>Jason.</u> On deck at once you'd better dance—
        To morrow pr'haps you'll loose your chance
        Be off to Bath or Wales or France—
            If you have me with Creusa
        You'~~d~~ ve shown your teeth—you'll bite I know
        Take my advice ~~**~~ be calm and go.
            Policeman Three
            Of Division B.
        Has his eye on folks disliked by me
            Or abhorr'd by the fair Crëusa.
              (<u>exit</u>)

196 SD] *LC* alone
199 Irish!] *C (Irish)*
Italiano!] *LC (Italiano)*
200–205] *not in LC*
206 fellow's] *LC (fellows)*
213 'Dusa!'] *LC* ~~Deusa~~ 'Dusa—!'
ah!] *LC (a)*
Ha, Creusa!] *(Ha! Crëusa!)*
214 of] *LC* to
216 SD *Draws*] *LC* drawing
218 cup] *LC* cap
220] *LC* ~~Hooray Hooray Hoooray I'll do it.~~
 ~~/dances~~
 ~~Exit Creusa—She conceals~~
 ~~knife~~
~~Creusa. Fly! wretched individual~~
I've thought—I've plann'd—I have resolv'd—
—I'll do it—:
I feel as ******* as Punch—
 ⌞ Root too—too too it!
221 SD *L.1 E.*] *LC* R
knife.] *LC* knife hastely.
222 individual?] *this edn*; *LC* individual; *1856* individual?
matter?] *(matter)*
226 What] *LC* ~~I fly~~ What
Why?] *LC* ~~What for?~~—Why?
227 SD] *not in LC*
guy!] *LC (Guy)*
228 SD] *LC* /draggin her R.)
229 SD *murmurs ... C.*] *LC* murmuring
231.1 SD *Creusa*] *LC* ~~Med~~ Creusa
R ... E.] *not in LC*
231.2 SD *enters ... C.*] *LC* enters C,
enters...E.] *LC* Jason L
232 SD] *not in LC*
236 SD] *not in LC*
237 SD *(L.)*] *not in LC*
lose] *LC (loose)*
239 so.] *LC* so!

241 So, with] *LC (So with)*
241.1 SD *L.C.] not in LC*
241.2 SD] *not in LC*
Rocket ... (All.] *LC* Orph. I'll to the king at once and let him know
                That you're a ******** already—
        Jason.   Go.
                Spread discord minstrel, stead of harmony.
                S*** that the marriage tie's no noose to me.
                What then? Let Creusa find a champion better.
                Though he gave fifty brides he'd be my debtor
                      Duet
                Jason. Of what's
241.3 SD *are] LC* ~~are~~ are
SD *C.] not in LC*
242 SD] *not in LC*
243 SD] *LC* Finale; *not in LC;* 1856 DUETT AND CHORUS | —CREON, JASON, ORPHEUS, CREUSA
244 beaming, love,] *LC (beaming love)*
245 gleaming, love,] *LC (gleaming love)*
253 night, Medea.] *LC (night Medea)*
254–255.1 SD] *LC* /<u>Exeunt all but Medea</u> *******-the <u>door when her</u>
255.2–3 SD] *LC* Medea sola/sings
256 SP] *this edn; not in LC;* 1856 SOLO.—MEDEA.
257 Don't] *LC* ~~Not~~ ^Don't^
258 time, now,] *LC (time now)*
259–260 operation. / Something] *LC* operation,
                ~~Nothing I shall shoot a little~~
                ~~Bullet or think t** too little~~
                Something
264] *LC* ~~In a * ** ** **~~ ^Drop **** some stuff^ in port a little
266 a] *LC* ~~ah~~ a
267 SD] *LC* Exit R /Exit R

1.3

0.1–2 SD *A ... C.] not in LC*
0.2 SD *banquetting] not in LC*
0.3 SD *seats ... H.] not in LC*
0.5 SD *bowing ... song.] not in LC*
1 SP] *this edn; not in LC; not in* 1856

1–3 SD *Chorus . . . C.*)] LC <u>Song.</u>
>(<u>Orpheus and chorus.</u>)
>(<u>Air "Crambambulee".</u>)
><u>Orpheus.</u> Crambambulee! a German observation
>Which means some kind of drink I'm told.
><u>Chrorus/rapping their goblets)</u>   Tra li ra!
><u>Orpheus.</u> No cause I see on this serene occasion
>>Why the remark quite good shouldn't hold
><u>Chorus.</u>   Tra li ra!
><u>Orpheus</u>   To bridal boasts our cups we drain
>>And sing, for want of better strain
>>>Cram—bim—bam—bu-lee!
>>>Cram—bam—bu—lee!
><u>Chorus.</u>

>   ⌊ <u>2ⁿᵈ verse</u>)
><u>Orpheus.</u>) *******
>><u>Me</u>- dea's gone- the ~~strong~~ ^bring waves to croſs over
>>Her boys are leſs in the new wife's care
>>>(Tra li' ra!)
>>I as a bard and also a philosopher
>>>My own disappointment nobly bear
>>>(Tra li ra!)
>>This marriage is'nt quite the thing
>>But still—as I'm engaged to sing—
>>>Cram bim bam & &.

f.39

>   <u>3ʳᵈ verse.</u>
><u>Orpheus/confidentially to the public</u>)
>I've sent to ask the Oracle of Phoebus
>>To guide my steps on this trying day.
>>>(Tra li ra!)
>>Waiting to get an answer to the rebus.
>>I've caused the license to delay.
>>>(Tra li ra!)
>><u>They</u> little think that I'm the bore—
>>>(<u>pointing over his shoulder</u>)
>>******* And so as I observed before,
>>>Cram—bim—bam—bu—lee!
><u>Chrous.</u>   Cram bam bu lee!

3 thy] *LC* ~~thy~~ your
4–5 understand. / But] *LC* understand.
> ~~But modern bards don't care for sense or rhyme.~~
> ~~Well as this meſsenger's behind his time~~
> ~~But that's no detriment to modern song~~
> ~~I hope this license won't be very long~~
> But

5 indispensable] *LC (*indispensible*)*
10 SD R.] *not in LC*
10–11 more. / Now] *LC* more.
> ~~Creon. Pretty s** said. So! Let the sports advance.~~
> ~~Something original a Pyrrhich Dance!~~
> ~~Ballet~~
> ~~The Pyrrhic dance from the Winter's Tale/ Princeſs')~~
>   =
> Creon. Now

11 cab.] *LC* (cab?)
12 me!] *LC* (me)
13 Some … vengeance] *LC* . Some ₍adverse₎ pow'r of ~~rights conjugal~~ ᵛᵉⁿᵍᵉᵃⁿᶜᵉ
15.1 SD L. … E.] *not in LC*
16 Oracle] *LC* (oracle)
16 SD] *LC* /A Meſsenger ₍entering L₎ gives him a letter).
17 SP] *not in LC*
Phobus's] this edn.; *LC* Phoebus; *1856* Phobus's
20 on] *LC* upon
24 son] *LC* Sun
28 SD] *LC* ~~We've sent her this oracular reply~~
  'Tell the astronomer to ~~axe his eye.~~'
  Enter Jason ˣ eagerly with a paper
29 SD] *not in LC*
Dearest, behold] *LC* (dearest behold)
31 Come, let] *LC* (Come let)
haste, our] *LC* (haste our)
32–33 canonical. / What] *LC* canonical
> /All rise to go & Jason offers arm to Creusa)
> /suddenly changing his tone)
> What

33 SD] *not in LC*
34 SD] *not in LC*

35 SD (C.)] *not in LC*
it] LC it!
savour.] LC (savour)
37 SD (*harshly ... R.*)] *not in LC*
37–38 hush! | Methinks,] LC hush!

                        Jason./******ing)

                        ~~I*** **** as if I were about to rush~~
                        ~~**** *****~~

                        Methinks

39 misery.] LC (misery)
40 SD] *not in LC*
41 go!] LC (go)
43 be] LC a̶ be
44 string;] LC (string!)
45 Hence!] LC (Hence)
46 prevent—] LC (prevent?)
46.1 SD] LC <u>Turning to go, he sees Medea standing at his elbow. She has entered from back</u>)
46.2 SD–47 SD *consternation.*) / (*C.*)] LC consternation)

                        Guests. ********&

                        <u>Creon Creusa</u> Jason. Medea.   <u>Orpheus</u>
                        Forgive a poor lone creature's
                                └ schemings pray
                        I really couldn't keep myself away
                        You've been so thoughtful of my wants & ailings
                        So very lenient to my little failings—
                        *****/~~aside~~)

47 L ... so!] LC /<u>who is close to him</u>)   Just so!
        ~~I******* right tr**** *******off I'll go~~
        I see—   /<u>moves away</u>)
48 SD (*aside R.*)] LC /aside
row ... R] LC row ~~I've naught~~ I'll go!
                        ~~to do with it~~
            ~~I will ****** Phoebus self to help them through with it.~~
                (exit)
49.1 SD (*C ... C.*)] LC <u>to Creon</u>
SD (*Goes ... H*)] *not in LC*
49.2 SD] *not in LC*
49.3 SD] LC <u>humbly</u>

ludship] *LC* (lordship)
50 you ... in] *LC* you're not ab, — in
ship?] *LC* (ship)
51 usage] *LC* e**** usage
lenient,] *LC* (lenient)
53–56] *LC* ~~Forgive a woman's humble artful dodging~~
      ~~By which I'm left my ship board & ship lodgings~~
      ~~You ** on such a very blifsful day~~
      ~~Surely couldn't take myself away~~
      ~~I've been so kindly treated on all sides~~
      ~~Equally on the bridegrooms and the brides~~
      ~~You've been so thoughtful of my wants and ailing~~
      ~~So very lenient to my little failings~~
      ~~Quite undeservedly as one might say~~
      ~~I really couldn't keep myself way═~~
      ~~"******^ aid I" I'm bound to-day═~~
      ~~***** after**** to throw a shoe~~
      ~~If only the conventional old shoe═~~
59 it's] *LC* 'tis
to] *LC* but to
60 'And] *LC* ~~Or~~ ^'And
an] *LC* and
60.1 SD] *LC* (&)
em!] *LC* (em)
60.2 SD] *not in LC*
61 SD *and...C.*)] *not in LC*
63] *LC* ~~For one of your own sons a body'd take you═~~
 ~~Like *** Like~~ Like one of his own sons ^I vow—but then
64 men;] *LC* (men)
65 by;] *LC* (by)
66] *LC* ~~Tis to****s pity and I can't think why!~~
   ~~I've nothing **═ &~~ ^but can't imagine why!
   ~~I won't detain you from your duties ******~~
   ~~I've the~~
   It's odd but so it is—I wonder why?
68 SD] *LC* ~~You/~~(producing a veil)
69 When] *LC* If ^When
kirk,] *LC* (kirk)
70 *work.*] *LC* (work!)

Precisely!] *LC* (Precisely)
73] *LC* O̶h̶!̶ give it me!—/******** admiring the veil)
marriage!] *LC* (marriage)
SD *quickly*] e̶x̶* quickly
74 yet!] *LC* (yet)
75 altar!] *LC* (altar)
76 it!] *LC* (it)
name!] *LC* (name)
77.3 SD] *LC* —/going)
77–78 word! / I] *LC* word!

         /music commences piano)
            I

81 SD *R*] *this edn; not in LC; 1856 | B*
Oh!] *LC* (Oh)
charity!] *LC* (charity)
82 life!] *LC* (life)
82–83 vulgarity / Well] *LC* vulgarity

         W̶o̶u̶l̶d̶ ̶q̶u̶i̶t̶e̶ ̶r̶e̶t̶a̶r̶d̶ ̶t̶h̶e̶ ̶p̶r̶i̶n̶c̶e̶l̶y̶ ̶e̶d̶u̶c̶a̶t̶i̶o̶n̶
         O̶f̶ ̶w̶h̶i̶c̶h̶ ̶y̶o̶u̶'̶v̶e̶ ̶l̶a̶i̶d̶ ̶a̶l̶r̶e̶a̶d̶y̶ ̶t̶h̶e̶ ̶f̶o̶u̶n̶d̶a̶t̶i̶o̶n̶—
         Yet

83 Ah!] *LC* Oh!
84 me!] *LC* (me)
welcome!] *LC* (welcome)
SD *at . . . Medea*] *LC* back, R)
85 *out*] *LC* o̶u̶t̶ off
90 wail.] *LC* (wail)
92 spontaneous.] *LC* (spontaneous)
96 tinder.] *LC* (tinder)
97–103] *LC*

    N̶o̶w̶ ̶f̶o̶r̶ ̶t̶h̶e̶ ̶b̶o̶y̶s̶ ̶I̶ ̶h̶a̶d̶ ̶h̶i̶m̶ ̶n̶i̶c̶e̶l̶y̶ ̶t̶h̶e̶r̶e̶)
    I̶'̶v̶e̶ ̶g̶o̶t̶ ̶o̶u̶t̶s̶i̶d̶e̶ ̶a̶ ̶d̶r̶a̶g̶o̶n̶ ̶c̶h̶a̶r̶i̶o̶t̶ ̶a̶n̶d̶ ̶****
    (Looks off R)
    Those well know steps! My boys (cheeking herself)
    My boys—not they—
    They are the sons of Jason—I must say
    That to myself—all tenderneſs to smother
    T̶o̶ ̶b̶e̶a̶r̶ ̶t̶h̶e̶m̶ ̶o̶f̶ ̶b̶r̶i̶d̶e̶ ̶a̶n̶d̶ ̶s̶o̶n̶s̶ ̶b̶e̶r̶e̶f̶t̶
    W̶i̶t̶h̶ ̶n̶e̶'̶e̶r̶ ̶a̶ ̶****̶ ̶t̶o̶ ̶c̶a̶r̶e̶ ̶f̶o̶r̶ ̶h̶e̶'̶l̶l̶ ̶b̶e̶ ̶l̶e̶f̶t̶—
    D̶o̶o̶m̶'̶d̶ ̶i̶n̶ ̶h̶i̶s̶ ̶o̶w̶n̶ ̶s̶o̶c̶i̶e̶t̶y̶ ̶—̶t̶o̶ ̶p̶i̶n̶e̶—

~~I do believe he'd just as son have mine!~~
~~They come—Lycaon and his little brother~~
103 SD R. . . . E.] LC (R) they are
105 I'll . . . them!] LC ~~*************~~ I'll try them
106 SP LYCAON] LC ~~Melanthe.~~ Lycaon
fly.] LC (fly)
107–111] LC ~~Mel. Wretched! Oh that we're not! I've got a poney~~
~~He's just been getting shod~~
~~Medea.**   Affecting proof!~~
~~Shod is he? it's for me to pad the hoof~~
~~But to your mother have ye nought to say?~~
108 SP LYCAON] LC Mel.
oh,] LC (Oh)
pony;] LC (poney)
109 shod!] LC (shod)
110 he!] LC (he?)
hoof!] LC (hoof)
111] LC But to your mother ~~have ye nought~~ to say?
112 SP LYCAON] LC Mel.
Oh. . .we've] LC ~~Lots! we have~~ Oh, no! we've
114 As . . . it] LC ~~Talking of dinner~~ As we are talking of it
Well] LC Well? ~~I ******* my son!~~
114.2 SD R. . .E.] not in LC
114.3 SD] not in LC
116–117 tarts! / One] LC tarts!
~~With beef, enroled them~~ neath *** ~~her fl*g (and master'd).~~
~~Taken them into custody with custard!~~
118 mamma to] LC mamma ~~have you~~ to
119 Yes . . . this!] LC Melan. ~~There's my old cricket bat—~~
Lycaon. Eh! Stop here's this? ~~I've got a boat~~
The mast is broken— ~~St**~~ though here's a note
119.1 SD scroll] LC one
119.2 SD (Reads.) What?] LC reads) ~~Dearest Madam~~? What?
122 feelings] LC ~~f*llings~~
harry,] LC (harry)
124.1 SD astonished, then] LC astonished, at, then
124.3 SD who . . . side] not in LC
125 Mamma!] LC (Mamma)
pray?] LC (pray)

127 hands, there's] *LC* (hands there's)
seething,] *LC* (seething)
128 breathing.] *LC* (breathing)
130 'Twasn't] *LC* ('twas not)
he.] *LC* (he!)
SD *without*] *LC* <u>outside</u>
SD *gradually increasing*] *LC* increasing gradually
131 past time] *LC* past the time
133] *LC* ****************
      This way my babes
133 SD *down, R.,*] *LC* <u>at foot of a column L</u>
134 Round] *LC* R̶o̶u̶n̶d̶ Round
135 thunder!] *LC* (thunder)
135 SD] *LC* <u>Enter Creon and Populace at</u> back
136 asunder.] *LC* (asunder!)
138 children!] *LC* children! (<u>The crowd rush towards he</u>r)
138.2–3 SD *with . . . horror*] *LC* <u>in horror</u>
on steps, C.] not in *LC*
138.4–5 SD *the . . . dead*] *LC* the Children are not seen by the public)
SD *apparently*] this edn; not in *LC*; *1856* | *apparently*
138.5 SD *R.U.E.*] *LC* <u>at back</u>
drawn] *LC* <u>the drawn</u>
138.6 *but is*] not in *LC*
the Populace] *LC* <u>two of the</u> Populace
139] *LC* <u>Creon</u>. Back for your life—
      Jason. (struggling)   Her life to me is due.
159 SP] *this edn; not in LC; 1856* MEDEA AND THE CHARACTERS.

5

Electra in a New Electric Light

Francis Talfourd

(1859)

Electra in a New Electric Light was first staged at the Haymarket Theatre in London on 25 April 1859. The present edition is based on the 1859 printed copy published by Thomas Hailes Lacy, collated with the LC unbound manuscript, BL Add MS 52982 C, held at the Lord Chamberlain's Plays Collection at the British Library.

For biographical information on F. Talfourd see the introduction to *Alcestis*.

Manuscript paratext

f. 1

   Electra

1859 in a new

   Electric Light— an

Mss received _____. April 19

   original claſsical Extravaganza

License sent _____ April 19

S^{cl}- Council Chamber

    W.D. Donne

Lacy's edition paratext

ELECTRA IN A NEW ELECTRIC LIGHT. An entirely new and
Original Extravaganza,
In ONE ACT
By
FRANCIS TALFOURD, Esq.

Author of
*Atalanta, Pluto and Proserpine, Abon Hassan, Ganem, Macbeth
Travestie, Shylock, Alcestis, the Strong-Minded Woman,
Black-eyed Sue, By Special Appointment, March of
Intellect, Jones the Avenger, Mammon and Gammon,
The Heart-wreck, Rule of Three, &c, &c*
Past Author of
*Sir Rupert the Fearless, La Tarantula, Leo the Terrible, Godiva,
Thetis and Peleus, Spirits in Bond, Princesses in the Tower,
Willow Pattern Plate, &c., &c., &c.*

ELECTRA
First performed at the Theatre Royal, Haymarket,
on Easter Monday, April 25th, 1859.

The Overture and Incidental Music composed and arranged by Mr. SPILLANE. Scenes 2, 3 & 5, by Mr. O'CONNOR. Scenes 1, 4 and 6, by Mr. G. MORRIS. The last Scene invented and executed by Mr. FREDERICK FENTON. The Costumes (derived from most Authentic Sources) by Mr.

---

19 **Mr. Spillane** Spillane also composed and arranged the music for Talfourd's *Pluto and Proserpine*, first performed at the Theatre Royal Haymarket in 1858. The scene painters G. Morris and Mr. O'Connor, the costume designers Mr. Barnett and Miss Cherry, and property master Mr. Foster participated in the production of the two plays.

21 **Mr. Frederick Fenton** the scenic artist Frederick Fenton (1817–1898) was known for his elaborate settings. The 1853 Sadler's Wells production of *A Midsummer Night's Dream*, for example, was praised for Fenton's inventiveness in the use of the gauze (Baugh, 'Stage', p. 322).

Barnett and Miss Cherry. The Properties by Mr. Foster. The Machinery by Mr. Oliver Wales. The Piece produced under the Superintendence of Mr. Chippendale.

THE ARGUMENT
Agamemnon, having confided the guardianship of his kingdom to Ægisthus during his absence at the siege of Troy, returns to resume his sovereignty. His wife, Clytemnestra, conspires with Ægisthus, for whom she has conceived a passion, and they, lying in wait for the king as he is leaving the bath, barbarously slay him with an axe (an-acc-ident which possibly anticipated for him his Homeric title Ἀν-αξ ἀνδρων Ἀγαμέμνων) The guilty parties are married, and Ægisthus usurps the throne of Argos, to the exclusion of the rightful heir, Orestes. Electra, however, true to her father's cause, and fearful for the safety of her brother, sends him away privately to the court of his uncle Strophius, king of Phocis, until he shall be of years to avenge their father's death, and claim his rights. Seven years elapse, at the expiration of which, indeed, on the anniversary of the marriage of Ægisthus, the present drama opens. The people are crushed beneath the despotic sway of Ægisthus, who, in his turn, bows in slavish submission to the will of his strong-minded lady, while both combine to render wretched the life of Electra. She, unswerving in her loyalty to her father's cause, is awaiting the expected return of Orestes, who, having spread a report of his own death at a chariot race, the more easily to gain admission to the palace, arrives with his friend Pylades at Mycenæ;— they have provided themselves with a funeral urn, supposed to contain the ashes of Orestes, to give additional probability to their story—they are hospitably received, as the bearers of welcome tidings. Orestes then discloses himself, but is spared the personal infliction of vengeance on the usurpers by the intervention of Nemesis, who contrives

that they themselves are made the instruments of their own destruction.

CHARACTERS

ÆGISTHUS *King of Mycenæ, who, if not overwise, is decidedly a shrew'd one, and who, though the accredited leader of the band, is content to play second fiddle to his Monster Consort,* Mr. COMPTON.

PHILARIO & LYCUS *Courtiers,* Mr. BRAID & Mr. CLARK.

ORESTES *Son of Agamemnon and Clytemnestra—the rightful heir, and forlorn hope of the family,* Miss M. TERNAN. (Her first appearance here.)

PYLADES, *Son of Strophius, King of Phocis, his fast friend and fellow traveller,* Miss F. WRIGHT.

CHIEF HUNTSMAN, Mr. MOYSE.

HERALD, Mr. WEATHERSBY.

---

25 **Mr. Chippendale** William Henry Chippendale (1801–1888), actor (*ODNB*). In 1853 he made his début in London at the Haymarket Theatre, where he became famous for his comic business and also acted as stage manager (Pascoe, *Dramatic*, pp. 83–84).

32-4 Pun with the common Homeric formula ἄναξ ἀνδρῶν Ἀγαμέμνων (leader of men, Agamemnon); ἄναξ is split into Αν-αξ ('an ax'), in order to comically allude to the death of Agamemnon explained in lines 32–33.

39 **Phocis** region in ancient Greece which included Delphi. Orestes was sent to stay with Strophius, King of Phocis when Agamemnon was slain.

41 **Seven years** Aegisthus and Clytemnestra ruled over Mycenae for seven years until the adult Orestes arrived to revenge the death of his father Agamemnon. For reasons of comedy the violence of Orestes over Clytemnestra is toned down in Talfourd's burlesque. One hundred years earlier, Voltaire's tragedy *Oreste* (1750) had already eased the cruelty of the murder.

43 **despotic** Aegisthus is usually depicted as a person with a feeble temperament following the classical tradition. Part of the comic effect of the character in Talfourd is the contrast between his public despotism and his private submission to Clytemnestra.

45 **strong-minded lady** predating the fin de siècle New Women, strong-minded women were determined women who played social roles usually adopted by men. See pp. 33–36.

49 **chariot race** in Sophocles, Orestes is said to have died during the Pythian games.

63-4 **Monster Consort** Clytemnestra, see 45n.

67-8 **Miss M. TERNAN** probably Maria Susanna Taylor (neé Ternan, 1837–1913). The third daughter of the actors Thomas Lawles Ternan and Frances Eleanor. Her sister, Ellen Lawless (Nelly) Ternan, made her adult début on stage in 1857 at the Haymarket. Soon after that she started a relationship with Charles Dickens (*ODNB*). Together with Miss E. Weekes, Compton, Chippendale, the dancing of Miss Louise Leclercq and the scenery by Fenton, she successfully took part in various comedies, burlesques and fairy romances at the Haymarket Theatre.

CLYTEMNESTRA, *Late wife of Agamemnon, married to Ægisthus—so unnatural a mother that she cannot bear her own children: whose conduct, though by no means correct, is that of a very decided lady,* Mrs. WILKINS.

ELECTRA, *The strong-minded Daughter of Agamemnon and Clytemnestra, who looks forward to the removal of her present Sovereigns as the termination of her present sufferings,* Miss E. WEEKES.

CHRYSOTHEMIS, *Her Cousin—in love with Orestes,* Miss L. LECLERCQ.

NEMESIS, *the Spirit of Retributive Justice,* Mrs. GRIFFITHS.
Courtiers, Lords, Ladies, Attendants, Citizens, Dancing Girls, &c.

Scene I. MYCENÆ AND ITS VICINITY
    HALL OF AUDIENCE IN THE PALACE
        Congratulatory Offerings on the Anniversary of the Royal Nuptials— The Tyrant and (*sed longo proximus intervallo*) the Husband —Domestic Afflictions—Introduction of the "green-eyed monster," and its consequences—Departure for the Chase.

Scene II. A CHAMBER IN THE PALACE
        The Cousins—Mother and Daughter—Recriminations.

Scene III. SACRED GROVE OF CYPRESS
        With distant view of Mycanæ. Return of the Wanderer — The Urn— The Love-Test—Brother and Sister— A Noble Sportsman in difficulties.

Scene IV. THE CURTAINED GALLERY
        The Rejected Suitor—The Bargain—Illustrious Visitors.

Scene V. GREAT SQUARE OF THE CITY
        During a Fete. A Classic Divertissement, Invented and arranged by Mr. LECLERQ, and supported

by Miss Louise Leclerq, Mr. C. Leclerq, and Mr. A. 105
Leclerq, Master D. Carroll, and the Ladies of the
Corps de Ballet. Consisting of Mesdames McLewee,
Desborough, Harrison, Henrade, Lewis Kendall, Russell,
Matthews, E. Harrison, Pool, Perry, and Vernon.
Affecting loyalty of a free and grateful people—The 110
Proclamation—The Challenge—The Last Hope.

Scene VI. THE WRESTLING MATCH. ANTE CHAMBER IN THE PALACE
Wherein the hand of Fate sets the puppets dallying.

Scene VIII. BANQUET HALL
The 'bitter cups'—The biters bitten. 115

THE NEMESIS
An entire change of Minstry, and Dissolution of the
House.

RESTORATION OF ORESTES
And his release from the threatened persecutions 120
of the Furies, sanctioned by a

CONGRESS OF THE FOUR GREAT POWERS
Of Earth, Sea, and Air,—through whose mediation it
is humbly hoped, a

LASTING AND NOT DISHONOURABLE PIECE 125
MAY BE HAPPILY CONCLUDED!

---

76 **very decided lady** see 45n.
77 **strong-minded** see 45n.
80 **Miss E. Weekes** Eliza Weekes made her first appearance at the Haymarket Theatre, as Madame Galochard, in Charles Selby's *The King's Gardener* in September 1858 (*The Era*, 9 January 1859, p.13). She was the daughter of Richard Weekes, the comic actor who became famous for his delineations of Irish characters. She was praised both for her acting and her singing techniques and was part of the successful performers that John Baldwin Buckstone gathered together at the Haymarket Theatre during his management between 1853 and 1878.
81 **Cousin** note that Chyrsothemis is Orestes' sister in the classical tradition.

88–9 **sed ... intervallo** 'but next at a long distance', from Virgil's *Aeneid*, V.320.
90–1 **green-eyed monster** jealousy (*OED*, 'green-eyed', *adj*. 2b).
96 **GROVE OF CYPRESS** groves, caves and grottoes were places for wonderful encounters and magical plots in nineteenth-century literature. Examples abound from recreations of *The Babes in the Wood* to William Dimond's opera *The Nymph of the Grotto* (1829), for example.
102 **GREAT SQUARE** the scene imitates the popular entertainment of the time usually found in street fairs. See for example *ILN* No.51. Vol. II, Saturday 22 April 1843, pp. 269–270.

List of Roles

ÆGISTHUS	*King of Mycenæ*	
PHILARIO & LYCUS	*courtiers*	
LADY CLYTEMNESTRA	*late wife of Agamemnon, married to Ægisthus*	5
NEMESIS	*goddess*	
CHRYSOTHEMIS	*Electra's cousin*	
HUNTSMAN		
ELECTRA	*daughter of Agamemnon and Clytemnestra*	10
ORESTES	*son of Agamemnon and Clytemnestra*	
PYLADES	*son of Strophius, King of Phocis*	
HERALD		

Courtiers, Lords, Ladies, Attendants, Citizens,   15
Dancing Girls, and Huntsmen

1 ÆGISTHUS Aegisthus is the son of Thyestes who survives to avenge the deaths of his brothers at the hands of Atreus. Atreus had killed Thyestes' other sons, and cooked and served them up for their father to eat. When Agamemnon led the Greek expedition to the Trojan War, his wife Clytemnestra and Aegisthus became lovers. Together they murdered Agamemnon on his return home along with his Trojan captive Cassandra. The myth was a popular subject in fifth-century BC tragedy. This burlesque plays on the traditional weak figure of Aegisthus in contrast with the powerful Clytemnestra.

2 PHILARIO & LYCUS Philario is a friend to Posthumus Leonatus in Shakespeare's *Cymbeline*, which was successfully staged throughout the nineteenth century. He is also a character in Henry Hart Milman's tragedy *Fazio, or the Italian Wife*, which was first performed as *The Italian Wife* at the Surrey Theatre in London (Nicoll, *History*, pp. iv, 256). There is also a tradition of Lycus as a minor character; for example, he is an emissary of Aegisthus' in Peter Bayley's tragedy *Orestes in Argos* (1825).

4 CLYTEMNESTRA Daughter of Tyndareos, king of Sparta, and Leda, and sister or half-sister of Helen and the Dioscuri. Clytemnestra was also the wife of Agamemnon, king of Mycenae. Mother of Iphigenia, Electra, Chrysothemis and Orestes. Here Orestes and Chrysothemis are cousins in order to facilitate the love plot of the burlesque. Here, Clytemnestra is in the line of modern refigurations which emphasize the powerful and manly character of the myth.

6 NEMESIS Nemesis is a Greek goddess personifying retribution. She is personified in Hesiod's *Theogony*. She is ruthless, the avenger of *hybris* and therefore akin to the Erinyes, who pursue Orestes in Aeschylus for his matricide. Here Nemesis performs the role of the divinity who controls the lives of mortals. She is also a female attendant in Peter Bayley's tragedy *Orestes in Argos* (1825).

7 CHRYSOTHEMIS Daughter of Agamemnon and Clytemnestra and sister of Orestes, Electra and Iphigenia. In Sophocles' *Electra*, Chrysothemis serves as a foil to Electra's courage, since she is constantly urging for caution in order to keep up their status quo. Here Chrysothemis is cousin of Electra and beloved of Orestes.

9 ELECTRA Daughter of Agamemnon and Clytemnestra, and sister of Orestes, Iphigenia and Chrysothemis. In fifth-century tragedy she plays a central role in Orestes' vengeance on Clytemnestra and Aegisthus for the murder of their father Agamemnon.

11 ORESTES Son of Agamemnon and Clytemnestra, and brother of Electra, Iphigenia and Chrysothemis. He killed his mother and her lover to avenge the death of his father. Here Orestes is Chrysothemis' cousin and suitor to keep the humorous love plot of the burlesque.

13 PYLADES Pylades is a silent character in Sophocles' *Electra*; Orestes travels with Pylades and the Paedagogus, who spreads the news on his death. Pylades has a more prominent role in Euripides' *Iphigenia in Tauris*, yet the pre-eminence of Pylades in Talfourd is probably inspired by Voltaire's *Oreste* (1750) and Alfieri's homonymous tragedy (1783), which are also a source for Peter Bayley's *Orestes in Argos*, first performed at the Covent Garden Theatre in London in 1825 (Nicoll, *History*, pp. iv, 262). Also consider that the playwright is not constrained by the Greek convention of only having three speaking characters on stage.

1.1 *Hall of Audience in the Palace of Ægisthus —through the columns at back, a view of the City of Mycenæ.* ÆGISTHUS *discovered seated on his throne, surrounded by* COURTIERS. *A* PROCESSION *appears, L. U. E. from behind the columns, bearing costly gifts, and enters C. to the following.*

Opening Chorus.

AIR

Le petit Tambour.

> On this auspicious day, great king,
> >   Our homes we all forsake
> Thus freely at your feet to fling
> >   What else your hand would take.
> These tributes to your sovereign sway 5
> >   Vouchsafe, sire, to accept,
> For loyalty must give away
> >   What prudence would have kept;
> 'Tis thus we come to pay our court,
> >   Though traitors' lips may say 10
> The privilege is dearly bought
> >   When there's so much to pay.

COURTIERS
>   Long live the King!

ÆGISTHUS
>   With gratitude we take your generous proffers,
>   Yet, 'ere we can dismiss them to our coffers, 15
>   Be sure the precious gifts upon us pressed,
>   Have touched our *heart* before they reach our *chest!*
>   Tis, as 'tis obvious you are all aware,
>   Both by your presence here, and presents there,
>   The anniversary of that happy day 20
>   When Clytemnestra gave her hand away,
>   Threw me the reins of government, indeed,
>   For, from our bridal I've *reigned in her stead*.

PHILARIO
>   We trust no anniversaries, dread sovereign,
>   Less happy round the royal head are hovering.   25

ÆGISTHUS
>   A cordial wish in which we sympathise,
>   And hope we mayn't see *any worse arise*.
>   Meantime proclaim a general holiday,
>   That all may give their loyal feelings play
>   By general joy in every direction—   30
>   In one outburst of unrestrained affection.

PHILARIO
>   Pardon, dread king, you've made a slight mistake
>   We fear the vulgar rabble scarce partake
>   The loyal sentiments which animate us
>   But, rather—

ÆGISTHUS   Yes we know, they rather hate us—   35

PHILARIO
>   Sire, Agamemnon, it must be confessed, is,
>   With aching hearts remembered, and Orestes
>   Whom, if he should return, they swear they'll make King.

ÆGISTHUS
>   These aching hearts shall find their head is a-king!

Enter one of CLYTEMNESTRA'S LADIES, *L.*

LADY
>   Most gracious sovereign—

ÆGISTHUS
>   (*starting up angrily*) How now? What means   40
>   this insolent intrusion?

0.7 SD 'Le petit tambour de la Garde Nationale'. French air and duet composed by Jean Théodore Latour (1766-1837) in the early nineteenth century. Latour was resident pianist for King George IV.

20–1 The play starts on the anniversary date of the nuptials between Aegisthus and Clytemnestra. The marriage itself is supposed to have taken place after Agamemnon's death.

36–8 The oracle of Delphi ordered Orestes to return home to avenge the death of his father.

LADY   Sire, the queen's
         Desirous you'll be good enough to say
         If you mean to sit preaching there all day—
         Because, when you have nothing else to do
         She would be glad to have a word with you.   45
ÆGISTHUS (*with change of manner*)
         The playful dear! how quaintly she reveals
         The jealousy she of our absence feels!
         But she's so fond of us we must excuse her,
         Besides there's nought in life we can refuse her.   *Exit Lady, L.*
         (*aside*) At least a long experience tells me so,   50
         (*aloud*) All which considered, p'r'aps you'd better go.
         (*Chorus repeated—procession goes off, R. U. E.—courtiers exeunt, L. U. E.*)

                    Enter CLYTEMNESTRA, *L.*

CLYTEMNESTRA
         How fares my gracious lord?
         (*with change of manner*)   Oh! so they've left you?
         I thought you'd company—pray what's bereft you
         Of common sense, (you'd not too much to start with
         Certainly, none you could afford to part with,)   55
         That these last three nights you have left your bed
         To indulge in restless wanderings over head?
ÆGISTHUS
         Though my arising may to you seem queer,
         Your own horizon's anything but clear,
         The seeds of revolution, taking root,   60
         Promise to both of us an early *shoot;*
         Our cutting off their late king with a hatchet,
         Returning from the bath, the rebels snatch at
         As cause against us—and exclaim, in wrath,
         He got his head shaved when he went to Bath!   65
CLYTEMNESTRA
         With honeyed words, I have disguised the facts.

ÆGISTHUS
    Words won't avail, they'll judge us by our *axe;*
    In nightly visions, Agamemnon's shade
    Calls on his son for vengeance!
CLYTEMNESTRA   What! afraid
    Of a night phantom?
ÆGISTHUS   I don't mean a pun,   70
    'Tis not the *shade* I fear—it is the *son!*
    And there's the daughter too—the girl, Electra—
    I always pop on when I least expect her
    Laden with curses, every sort and size
    For application to my head and eyes;   75
    I wish, unless her language she can soften,
    That peerless orphan would appear less often.
CLYTEMNESTRA
    Broken of that, she soon to us will bend herself.
ÆGISTHUS
    She may be broken, but will never mend herself;
    Besides, her dress is—where got I can't tell,   80
    Apparel quite without a parallel:
    Wherein she wanders forth at early morn,
    Unkempt, uncinctured, with her stockings torn,
    In her hand offerings, in her eye a tear
    To *imbrue* her father's lamen- *table* beer.   85
    Chrysothemis is of another sort,
    On politics she never wastes a thought.

---

62   **hatchet** Aegisthus recounts the killing of Agamemnon according to Seneca.

65   **Bath** both referring to the bathtub where Agamemnon was killed in Aeschylus' *Agamemnon* and to Bath, a watering place or spa and common holiday resort during the nineteenth century.

68   **nightly visions** allusion to Clytemnestra's dreams in Aeschylus' *Choephori* and Sophocles' *Electra*. The fact that the visions are Aegisthus's in Talfourd reinforces the caricature of the character. Also consider the high recurrence of ghostly visions in the entertainment of the age, which would be a common referent for the audience (see Zeitlin, 'Study', pp. 361–378).

80–3   Electra is dressed in permanent mourning for the loss of her father and the apparent loss of her brother according to the classical tradition. Reflecting the distress of a female character through slovenly clothing and hair is also commonplace in nineteenth-century literature.

86–7   Chrysothemis is the counterpart of Electra inasmuch as she represents the 'angel-in-the-house' as opposed to the strong-minded woman.

CLYTEMNESTRA
    I doubt if she's a thought to waste, unless
    It be upon the fashion of her dress.
    Thus different ways, each in her duty flags,   90
    One's *over dressed,* the other *done to rags.*

ÆGISTHUS
    Chrysothemis I'm sure is worth a dozen
    Of her pale, slipshod, sentimental cousin.

CLYTEMNESTRA
    A worthless minx! (*Chrysothemis is heard singing without.*)

ÆGISTHUS   Hark! here's the dear child coming,
    An opera tune most *opera-tunely* humming;   95
    You called her worthless, and you were not wrong,
    Since she is going now for an old song.

Enter CHRYSOTHEMIS, *R U E. down C., a bunch of violets in her hand, singing and dancing.*

AIR

By the margin of fair Zurich's Waters.

As the morning looked fair in all quarters,
        And I knew
    A bank where these lie-a-beds lay,   100
These the fairest of fair Nature's daughters
        That on it grew,
    I gathered and brought them away!
    And you'll own no one bolder can be,
        For it don't with my practice agree   105
    To rise at this time of the day;
        Aye, aye, you
    May stare—but the duty to pay
    I owe you—I owe you—on this happy day,
    I owe you—I owe you—drove all sleep away!   110

(Nemesis rises invisible behind Clytemnestra,
L. C., and speaks through tremulous music.)

NEMESIS

Now is the time, all my resources rallying,
To pull the wires and set these puppets dallying,
Anticipate the tyrant's crime-earned woes,
And hasten matters to their fated close;
My mission I at once will set about, 115
True men come by their own when knaves fall out.
Come, Jealousy—obedient to my will,
Thy subtle poison through her veins distil!
(Nemesis sinks—Clytemnestra appears inoculated with a new feeling—
she observes Aegisthus and Chrysothemis with distrust.)

CLYTEMNESTRA

(*aside*) What are they saying? I'm inclined to think
A nod accompanied by such a wink 120
Means something!

ÆGISTHUS (*receiving the bunch of violets from Chrysothemis*) Are these violets for me?
You're not forgetful of the day I see.

CHRYSOTHEMIS

Oh no, I found them nestling in their beds
This morning, and they raised their modest heads,
Blushing to find that I was up before 'em. 125

CLYTEMNESTRA

(*aside*) Violets should blush which violate decorum.

CHRYSOTHEMIS

They are the prettiest that I could gather.

CLYTEMNESTRA

(*aside*) Ogling! he's old enough to be her father!
(*aloud*) When you've quite done exchanging compliments,

97.4 SD Song composed by Charles Dance. It refers to the love of a youth for a young lady (Thiselton-Dyer, *Folk-lore*, p. 161).

100 **lie-a-beds** idle persons (*OED, n.*).
111–18 see List of Roles, 6n.
128 **Ogling** 'the giving of admiring, flirtatious, or lecherous looks' (*OED, n.*).

Perhaps you'll explain this matchless impudence! 130
Flirting before my face.
CHRYSOTHEMIS (*astonished*) Flirting? oh, aunt—
ÆGISTHUS
I can't imagine—
CLYTEMNESTRA No, of course you can't,
You never can—
CHRYSOTHEMIS Harm, aunt, I ne'er met any—
ÆGISTHUS
And I had no idea—
CLYTEMNESTRA You haven't many.
CHRYSOTHEMIS
But I assure you—
CLYTEMNESTRA Yes, you'll soon the folly see, 135
Of such assurance with so little policy.
ÆGISTHUS (*C., deprecating*) My love.
CLYTEMNESTRA Oh don't love me!
ÆGISTHUS Your word is law,
I promise not to do so any more,
Though I don't yet quite see her crime's immensity.
CLYTEMNESTRA
Good *evidence* of your own *heavy density*! 140
And pray where is Electra?
CHRYSOTHEMIS In her room,
Weaving a chaplet for her father's tomb,
Content, she says, for happier times to wait,
And bend, in mute submission to her fate.
CLYTEMNESTRA
Bid her *unbend* herself and come here *straight*,
Exit Chrysothemis, R. 145
Such shameless conduct would a saint provoke.
ÆGISTHUS
(*aside*) It won't touch *you* then.
CLYTEMNESTRA What?

ÆGISTHUS   I only spoke.
      Nothing's *occurred* to make you thus give *way*.
CLYTEMNESTRA
      That girl shall married be without delay.
      Now, as I've family duties to attend to,   150
      We'll this discussion put at once an end to.
      You'll join the hunt.
ÆGISTHUS   I hunting go?
CLYTEMNESTRA   Of course.
      I've taken care to order round your horse,
      For idle men are always in the way at home.
ÆGISTHUS
      I'll be so quiet if you'll let me stay at home.   155
CLYTEMNESTRA
      You used to like the chase!—I see I—
ÆGISTHUS   The fact is,
      Of late, my dear, I've got so out of practice
      Since we've been married, long experience teaches
      I've never worn, nor am to wear the breeches.   *The sound of horns.*

Enter HUNTSMEN *and* RETAINERS *through centre arch from L. U. E.*

HUNTSMAN
      Will't please your majesty to join the sport?   160
      Your thoroughbred is saddled in the court
      Champing his bit
ÆGISTHUS   Oh! that is a decider,
      For I am not a bit a *champi'n* rider;

---

142   **chaplet** garland of flowers (*OED, n.* 1a).
149   **married** see pp. 14, 26, 28.
152–77   The fragment exemplifies Aegisthus's feeble character as opposed to Clytemnestra's strong-mindedness. A recurring refiguration of a parallel couple in English literature is in Shakespeare's *Macbeth*. Francis Talfourd's *Macbeth Travestie* (1850) follows in the line of this tradition.

159   **breeches** another allusion to the effeminate character of Aegisthus. 'Breeches roles' were interpreted by actresses wearing men's clothing. Yet the role of Aegisthus in the 1859 performance was interpreted by Mr. Compton. The pun therefore is twofold.

>   The clouds are threatening too, and seem to say
>   Our marriage morn will prove a *wettin'* day 165
>   From which, excuse me, I'm induced to dread
>   A *quartan* ague from my thorough *bred*.

CLYTEMNESTRA
>   No, go you must; your thoroughbred 'tis clear
>   Is *needed* to prevent your *loafing* here.
>   Why, Agamemnon rode! they'll say in scoff, 170
>   From him to you was a sad falling off.

ÆGISTHUS
>   'Twixt you and me, and probably my steed,
>   I feel there'll be a *falling off* indeed.
>   But here goes!

CLYTEMNESTRA   Shrewdly answered,

ÆGISTHUS   You're too good,
>   With such a wife the husband must be *shrew'd*. 175

CLYTEMNESTRA
>   The dinner hour for seven o'clock we fix,
>   So mind you don't return, at least, till six.   *Exit, L. 1 E.*

ÆGISTHUS
>   Now since we've got our work cut out before us,
>   We'll make believe we like it in a chorus.

SONG AND CHORUS

AIR

Kiss me Quick and go, my Honey.

>   A southerly wind and a cloudy sky 180
>   Proclaim a hunting morn,
>   The deadly breeches I must mount
>   I've not for seven years worn;
>   I ventured once to plead excuse,
>   She kicked me out of bed, 185

  And while I struggled with my boots,
    Now what do you think she said?
  Oh cut your stick and go, my hubby,
    Cut your stick and go;
  Don't rub your eyes, but I advise   190
    You cut your stick and go.
  And now the royal hunt is up,
    I must get up *as-well,*
  And clamber up that thoroughbred
    From which last time I fell;   195
  I never can forget that day
    They picked me up for dead—
  And yet to-day I can't say nay,
    You all heard what she said.
  Then let's be quick and go, my honeys,   200
    Let's be quick and go,
  As't must be done, we'll call it fun,
    So let's be quick and go. *Chorus repeated and exeunt, R. U. E.*

1.2 *A Chamber in the Palace. Music—Air, 'The Miller of the Dee,' very slowly.*

  Enter ELECTRA, *L., her hair dishevelled, her dress torn
  and disarranged, shoes unsandaled and down at heel.*

ELECTRA

  Another day has passed, and yet another
  Brings with its light no tidings of my brother.

---

167 **quartan ague** fever recurring periodically.
179.3 SD Song composed by Silas Steel and Fred Buckley in 1856. It illustrates 'a new style of courtship pressed increasingly into genteel songs, one in which the couple enjoy close proximity and physical contact in recognizable surroundings' (Finson, *Voices*, p. 44). The song is comically used here as sung by Aegisthus with reference to Clytemnestra's abuses on him.
0.1 SD Song by Charles Mackay (Mackay, *Collected*, pp. 221–222).

0.2-3 SD Sophocles refers to Electra's signs of mourning in l.91. In l.359-362 the contrast between the two sisters is in the way they enjoy the wealth of the family. As unorthodox characters, madwomen, femme fatales and gypsies are usually depicted with dishevelled hair in Victorian literature and arts. Therefore, following the aesthetics of the nineteenth century, Electra's uncared for look not only matches her mourning but also her insubordinate temperament.

While poor Electra, wearied of expecting,
By all neglected, and herself neglecting,
Resembles much as classic heroine can 5
The well-known slip-shod, Good-for-Nothing Nan;
These locks of gold, when servants on me waited,
Used to be carefully *electra-plaited,*
Now all dis-*Sheffield* down my shoulders flow—
No friendly comb'll make them *comb-il-faut;* 10
Where a 'deserted auburn' they remain,
I fear not 'loveliest even of *the plain.*'

Enter CHRYSOTHEMIS, *R.*

CHRYSOTHEMIS
    Oh, aunt's in *such* a temper!
ELECTRA   *In* at last?
    She has been out of it for some time past.
CHRYSOTHEMIS
    And what I can have done I'm sure I'm *not* aware. 15
ELECTRA
    What matter.
CHRYSOTHEMIS (*hesitating*) Only—
ELECTRA (*contemptuously*)   True, I had forgot you were
    A little sycophant!
CHRYSOTHEMIS   I am, I vow,
    More than a little *sick of aunt* just now.
ELECTRA
    If then you don't her indignation fear,
    Enlist in my cause as a Volunteer. 20
CHRYSOTHEMIS
    Join a forlorn hope? No, I thank you dear,
    When I my own light company can choose,
    Pray, why should I exchange into the *blues*?
    No, a fast life for me! 'Laugh while you may'
    Has ever been my motto.

ELECTRA   Have your way,   25
    But you mistake to call a gay life *fast*,
    That must be *slow*, that's without trouble *passed*.
CHRYSOTHEMIS
    Here comes my aunt? I'd best retire, since she
    Has taken an antipathy to me.
ELECTRA
    Where's all that courage that you talked about?   30
    Meet her at once, and boldly face it out.
CHRYSOTHEMIS
    Meet her? a lighted candle you might as
    Well introduce to an escape of gas!
    There'll be a blow up if we meet—discreeter
    'Twill be to turn myself off, at the *meet-her!*   *Exit, R.H.*   35
ELECTRA
    So, all desert me!

5–6 Metatheatrical reflections abound on the Victorian popular stage. Here Talfourd manifests the anachronistic nature of burlesque by juxtaposing the portrayal of a classic heroine with a popular stereotype of the time. See 6n.

6 **slip-shod** careless (*OED*, *adj.* 1).
Good-for-Nothing-Nan the one female protagonist in John Baldwin Buckstone's *Good for Nothing* first staged at the Theatre Royal, Haymarket in 1851 (Nicoll, *History*, pp. v, 287). Nan is an orphan girl brought up by two brothers who pay little attention to her education. The play manifests the development of the character from a tomboy to an educated young girl. The following review in *The Musical World* makes the links with Electra explicit: 'Such domestic matters as combing her hair, washing her hands, and other enforced requisites of society, are not held in absolute regard by Nan, who inclines to the normal state of nature' (1851, Vol. 29, p. 88).

8 *electra-plaited* pun. *Electroplate*: to colour with electrolysis (*OED*, v.). *Plait*: to braid (*OED*, v.).

9 **dis-*Sheffield*** pun for dishevelled. The Sheffield plate was a 'plate made of copper coated with silver by a special process brought to perfection in Sheffield' now disused (*OED*, *n.* 1a). It was generally replaced in the mid nineteenth century with electroplating processes.

11 **'deserted auburn'** allusion to Oliver Goldsmith's poem 'The deserted village'. The poem became popular at the time of publication as it evoked the romantic spirit of the vanishing of existence. Goethe was one of its admirers (Rousseau, *Oliver*, p. 113).
auburn golden brown (*OED*, *adj.*).

12 **'loveliest … plain.'** first line of Goldsmith's poem 'The deserted village': 'Sweet Auburn! loveliest village of the plain'. Thomas Hood (1799–1845) used the line in 'The Progress of Art' as follows: 'How Beauty's cheek began to blush; /With lock of auburn stain— / (Not Goldsmith's Auburn)—nut-brown hair, /That made her loveliest of the fair; /Not "loveliest of the plain!"'. Electra's is a punning reference to her hair, which is not fair but the opposite.

24 **'Laugh … may'** song by Charles Morris (1745–1838), army officer and songwriter. Many of Morris's songs were set to popular tunes even in the nineteenth century. First published in 1786 as *A Collection of Songs by the Inimitable Captain Morris*, countless new editions of his lyrics were revised until the late Victorian period (*ODNB*).

32–5 Gas light was the cause of numerous accidents in theatres throughout the nineteenth century.

Enter CLYTEMNESTRA, *L.*

(*coldly to Clytemnestra*) Pray may I solicit
The cause, ma'am, of this unexpected visit?

CLYTEMNESTRA
Electra, you've your father much offended;

ELECTRA
About my father, least said soonest mended;

CLYTEMNESTRA
Oh, you allude to fables long refuted. 40

ELECTRA
It was, ma'am, to all-you-did I all-u-ded,

CLYTEMNESTRA
My own child! must I lectured be by her?

ELECTRA
I am Electra! not a lecturer.

CLYTEMNESTRA
Besides, what's done is done—

ELECTRA That's very true,
But much that's not done, yet remains to do. 45
Then let Ægisthus triumph while he may,
Work his own will, and exercise his sway,
Till the gods, pitying this distracted land,
Summon Orestes to arrest his hand.

CLYTEMNESTRA
Your brother? Sure you've heard the news? he's dead, so 50
Will never trouble us.

ELECTRA It has been said so!
Yet cannot I forget a certain oracle—

CLYTEMNESTRA
Asserting an untruth, for, from his curricle
Which threw him out, a lifeless corse he fell,
Throwing out, o' course, the prophecy as well; 55
Meantime, what ails you, that you needs must rove,
Despite our orders, to the cypress grove!

Pluck my choice flowers into wreaths to twine,
And spill, while in the wood, our bottled wine?

ELECTRA
 'Twas a libation,

CLYTEMNESTRA   Yes, but you forget
You took the claret from the cellaret
To waste upon these empty demonstrations,
I've scarcely patience with your scarce libations.

ELECTRA
It was not I—so that reproach may spare it—
Who was the first to tap my father's claret.
Have you no tributes to bestow? I pity you.

CLYTEMNESTRA
I wish you'd *try boots,* for your shoes don't fit you.

ELECTRA
E'en in my shoes my sympathy's revealed
With him whose soul you sent down unan-*healed.*

CLYTEMNESTRA
Still the old tune and words!

ELECTRA   'Twill be the same,
Until Orestes shall his birthright claim,
Then will I change my note, and sing, I swear,
A different tune, in fact, the rightful *heir!*
Now I'll a walk take, this dispute to end,
And seek the change of air you recommend.

CLYTEMNESTRA
Was ever queen plagued with a child like this?
I may say two, for there's Chrysothemis;

50–1 In Sophocles' *Electra* it is the Paedagogus, Orestes' attendant, the one who spreads the news of his death.

52 **oracle** the Delphic oracle ordered Orestes to avenge his father. See *Antigone*, 288n.

53 **curricle** a two-wheeled carriage (*OED, n.* 2).

60 **libation** 'ritual pouring of water, wine, oil, milk, or honey in honour of gods, heroes or the dead' (Roberts, *Dictionary*, p. 419).

	Henceforth I shall enjoy no peace of mind	
	Until I see her marriage contract signed,	
	So will for Lycus send, without delay,	80
	(*to Electra*) I've no more time to waste on you. *Exit angrily, L.*	
ELECTRA	Good day!	

And where is he for whom so long I've striven?
Would I could be assured he's even living!
Kind Destiny, his guardian to the last,
Watch o'er him on *what shore* soever cast,   85
And, Fortune, though disaster strive to floor him,
Rest o'er his arms till you to mine *restore* him!

SONG—AIR

Willie, we have missed you.

Oh! brother, would I knew, dear,
    Where 'tis you roam;
They do not tell me true, dear,   90
    Who say you'll ne'er come home.
I'm sure the cruel fate
    Which makes their hearts rejoice
Can ne'er have overtaken you,
    For there's a still small voice   95
Whispering solace to my heart
    To dispel its midnight gloom!
Orestes, we have missed you,
    Pr'ythee, hasten home.
My dreams are all about you,   100
    For all the hopes I rear
Of vengeance, are, without you
    Quite desperate, I fear.
Patient I wait and watch,
    Cheered by that hope's faint ray   105
You'll homeward turn your footsteps

>   And wipe my tears away,
>   For my efforts are in vain
>   While you delay to come,
>   Orestes, I have missed you,   110
>   Hasten—hasten home!   *Exit, R.*

1.3 *The sacred Grove of Cypress, through which runs a path supposed to lead to the Tomb of Agamemnon; open country, R.*

Enter ORESTES *and* PYLADES, *L., the former bearing a cinerary urn.*

ORESTES
> Thus far into the bowels of the land,
> A process only miners understand—
> Have we marched on. Behind us Argos lies.

PYLADES
> To see it one must needs have Argus eyes.

ORESTES
> Close here—Mycenæ, (*pointing, R.*)

PYLADES
>   Then you tread the earth   5
> Once more of the fair land that gave you birth.

ORESTES
> True, but I can't much gratitude evince,
> I've given it such a wide berth ever since,
> Nor would I venture now, but for the rumour
> That I am dead—we'll that delusion humour;   10

---

85   **soever** whenever (*OED*, adv. 2).

87.2 SD Popular song by Stephen Collins Foster, leading songwriter in nineteenth-century America and author of famous hits such as 'Oh! Susanna' (Milligam, *Stephen*, p. 86).

0.1   SD **Grove of Cypress** see Lacy's edition paratext, 96n.

2   **miners** burlesque was full of topical references to trades and new mechanical devices. Coal was an important source of power in Victorian England.

4   **Argus** Argus Panoptes; the epithet clearly manifests that he is an all-seeing character. Argus Panoptes was the guardian of Io killed by Hermes. Io was loved by Zeus. Hera, in revenge, turned her into a white cow under the surveillance of Argus, whose many eyes never slept all at the same time. Zeus sent Hermes to rescue Io. Hermes put Argus to sleep with his stories and cut off his head.

> Indeed, to make maternal instinct duller,
> I'll swear I *died* myself to give it *colour*.

PYLADES
> What! at your own death be the undertaker?
> But there's your mother, can you hope to make her
> Deaf to the voice of nature?

ORESTES
>   There's no danger,   15
> For seven years I've play'd the Son and Stranger,
> And luckily, this cinerary urn
> Supposed my ashes to contain, will turn
> Suspicion from my person:—once we've gained
> Credence, and footing in the house obtained,   20
> We then may stand at ease, or I shall, rather,
> Move one step nearer to remove one step-father,
> Who in the downfall of our house will glory,
> First floor'd by our one ready-furnish'd story.

PYLADES
> But should he doubt the urn, and perhaps begin to   25
> Think it a case that should be well look'd into,
> He, our returns will smoke, and truly say
> 'Tis mere sham dust and not your genuine clay;
> The plot's found out by but the cover lifting,
> For yours are ashes that will not bear sifting.   30

ORESTES
> He'll never *go to see*—how can he, pray,
> While we contrive to keep him at *Urn Bay*.

SONG—AIR

Oft in the Stilly Night.

> Soft if not silly quite
>   You must I fear have found me,
> If you think I can't bring off right   35
>   The troubles that surround me.

> Dispel your fears my boyhood's years
>   My manhood will betoken,
> Or that they'll learn aught from the urn
>   Which will remain unbroken.   40
>   Soft if not silly, &c.
> I shall remember all
>   The lies we have link'd together—
> When I recount my fall,
>   I doubt most shrewdly whether   45
> They'll take to task, or think to ask
>   The how, or when, or wherefore,
> Quite satisfied that I have died,
>   The only fact they care for.
>   Soft if not silly, &c.   50

PYLADES

(*looking off R.*) But who comes here, with votive offerings laden?

ORESTES

(*with indifference*) Some pious peasant.

PYLADES   No—a glorious maiden!

What dignity and grace in every movement,
Although her costume might bear some improvement:
In mien a princess, though apparelled humbly.   55

ORESTES

I see, she's coming—I don't see she's comely.

PYLADES

That taper waist!

ORESTES (*staying him*)   Yes—taper's a good name;
Don't burn your fingers at that taper's flame.
(*Becomes interested as he recognizes his sister Electra advancing.*)
Stay! (*clutching the arm of Pylades*)

---

16 **seven years** see Lacy's edition paratext, 41n. Orestes recalls the plot set at the beginning of Sophocles' *Electra*.

32.2 SD Song by Thomas Moore (1779–1852) (*ODNB*; Griswold, *Poets*, p. 166). James Joyce alludes to this song in *A Portrait of an Artist as a Young Man* (see Bowen, *Musical*, p. 38).

PYLADES   Hey!
ORESTES   Aye!
PYLADES   Why?
ORESTES   No.
PYLADES   Oh!
ORESTES   It cannot be!
    That form! yes—I am not deceived! 'Tis she.   60
PYLADES
    No doubt I shall agree to all you've stated,
    If you will take the trouble to translate it.
ORESTES
    My sister—yet I mustn't yet embrace her!
PYLADES
    I'll act as proxy for you.
ORESTES   I dare say, sir.
    If to the good cause loyal she remain   65
    As yet we know not, so, to ascertain
    Rehearse our story of the urn, my friend,
    And coil a tail about my hapless end;
    While I, to make her disposition clear,
    Conceal myself, and thus get a *hide-here*.   70
PYLADES
    Sure, with an empty jar you would not mock her?
ORESTES
    Not being a *laden* jar it need not shock her! *They retire, L. U. E.*

Enter ELECTRA, *R. U. E., bearing votive offerings for the tomb.*

SYMPHONY—SONG.

AIR

Nothing More.
    I've the matter fairly pondered,
        And its many pathways seen,

But I scarcely know which road leads 75
    To the vengeance that I mean.
For what can a lonely maiden,
    With a task that brimming o'er
With difficulty do, but ask
    For her brother, and nothing more? 80
With no advice to guide me,
    I must still go blundering on,
Till I fear the hour for action,
    Long arrived will soon be gone.
Let me hear the welcome music 85
    Of his footfall on the floor—
'Tis surely not too much to ask
    Only this, and nothing more.
Thus for weeks and months I'm brooding
    O'er hopes too long deferred; 90
Orestes promised to return,
    I know he'll keep his word,
Could I but see him face to face
    With his worthless pa-in-law—
That party would like nothing less, 95
    And I'll ask nothing more.

ELECTRA

(*Kneels, C.*) Ye gods who rule the destinies of kings,
Look down upon this dreadful state of things!
If for misdeeds ye retribution purpose,
Let fall your lightning on these proud usurpers. 100
Our country groans, so ruthlessly they bleed her;
While the inhabitants, without a leader,
Stir not to staunch her wounds!—there's not a man

72.5 SD This ballad dates from 1856 with music by William Winn and lyrics by J. B. Rogerson. It was widely performed in the popular theatre of the nineteenth century, for example in William Brough's *The Gipsy Maid* (1861) (Davis, *Broadview*, p. 307).

>   Will be the spirited *leader of the van;*
>   Though factious citizens in gloomy knots,   105
>   *Sit as hens* brooding o'er their half-hatched plots;
>   E'en knowing blades with hunger, through the town
>   Become sharp set, for taxes grind them down.
>   Lycean Phoebus, (*Kneels.*) make these patriots bolder,
>   The rebel fires which in each bosom smoulder,   110
>   Into a blazing conflagration fan,
>   And send me, I implore thee!—a young man.
>   (*Observing Pylades, who approaches, L. C, bearing the urn.*)
>   (*aside*) Good looking, too—and I in such confusion!

PYLADES
>   Pardon this unintentional intrusion,
>   Fair lady, and be sure I no offence meant.   115
>   (*aside*) That's pretty well, I think, for a commencement,
>   (*aloud*) I'm to Mycenæ bound, where they expect me.
>   But fear I've missed the path—can you direct me?

ELECTRA
>   (*pointing, R.*) This spot a plain view of the city yields;
>   There is a nearer path across the fields,—   120
>   You'll have to ford a brook, through, by that way,
>   But if you can't afford, nor brook delay,
>   You'll find the distance will by half be shortened.

PYLADES
>   Thanks, ma'am, the news I bear is most important,
>   From Strophius, King of Phocis.

ELECTRA   Ha! I presage   125
>   The worst news of Orestes in that message;
>   Speak—and allay an anxious sister's fears.

PYLADES
>   Alas, I can but answer with my tears;
>   My assistance, like *a cistern's* full of water!
>   But if you be great Agamemnon's daughter,   130
>   You'll mutely bear this new affliction.

ELECTRA   Who
    Can be at once a *mule* and *bearer*, too?
    But come, the sad particulars disclose.
PYLADES
    'Tis pity—but I promised, and here goes:
    (*Sings.*)

                        AIR

                The Bold Dragoon.

It was a sad affair that befell that smart young man,—   135
Not a maid but stole a glance at him as through the lists
    he ran,
With his harness light and horses bright, and garbed as
    choicest taste equipped 'em,
He took the lead and kept it too, so swiftly round the course
    he whipp'd 'em.
            Crack went the lash, ri, tol, &c.

But turning round to take a look what made his rivals lag,   140
His horses made a sudden swerve, and touched the turning
    flag;
Then like a rocket from the shock (such cruel grief the gods
    can send us),
He spun up there into the air, and came down a most
    tremendous
            Whack on his back, fol lol, &c.

---

104 **van** to lead the van (*OED*, n.², 2b). 'Van' as an abbreviation of 'Vanguard' (*OED, n.*).
106 **Sit as hens** to brood, to incubate, to couve (*OED, v.*).
108 **taxes** the burden of taxation was a major political concern throughout the nineteenth century. Electra here explicitly comments upon a social problem related to the public sphere that 'strong-minded women' were so eager to conquer.

125–60 In Sophocles' *Electra* she first learns about the death of Orestes from the Paedagogus, Orestes' attendant.
134.3 SD 'The Bold Dragoon or the Plain of Badajos'. Song by Walter Scott written in 1812. The song was written shortly after the battle of Badajoz for a yeomanry cavalry dinner and first published in 1814 (Scott, *Poetical*, pp. 637–638). Talfourd transplants the words of the Paedagogus to the lyrics of this popular martial song.

It was a sad reverse the most impartial will declare, 145
For the right heir unto the throne to be thrown right unto
   the air,
But so it was, and all because he would not keep his eyes before him,
He fell a corse upon the course, from which home of course they
   bore him,
            Back in a sack, fol, lol, &c.

For your better understanding, I must tell you that the Phocians 150
About the mode of burial have most eccentric notions;—
His ashes burned, were then inurned, for into this funeral vase I
   swept 'em,
And thinking as his sister, you might like to see 'em, kept 'em.
            Packed, fol, lol, &c.

ELECTRA
   This vessel, then?
PYLADES (*aside*)   I of the trick repent— 155
   (*aloud*) The man you mean is in this monument!
   Although in this form you might not have known him
   But as *de mortuis nil nisi bone-um*
   I as his best friend for his dust contracted,
   And in this urn hermetically packed it! 160

ELECTRA
   Alas! I was prepared for this, because
   I knew Orestes had been in the *vars*.
   Let me look on the sad memorial, pray—
   Fie—a tea-urn.
PYLADES   Do not t-urn away,
   Not having time the matter to discuss, 165
   A tea urn seemed a fit *sax-coffee-gus*.
   Besides, the mode of burial I thought a-
   Ppropriate, for one so often in hot water!
   And so to soothe a sister's pious yearnings,
   I have saved up all your brother's little urnings. 170

ELECTRA
>	Kind thoughtful friend, I pray you give it me,
>	Let me embrace the vase that once *vas* he.
>	And what you ask, I promise without fail!

PYLADES
>	An urn's a steam vessel, not meant for sale,
>	Take it, and welcome.
>	(*Gives it to her and retires up to Orestes.*)

ELECTRA   How old feelings rush up,   175
>	And to my eyes unbidden fountains gush up!
>	I as 'twere yesterday remember well
>	What miseries his infancy befell,
>	The painful cutting of his earliest tooth,
>	And other *incidental* to his youth, 180
>	This urn appropriately suggesting three things
>	His infant *cough, hiccups,* and baby *teethings*.
>	More clearly still back on my memory flow
>	The *souvenirs* of *seven years* ago.
>	When I from tyrants' menaces to snatch him, 185
>	Sent him abroad, for fear they should dispatch him.
>	And thought a tardy vengeance to enjoy,
>	Bringing my hopes to anchor round that boy,
>	Now since harsh fate removes the channel's mark,
>	All my small craft must founder in the dark. 190
>	(*Orestes rushes to her from his concealment, R. U. E.*)

---

158 *de ... um* 'of the dead, nothing unless good', Τὸν τεθνηκότα μὴ κακολογεῖν (from Diogene, Laerci 1, 3, 70. A. 852. D. 575. G. 586. H. 1803. S. 1885). Also old saying in English: Never speak ill of the dead.
     bone-um pun 'bones' and 'bene/bonum'.
162 **vars** pun 'vase' (*OED, n.* 1b). Also 'wars' as in 'hostile contention' (*OED, n.*¹).
166 **sax-coffee-gus** sarcophagus.
167–8 **a- Ppropriate** word split for the pun.
170 **urnings** pun with 'earnings'.
172 **vas** was; pun with 'vase'.
174 **steam vessel** allusion to topical objects recurrent in Victorian burlesque. For comic reasons, the steam vessel here refers both to a vessel, a container for holding steam (*OED, n.* 1) and to a 'steamboat' (*OED, n.* 2).
184 **seven years** see Lacy's edition paratext, 41n.

ORESTES
    (*C.*) Not so, dear sister.
ELECTRA   Pray who are you, sir?
    I'd but one brother.
ORESTES   Can't you then infer?
ELECTRA
    'Tis hard, this contradiction as I view it
    To reconcile.
ORESTES   I *reckons I'll* soon do it.
ELECTRA
    It is—it is'nt! Yet that well known voice.   195
    Yes—no.
ORESTES   You have the privilege of choice.
ELECTRA
    Orestes! (*Throws herself into his arms.*)
ORESTES   Oh, rest easy on that head,
    In spite of all this gentleman has said
    Upon my word and honour I'm not dead;
    But for a further proof my tale is true—   200
    Observe my linen.
ELECTRA   Marked Orestes, too!
ORESTES
    Well, never mind the number.
ELECTRA   Oh! my brother.
    Even without these proofs 'twere hard to smother
    The inward voice that whispers your recovery.
ORESTES
    True, 'tis the invoice marks the goods delivery.   205
ELECTRA
    But, why deceive me?
ORESTES   I apologize;
    That dust was meant to throw in other eyes,
    Though first we tried its influence on you,
    To find you, as we reckon'd, staunch and true;

> But, since you seem to stand, like strangers ill at ease,   210
> I'll introduce you—there—my sister—Pylades,
> Our trusty colleague.

PYLADES (*to Electra*)   Put me to the proof
> I'll think no *feat* too great in your *behoof*.

ORESTES
> Now what's the news at home? Have they been starving you?
> You look so ill—and who's this upstart parvenu   215
> So unlike our own Agamemnon?

ELECTRA   True.
> He's very different from the *Pa ve knew*,
> But I must own, although they treat me vilely
> From morn to night I'm *rated very highly*.
> While prying eyes all secrecy deny us,   220
> Making the court a court of *nice eye pry us*.

ORESTES
> Let vengeance which has *long lain* dormant, burn in
> My breast! It's a *long lane* that has no turning.
> So now *en route* and forward as we trudge it,
> You can unfold the rest of the home budget.   225
> (*A bugle sounds distant, L. U. E.*)

ELECTRA
> A horn! the hunting party! I doubt whether
> It will be prudent we be seen together.

ORESTES
> You're right—if to the palace you precede us,
> We will be up and doing when you need us.   *Exit Electra, R.*
> (*Orestes and Pylades retire a little, R., looking after Electra.*)

---

201 **anagnorisis.** The recognition scene between Electra and Orestes is essential for the plot of the three Electra tragedies: Aeschylus' *Choephoroi*, and Sophocles and Euripides' homonymous *Electra*. The variation of the recognition motifs between the three playwrights imply different theatrical and gnoseological attitudes.

213 **behoof** benefit (*OED*, *n.*).

217 **Pa ve knew** Pa (Father), Ve (funny Germanic or Jewish pronunciation of 'We') Knew, thus mimicking Orestes' 'parvenu' of line 215.

> ÆGISTHUS *enters, L.U.E., through the thicket—he is habited in the costume of the chase, torn, wet and dirty—he sounds a horn.*

ÆGISTHUS
>Amid those branches I have lost my route, 230
>I play a trump, but no one follows suit!

ORESTES
>(*advancing, R.*) May we enquire, sir, what disaster's fretting you?

ÆGISTHUS
>(*C.*) Oh, gentlemen, I've lost my way, my horse, my retinue!
>(*Sounds horn.*) In vain I blow—the birds, with echoing throats
>Alone will take up my dishonoured notes. 235

PYLADES
>(*L.*) Birds? Fast men blow the post-horn for a *lark*.

ÆGISTHUS
>That is a *horni-tho'-logical* remark,
>But don't apply to my case, for in me
>You an unhappy hunting party see.
>'A southerly wind and cloudy sky proclaim 240
>A hunting morning'—and so, out we came:
>We reached the park—the hounds *threw off*, of course,
>A movement which was followed by my horse.

ORESTES
>You were unhorsed!

ÆGISTHUS
>The animal was vicious;
>Indeed, the whole day has been unhorse-spicious! 245
>On flew the hounds, and yelping through the park,
>Left me a *tarrier*—with a loss of *bark*.
>I, while the others kept their seats in clover,
>Was such a *green* that I was *grazed all over*.

PYLADES
>They left you in the slough of despond here? 250

ÆGISTHUS
>Worse—it was in the slough of that pond there;
>A situation I did not desire—

You see there's no occasion to *add-mire!*
(*Turns round and shows himself covered with mud.*)
Galled by the saddle, sadly I remained
In water, that was not—as I was—*strained*.   255
Fearing a ditch additional to meet,
Where I might my *Graze Elegy* repeat;
Till finding mine a sinking situation,
Like a great man, I rose with the occasion,
Went wandering on amid these tangled trees,   260
Until I thought *wanders* would never cease!

PYLADES

If you're fat-igued, on us you'd better *lean*.

ORESTES

We'll be your guides, though doubtless when you're seen
By the street boys, you'll find you're guyed enough;
For they'll provide the *stares*—and show you up.   265

ÆGISTHUS

Thanks, friends; but first your names I fain would learn.

ORESTES

You'll give us your address, sir, in return?

ÆGISTHUS

Of course—my costume so to seed has run,
I'd gladly change address with any one.

---

236 **post-horn** formerly used to announce arrival (*OED*, *n.* 1a).

240-1 '**A ... morning**' first lines of the popular hunting song 'A southerly wind', also known as 'The Fox Chase'. It is mentioned in countless popular books and magazines of the time, for example, 'Fox Hunting', Chambers, *The Book of Days: a Miscellany of Popular Antiquities*, vol. 2, 2 vols. p. 489, October 24, 1864; Foster, *The Perennial Calendar, and Companion to the Almanack; Illustrating the Events of Every Day in the Year*. London: Printed for Harding, Mavor, and Lepard, 1824, October, p. 557. In 1883, the American Thomas Moran first exhibited a landscape etching entitled after this song at the Art Department of the New England Manufacturers' and Mechanics' Institute, Boston.

250 **slough ... despond** after John Bunyan's *The Pilgrim's Progress* (1678).

257 ***Graze Elegy*** punning reference to Thomas Gray's *Elegy Written in a Country Churchyard* (1751).

TRIO

AIR

LAUGHING TRIO

Rose of Castile.

ÆGISTHUS

 I am the king, ha! ha! 270
 Who got a fling, ha! ha!
 Over a thing, ha! ha!
 They call a Ha! Ha!

PYLADES

 He is the king, ha! ha!

ORESTES

 'Tis an odd thing, ha! ha! 275
 Fate should thus bring, ha! ha!
 Us together, ha! ha! ha! ha!

ÆGISTHUS

 While here we must amuse you, ha! ha!
 To the queen to introduce you, ha! ha!
 I shall be proud, ha! ha! 280
 If I'm allowed, ha! ha!
 Which I much doubt, ha! ha!
 Entres nous, but ha! ha!

PYLADES, ORESTES

 We shall be proud, ha! ha!
 If honoured so far, ha! ha! 285
 But, sire, this condescension.

ÆGISTHUS

    Ha! ha!
The matter pray don't mention.

PYLADES, ORESTES, ÆGISTHUS

 If he's your new papa, fate lends her aid so far.
 If he's my new papa, fate lends her aid so far.

Home you must come, ha! Ha! 290
You and your chum, ha! ha!

ORESTES, PYLADES, ÆGISTHUS

I need not go far for vengeance, ha! ha!
You need not go far for vengeance, ha! ha!
She may look glum, ha! ha! no matter, ha! ha!

Exit Aegisthus, supported by Orestes and Pylades, R. U. E.

1.4. *The Curtained Gallery.*

Enter CHRYSOTHEMIS, *R.*

CHRYSOTHEMIS

Orestes is returned! What joy! Yet he
May long ere this have quite forgotten me!
Does he still wear my portrait next his heart
With which he promised he would never part?
"Give me," said he, "your miniature, I pray, 5
To look on every *minute you're* away."
But did he *mean it sure?* or was the intent
Naught better than an empty compliment;
One of those bubbles men with soft soap blow
To please a woman's fancy, who, below, 10
Delighted sees the fairy globe mount higher,
Then like a dream, break, vanish, and expire?
Nay, I'll not think it—'twill not do to be
So hard on one who was so soft on me.
Here comes my aunt, and Lycus in her train, 15
To try his second-hand suit on again;—

269.4 SD Comic opera in three acts by William Balfe with words by Harris and Falconer, adapted from Adolphe Adam's *Mutelier de Tolède*. It was first performed at the Lyceum Theatre in London, 1857. (*ODNB*; Upton, *Standard*, pp. 19–21; White, *Register*, p. 79).

1–6 Orestes is Chrysothemis' brother in Sophocles. Miniatures were usually given as a token of love.

'Twas but this morn she for my coldness chid me;
I wish he'd run away with aunt, and rid me
Of both at once; but 'tis too much to hope
To merge the two bores in one *aunt elope!* *Exit, R.*   20

Enter CLYTEMNESTRA *with* LYCUS, *who appears anxious to escape, L.*

CLYTEMNESTRA
Come in! What do you fear?

LYCUS
                        'Twas but this morn
That she turned up her nose at me in scorn,
And though she didn't in plain terms refuse, she
Distinctly meant nay by her *ney-retroussee;*
While, singular but sympathetic fact,   25
My nose became disjointed by the act;
When love's in question, as you may suppose,
The man's ears ain't soothed by the lady's noes,
So please, I'll call again this day six months.
(*going, L.*)

CLYTEMNESTRA
No—if 'tis done, it must be done at once;   30
I'll send her to you, and remember 'Faint
Heart ne'er, &c.'—in bright colors paint
The joys that to a wedded life belong.

LYCUS
I can't paint well, but I can pitch it strong.

CLYTEMNESTRA
Wait while of your arrival I inform her!   35
And should she still continue cold, I'll warm her.   *Exit, R.*

LYCUS
I'll to the sticking place my courage screw,
And brace my nerves up for the interview. (*Sings.*)

AIR

Would she but name the day—Satanella.

    Oh, would she but name the day,
        Or let me mention it for her;   40
    If she would only say,
        Sweetheart, I am yours to-morrow!
    Why does she floor me so;
        Vex me with long delay?
    Leave me to sigh, heigho!   45
        Why can't she name the day?
    (*Makes great exertions to reach a very high note— Chrysothemis runs in, R., in feigned alarm.*)

CHRYSOTHEMIS

    What's happened? Dear sir, are you in much pain?
    You've over-reached yourself, I fear, to gain
    A high note, and are suffering from the *strain;*
    Still in my ears that piteous wail is ringing.   50

LYCUS

    (*Offended.*) What you call piteous wailing, I call singing,
    And there are many, tho' I may do badly,
    Who'd give their ears to sing as well, miss, gladly!

CHRYSOTHEMIS

    Their ears! that sacrifice would not much cost them,
    They'd like your music better when they'd lost them.   55

---

24 **ney-retroussee** 'retroussé' 'of the nose: turned up (attractively) at the tip. Also more generally: turned or curving upward' (*OED*, *adj.* and *n.*). Here used as in phrase 'to turn up one's nose at' (see 1.4.22).

31–2 '**Faint … &c.**' 'Faint heart never won fair lady', old proverb and also the title of a comedy by James Robinson Planché published in 1840 and first performed at the Olympic Theatre in London in February 1839 (Nicoll, *History*, pp. iv, 381).

38.3 SD Song in *Satanella*, opera by William Balfe (*ODNB*). *Satanella, or, The Power of Love* was first performed in December 1858 at the Covent Garden Theatre in London, only a few months before the first staging of Talfourd's *Electra* (White, *Register*, p. 79).

47–53 Metatheatrical references featuring songs and music, two key elements of burlesque.

LYCUS
    Oh, why thus jeer a heart's pure fond desire?
    You know 'tis dangerous to play with fire.

CHRYSOTHEMIS
    This morn I threw cold water on your suit,
    Enough to deluge you from head to foot,
    And put out every spark you else might nurture,   60
    Unless your suit were made of gutta percha.

LYCUS
    Put me to any water proof you will,
    So I *get a perch here* in your heart still.

CHRYSOTHEMIS
    You've had your answer, why thus persevere?
    If some one I could name were only here,   65
    And saw you teaze me, he'd occasion seize
    To right me properly and *cross your teaze*.
    If he the down-strokes of his round hand tries—

LYCUS
    (*interrupting*) He'd cross my teaze by dotting both my eyes:
    I understand—a system taught by *Smart*   70
    And who's this happy sharer of your heart?

CHRYSOTHEMIS
    (*aside*) How foolish! his suspicion I've incurred.
    (*aloud*) 'Tis nobody.

LYCUS (*incredulously*)   Nobody? On my word,
    I wish that I were nobody.

CHRYSOTHEMIS   Ne'er fear, it
    May come in time, you are so *very near it*.   75

LYCUS
    Madam! But, I'll my indignation swallow
    Though it should choke me.

CHRYSOTHEMIS   Nay, that doesn't follow;
    Your indignation has so little menace in't,
    You couldn't swallow anything more innocent.
    (*Goes up and crosses, L.*)

Enter CLYTEMNESTRA, *R.*

CLYTEMNESTRA
    Well, is it settled?
LYCUS (*advancing despondingly, R.*) Yes; I think it's settled.
    Your majesty, the belle is too high mettled
    To chime in, as she's *told* with anything,
    Although she seems quite *clear* about the *ring*.
CLYTEMNESTRA
    (*Crosses to Chrysothemis.*) Why how's this? Do you dare
        dispute my will?
CHRYSOTHEMIS
    No, aunt, if you'll, by way of codicil,
    Let me choose whom I like and whom refuse.
CLYTEMNESTRA
    Well, but time presses and we've none to lose;
    To keep relations friendly I but see
    In this mate here material guarantee.
CHRYSOTHEMIS
    Your kindly project I've no wish to baffle,
    Hadn't you better put me up to raffle?
    A prize to wrestle for? (*aside*) A good idea,
    'Twill make the intentions of Orestes clear.
CLYTEMNESTRA
    (*C.*) Agreed—and to make sure the contest's fair
    To all, it shall be done upon the square,
    The public square, I mean, amid the games.
CHRYSOTHEMIS
    (*L.*) If none appear to urge his prior claims,
    I'll make my mind up to the worst,—that's you,
    (*to Lycus*) Or any one in short, I don't care who.

---

61 **gutta percha** 'The inspissated juice of various trees found chiefly in the Malayan archipelago' (*OED, n.*). Used as insulation during the nineteenth century.

69 **cross … eyes** 'Dot your i's and cross your t's'. Proverb. Make sure that everything is correct.

70 **Smart** probably Christopher Smart (1722–1771), English poet.

81 **mettled** high spirited (*OED, adj.*).

LYCUS

    (*R.*) Excuse me, madam, wrestling is an art   100
    Which of my youthful studies formed no part,
    Besides I'm delicate about the shins,
    And not so firm as might be on my pins,
    While shoes that pinch me, prudently admonish
    That I am for a wrestler much too *Cornish*.   105

CLYTEMNESTRA

    (*to him*) You run no risk, for, without my permission
    No one will dare appear in opposition.

LYCUS

    (*valiantly*) Under those circumstances I'll away
    And brace my sinews for the manly fray!   *Exit, R. 2 E.*

Enter ÆGISTHUS *dressed as in Scene I., with* PYLADES *bearing the urn, L.*

ÆGISTHUS

    (*timidly*) My dear, may I make bold to introduce   110
    An interesting stranger?

CLYTEMNESTRA (*aside to him*)   What's the use
    Of bringing home, to make our larder thinner
    Guests, when I'm not prepared to stand a dinner,
    E'en on the cheap plan that the Times would bring
    In vogue?

ÆGISTHUS (*aside to her*)   He's good news.

CLYTEMNESTRA (*aside to him*)   That's another thing.   115

ÆGISTHUS

    (*hypocritically*) Mentions your poor boy's death.

CLYTEMNESTRA (*aside*)   Then every dish
    Is his, if only the desert I wish
    Has fallen on Orestes! (*to Pylades*) Sir, you're welcome—
    My niece—(*Introduces him to Chrysothemis.*)
        you have some piteous news to tell? Come
    I know its purport, out with it, don't spare it,   120
    Besides I am strong-minded, and can bear it.

PYLADES

    (*Crosses to Chrysothemis.*) To coil it up then, in the smallest space,
    Your son was entered for a chariot race—
    The goal is near—a pillar intervenes,
    Smashing the chariot all to smithereens!   125

ÆGISTHUS

    I see—he shaved the post too closely, where
    Too close a shave *cut off his father's heir!*

CLYTEMNESTRA

    Excuse a mother's feelings—the essentials
    You've mentioned—may I ask for your credentials?

PYLADES

    That Death the '*graver* has *struck off the prince*   130
    This proof before all letters will convince. (*shewing the urn*)
    (*aside to Chrysothemis*) Be satisfied—Orestes is not far.

CLYTEMNESTRA

    To a mother's feelings this is a *sad jar*.
    Remove the mournful evidence, I pray,
    (*To Lady, who exits with urn, L.*)
    I've no time to cry over it to-day.   135
    The games require our presence.
    (*All move, L., as if going off.*)

Enter ELECTRA, R., *she is handsomely dressed—her hair neatly arranged, and her manner joyous.*

ELECTRA   What, mamma!
    Going without me?

---

105 **Cornish** 'Cornish wrestling' 'A local form of wrestling in which contestants, wearing loose canvas jackets, try to throw their opponent by grappling, tripping, and other techniques' (*OED*, *adj.* 2 and *n.*). Wrestling was also part of the Greek Olympic games.
114 **cheap ... Times** nineteenth century press was a source for the latest fashions of the day.
121 **strong-minded** see Lacy's edition paratext, 45n.
127 **heir** pun with 'air (hair).
131 **This ... letters** an impression taken from an engraved block or plate, before the ordinary issue is printed and before an inscription or signature is added (*OED, n.*).
136.2 SD **she ... arranged** the physical change reflects the change in the mood of the character.

CLYTEMNESTRA (*astonished*) Why, how changed you are!
>   This, for the ill-conditioned sloven miss
>   An unexpected metamorphose is.

ÆGISTHUS
>   True, dear—I, under favour be it said, 140
>   Ne'er met a more fast metamorphosed maid!
>   I fear I must be wandering in my mind.

CLYTEMNESTRA
>   You'll not stray far—the space is too confined.
>   (*to Electra*) Why, you are quite finely tricked out!

ELECTRA (*aside*) Yes, and you
>   Will soon find you are *finely tricked out* too! 145

CHRYSOTHEMIS
>   That flush of pleasure and joy-lighted eye,
>   Explain and say, my pretty coz—'cos why?

CLYTEMNESTRA
>   My daughter, sir. (*Introduces Electra to Pylades.*)

PYLADES (*to Electra, crossing to her*) Lady, I kiss your hand.
>   (*King and Lycus talk together.*)

CHRYSOTHEMIS
>   (*aside, watching them*) He does it too! Ah, now I understand
>   Her change of dress—'tis easy to infer, 150
>   These happy tidings must have *tidy-ed* her.
>   With that young man too she's in love, I see,
>   Which to those well oiled locks supplies the key.

ÆGISTHUS
>   Let us sad thoughts of past times chase away,
>   And mingle with the pastimes of to-day. 155
>   While that we have no false pride to attest,
>   Chrysothemis shall foot it with the rest.

QUINTETTE

AIR

Girl, I left behind me.

ÆGISTHUS
    The sports begun—let's see the fun,
        Front places are bespoken;
    What sight is there that can compare   160
        With seeing heads well broken?

CLYTEMNESTRA
    Young Lycus waits to lead the fetes,
        Then let's be off to find him;
    Twill cheer his eyes to see his prize—
        The girl he left behind him!   165

ÆGISTHUS, CLYTEMNESTRA
    Young Lycus, &c.

ELECTRA, CHRYSOTHEMIS
    I hope his pate may meet the fate
        To which our prayers consigned him,
    Before he tried to win as bride,
        The girl he left behind him.   *Exeunt [all], L.*   170

1.5 *The Great Square of the City during the Fete, The Stage is crowded with People engaged in various pursuits—Some are looking at the exhibition of a classical "Punch and Judy" R. C.; some are endeavouring to obtain wreath of*

---

147   **coz** 'abbreviation of cousin' (*OED, n.*).
153   **well oiled locks** see 1.1.80–83n and 136.2SDn.
157.3 SD Popular song which dates back to ca. 1758–1759. Also known as *Brighton Camp* or *Blyth Camps*. Early versions were played as military marches. It also became popular in the Revolutionary War and the Civil War in America (Erbsen, *Cowboy*, pp. 22–23).
      SD see Lacy's edition paratext, 102n.

laurel from the head of a greasy pole, C.; others are engaged witnessing the performance of a Strolling Company of Actors on a Thespian cart, L.; Two Players engaged in a contest, their partisans looking on encouraging them, R. The Scene opens to A BALLET DIVERTISSEMENT!

Enter PHILARIO, *R. U. E.*

PHILARIO

    (*pompously*) Their majesties approach! and bid me say,
    They give you leave for this once to display
    The loyalty which fills your hearts, no doubt,
    In one prolonged enthusiastic shout!
    (*Murmurs among the crowd.*)
    You seem inclined to take your time, I see;   5
    Perhaps you'd better take your time from me.
    Now, hip—hip—hip—Hurrah!
    (*The people groan.*) I was to add, if anybody feel
    A diffidence in answering this appeal
    With heart and voice, 'tis possible, instead,   10
    That gentleman will answer with his head.
    Take my advice, then, or you may repent it,
    Immediately be joyous and contented;
    Let your enthusiasm over *bile*.
    And mind you smile as you were wont to smile!   15

Grand March—Enter THE ROYAL PARTY, ÆGISTHUS, CLYTEMNESTRA, LYCUS *in the costume of an Athlete, with a cloak thrown over him;* CHRYSOTHEMIS, ELECTRA, *and* PYLADES *enter R. U. E, and come down to L. At the instigation of* PHILARIO *some of the* PEOPLE *faintly say, 'Hurrah,' in desponding unjoyous tones.*

ÆGISTHUS

    Thanks, friends, this genuine unbought applause
    Speaks volumes for the wisdom of our laws!
        (*cries of* 'Oh! oh!')

ÆGISTHUS

    (*fiercely*) Whoever 'oh's' will find he has to pay!

    (*mildly*) I did not catch that last remark.

PEOPLE (*faintly as before*)   Hooray!

ÆGISTHUS

    (*With feigned emotion*) Yes, these spontaneous outbursts of affection   20
    Are pleasant matter for a king's reflection.
    Pshaw! this is weakness!
    (*Brushes away an imaginary tear.*)   Doubtless you all know
    We are about our fair niece to bestow
    On the best wrestler, who, you'll understand,
    Must carry off the palm to win her hand;—   25
    But that you may all learn the stakes imperilled,
    We publish full particulars in the Herald.
    (*A* HERALD *advances, C., while a roped arena is formed round him.*)

HERALD

    Oh, yes! oh, yes! which means, oh, know you all
    'Tis my vocation to the lists to call
    Whoever ventures to pick up the glove   30
    Thrown down by Lycus for his lady love!
    Lycus, the Argos Gilliflower famous!

LYCUS

    (*aside to Clytemnestra*) Oh, dear! should any not an ignoramus
    Appear, I'm floored!

CLYTEMNESTRA (*aside to him*) On that head have no fear,
    Against my champion none will dare appear;   35
    Keep up your spirits.

---

15 SD The whole scene and Lycus dressed as an athlete exemplifies the anachronistic and lighthearted nature of burlesque.
25 **palm** 'branch' or leaf of palm tree worn as a symbol of victory (*OED*, $n.^1$, 2) and the inner surface of the hand (*OED*, $n.^2$). The winner of the contests in the Greek Olympic games were given an olive or laurel wreath.
27 **Herald** pun. A messenger and also reference to the names of various newspapers such as *Glasgow Herald*, *Southampton Herald* and *York Herald* which were published at the time.
29 **lists** tournament (*OED*, $n.^3$, 9a).
30 **pick ... glove** to accept a challenge.
32 **Argos Gilliflower** imitating the collocation with various attributes like English gilliflower and African gilliflower. The gilliflower is a native plant having flowers scented like a clove (*OED*, n. 3). Sometimes also used to refer to a woman (*OED*, n. 1).

LYCUS (*Re-assured.*) Thanks—on that condition
My pecker holds its usual high position.

HERALD
Three times I sound my trumpet! (*Sounds—a pause.*) No reply?
(*Lycus throws off his cloak and advances boastfully.*)

LYCUS
When once I stripped, I thought they would be shy!
Manner and style like mine not many men   40
Possess!—perhaps you'd better sound again.
They're much *too deep* for *soundings,* and they may
Take it as *sound* advice to keep away.
(*Herald sounds.*)

CHRYSOTHEMIS
(*to Electra aside*) With dread forebodings my sad mind oppressed is:
Alas! my only hope was in Orestes.   45
Why did I to this silly wager yield,
In full assurance he would take the field?
But he deserts me—

ELECTRA
(*aside to her*) Fie, you mustn't say so
All is not lost yet—prythee, don't give way so.

CHRYSOTHEMIS
And must I be that empty coxcomb's bride?   50

ELECTRA
You shan't be tied to him whate'er be-tide:
Let me entreat you to be pacified.

CHRYSOTHEMIS
Be pacified? The troubles that arise,
Could ne'er have come to *pass-if-I'd* been wise.

HERALD
None enters an appearance, sir;—all mute.   55

LYCUS
Then mine will be an undefended suit.
Wake all the town, and let the people know it
Is the last time of asking. Go it—blow it!
(*Herald sounds.*)

CHRYSOTHEMIS

(*aside*) That last blow is a last blow to my hopes.

ÆGISTHUS

No one will venture then within the ropes? 60

ORESTES *enters hurriedly, L. U. E., and makes his way through the* CROWD.

ORESTES

I will, sire, if it's all the same to you.

CHRYSOTHEMIS

(*to Electra*) 'Tis he! 'Tis he!

ELECTRA (*to her*)   Hush! List to my imploring,

Two more such *'Tis he's* will make up our *flooring*

CLYTEMNESTRA

(*aside*) 'Tis well! it matters little to my plan,

So she *be* married, *who's* the happy man. 65

ORESTES

(*to Chrysothemis*) How could you think I would forsake you, dear,

When 'tis for sake of you that I am here?

There is my gage, although I risk, I know,

A *par-a-dise* upon a single *throw!*

LYCUS

(*aside*) How very awkward! (*to Orestes with assumed superiority*)

Are you used to falling? 70

ORESTES

Wrestling with fate long time has been my calling

And in my college days I learned the charms

Of a good long pull at the Wrestler's Arms.

---

49   **prythee** I pray thee (*OED, int.*).
68   **gage** a pledge (*OED, n.*^{1}); also a pledge of battle, challenge.
71–3 Orestes humorously turns Lycus's threat into an anachronistic reference to his own university days when excessive drinking (pull, *n.*2g-long pull) might well have caused him to fall. The wrestling reference is cleverly maintained at start and finish. As a sport, wrestling became widely popular in London during the 1820s and 1830s (Collins, Martin & Vamplew, *Encyclopedia*, p. 283).

ÆGISTHUS
    We'll put you to the proof; so, clear the ring,
    And let them *trip* each other's *heal and fling*.   75
    You shall try but one fall.
LYCUS   Be that agreed.
ORESTES
    Now when you're ready, sir—

        SONG—AIR

    Come into the garden, Maud.

    Come into the ring, my lord,
      Since down your gage is thrown;
    Come into the ring, my lord,   80
      Though I'm not in fit state I'll own—
      In condition first-rate I'll own.
    But your wordy challenge is wafted abroad,
      And the trumpet defiance has blown,
    For our breeze of this morning proves,   85
      And the plan it our love it will try,
    'Twere sinning to faint in her sight whom one loves,
      Or instead—like a duffer—fight shy.
    It ain't in the light of a man she loves,
      She'll look on whoever says die.   90
    Come into the ring, my lord,
      Since down your gage is thrown;
    One of us will soon be floored,
      And the lady the victor's own!
    (*They wrestle—Lycus is thrown—shout.*)
ONE OF THE CROWD
    Well thrown, indeed.   95
    (*All the Crowd,* "Hoo— !"—*they are going to shout, but are stopped by the King.*)

ORESTES

    How do *you* feel?—*I'm* not warm at all
    So if you'd like to try another fall,
    We'll go 'best out of three.'

LYCUS (*rising*)   You're very kind.
    To come off second-best out of one, I find
    Is quite enough to put me out of breath,   100
    Best out of three to me were sudden death!
    (*Goes up to Queen—Boys take up ring.*)

ÆGISTHUS

    (*rising and coming down, R., to Orestes*)
    Since then your match her match with Lycus breaks,
    (*crossing to her*) I can't do less than offer you the stakes.
    (*Presenting Chrysothemis —Orestes crosses leaving King, R.*)

ORESTES

    An offer that's so handsome on its face
    I need, sire, no caressing to embrace.   105
    (*embracing Chrysothemis*)

CLYTEMNESTRA

    (*aside*) The girl's at last disposed of—that's a blessing!
    (*coming down, R. of King—Lycus R. corner*)
    (*aloud*) Since the engagement seems so very *pressing*,
    We'll set at once about the preparations;
    Meantime accept my best congratulations.

ELECTRA

    And mine.

LYCUS   And mine—for I don't see the fun   110
    Of breaking several ribs in gaming one.
    I pitched upon my head—

---

75 **heal and fling** 'highland fling', Scottish dance in which arms and legs are moved vigorously (*OED*, 'fling', *n.* 4a).

77.2 SD Section of *Maud* (1855) by Alfred Lord Tennyson. Talfourd reproduces the rhyme and metre of the poem.

79 see 68n.

ÆGISTHUS　　　　　　　　That's no hard case,
　　　You couldn't pitch upon a softer place.
　　　Stay! we must know the title of the winner.
ORESTES
　　　You shall be satisfied, sire, after dinner.　　　　　　　　115
ÆGISTHUS
　　　On to the banquet then, and after all
　　　Your yarn is spun, we'll wind up in a ball!
　　　　　March.—Exeunt R. U. E.—shouts and resumption of the music,
　　　　　　　and the Scene closes as the People go up the stage.

1.6 *Ante-chamber in the Palace.*

　　　　　　　　　Enter NEMESIS, C.

NEMESIS
　　　So far, so well; but much is yet to do.
　　　I really cannot tell if all of you
　　　Recall the old Greek rule of stage propriety—
　　　Which was—the audience having had satiety
　　　Of crime displayed and vengeance on it willed.　　　　　5
　　　Upon the stage the actors were *not* killed,
　　　But by some fanciful poetic means
　　　Were decently disposed of— off the scenes!
　　　Let none think we the grand old works despise,
　　　Which for your modern eyes we modernize;　　　　　10
　　　Since old Mycenæ then, my scenic art
　　　Displays—though you'll not find my scene a cart
　　　As in those days—we'll not in this depart
　　　From the old rule. So, though the guilty wife
　　　And husband both are doomed to end their life　　　　　15
　　　By changing poisoned cups, we'll leave the fumes
　　　To work upon them in their dressing rooms
　　　Behind the curtain. You'll enquire no doubt
　　　How this catastrophe is brought about.

Learn then the queen has fixed her admiration 20
On Pylades, who, at my instigation,
Appears to listen to her overtures,
(While poor Electra all the pangs endures
Of Jealousy). Whereat, the queen her mind up
Has made, her former partnership to wind up— 25
Will dose the king's cup—the mode well she knows it,
For, in her case, *experienta dose it.*
Meantime, here comes the interesting victim,
Looking as though some sense of wrong had pricked him
To meditate revenge. Of both I'll spoil 30
The future hopes, while, from this mortal coil
Both simultaneously slip their cables,
And each on each with your leaves turn the tables.
(*Nemesis retires up the stage.*)

Enter ÆGISTHUS, R.

ÆGISTHUS

This cat-and-dog life can't go on much longer,
The cat has proved so very much the stronger. 35
Would that we lived in times some yet may see,
When married folks can separated be—

3–8 In Greek tragedy characters are usually killed offstage. Nemesis enters here as *dea ex machina* and comments upon classical drama manifesting once more the concern of Victorian popular theatre for metatheatrical reflections.

9–10 Talfourd explicitly manifests that this is a comic refiguration of Greek tragedy.

12 **cart** medieval mystery plays were sometimes performed on a decorated cart. Carts were used as props and symbolically in Greek tragedy as exemplified in Aeschylus' *Agamemnon*.

14–16 **So ... cups** the motif of the cup is present in Euripides' *Ion*. Probably Francis Talfourd was acquainted with the tragedy as his father, Thomas Noon Talfourd, wrote a drama, *Ion* (1835), based on Euripides' homonymous play. Nonetheless, there are echoes of Claudius' and Gertrude's deaths in *Hamlet*, V, ii in this scene. Considering the introduction of Philario, a secondary character in Shakespeare's *Cymbeline*, probably the lines also refer to Cornelius' switch of the poison meant to kill the enemies of the Queen in Shakespeare's tragedy.

18 **curtain** the deaths are offstage. See 3–8n.

24 **Whereat** at which (*OED*, *adv.*).

27 ***experienta dose it*** pseudo-Latin for 'experience does it'.

36–7 Debates on separation and divorce filled the intellectual circles of the nineteenth century. Echoes in the literature of the time abounded as manifested in Charles Dickens' *Hard Times* (1854), for example. The controversial Matrimonial Causes Act, for example, was passed in 1857, only two years before the first performance of Talfourd's *Electra*. See pp. 12, 14, 28–9, 31.

>   I could prove cruelty 'mongst other wee sins,
>   And sue for a divorce, for *divorce* reasons.
>   Meantime, some means I must use to get rid o' her   40
>   And start again in life a jolly widower—
>   Make up to—whom? Aye! there's the rub!

NEMESIS (*Unseen by him, suggests.*)   Chrysothemis.

ÆGISTHUS
>   Chrysothemis? Why not? the notion's not amiss,
>   But there's a proverb not more trite than true,
>   Which treats about the old love and the new.   45
>   First, of the first dispose 'ere fix my choice on
>   A second—humph! what means to use though?

NEMESIS
>   (*as before*) Poison.   *Exit, L. 2 E.*

ÆGISTHUS   A good idea; yes, nothing can be clearer,
>   I'll drug her cup—South Attican Madeira—
>   'Tis fit for such a purpose I should choose   50
>   A wine that has no *character* to lose.
>   If she but take that draught, I am content
>   'Twill prove the rough draught of her *settlement*.

(*Sings.*)

AIR

Jolly Nose.

>   'Neath her nose—'neath her nose!
>   'Neath her nose at the banquet I'll manage to slip   55
>   A cup of South Attic Madeira,
>   With which if she ventures to moisten her lip,
>   She will not find her intellect clearer.
>   Where it grows—I suppose
>   Salt and senna may glow in the glass,   60
>   And rhubarb may crown the refection

>   So if but one drop to her palate may pass,
>   Though I scarcely conceive my fond wife such an ass,
>   She must pay for her strange predilection.
>   'Neath the rose—off she goes,   65
>   Without the least fear of detection!   *Exit, L.*

Enter ELECTRA, *R.*

ELECTRA

>   A warning this to all unmarried maidens is
>   Who list to Cupid's too seductive cadences,
>   That fickle, perjured Pylades who swore to me
>   Such oaths as never mortal swore before to me,   70
>   Is flirting with the queen in the back garden!

Enter NEMESIS, *L. 2 E.*

NEMESIS

>   Be comforted, my child.

ELECTRA (*astonished*)   I beg your pardon.

>   Are you aware, ma'am, these are private premises?

NEMESIS

>   No gates are strong enough to keep out Nemesis,
>   But to resume—your lover true remains,   75
>   'Tis but at my will he a passion feigns
>   For her.

38–9 see 36–37n. In 1857 women were allowed to divorce for offences such as 'incest, bigamy or gross physical violence' (Shanley, *Feminism*, p. 44). The words pronounced by Aegisthus emphasize the effeminacy of the character.

49 **South Attican Madeira** 'Madeira', wine from the Portuguese island of Madeira (*OED*, *n*.¹). 'South Attic', region in Greece. Talfourd again juxtaposes contemporary commodities with classical references.

53.3 SD Comic Victorian song. Lyrics by W. H. Ainsworth with music by G. H. Rodwell (Carpenter, *Songs*, p. 35). Popular at festive occasions. It refers to the effects of wine.

ELECTRA   Can this be true? or, am I dreaming?
NEMESIS
  This *new suit* that you dread's made up of *seeming*,
  When the work's done which I in hand have ta'en,
  The seeming shall come all unstitched again. 80
NEMESIS (*Sings.*)

AIR

Cheer up Sam.

  The sword of Fate suspended
   By justice over crime,
  Waits only for my signal
   To fall—and now the time
  Approaches—though deferred 85
   The long account to close,
  And give you at a word,
   A triumph o'er your foes.
  Cheer up, then,
   For to-day, 'ere the sun has gone down, 90
  For the past shall atone,
   And you will own
  You've more cause to smile than to frown.

ELECTRA
  (*Repeat*) I'll cheer up, ma'am,
  And won't let my spirits go down, 95
   For the kindness you've shown
  I'll freely own, &c. *Exeunt severally.*

1.7 *Grand Banquet Hall in the Palace—*GUESTS *seated at tables, which line the stage on either side—* ÆGISTHUS *and* CLYTEMNESTRA *at a table on centre trap—* ORESTES *and* CHRYSOTHEMIS *at extremity of table, R.—* PYLADES, ELECTRA, *and* LYCUS, *L.—Music.*

ÆGISTHUS

    (*rising*) My friends, although of speeches from the throne
    There are but few that kings can call their own,
    By ministers contributed each particle,
    I beg to say, mine is a genuine article:
    The toast I now propose with loud acclaim,   5
    (*Points to Orestes and Pylades.*)
    Is the illustrious visitors who came
    So lately to our Court,—drink we with zest
    These two last copies of the Welcome Guest!
    (*They rise to drink the health.*)
    (*aside*) She's left her goblet in my reach—that's capital!
    Hey, presto, pass!
    (*He exchanges his goblet for the Queen's, as he fancies, unobserved by her.*)

CLYTEMNESTRA (*aside*)   He's ta'en mine—ere he lap it all   10
    Another sovereign on the cypress mount
    Is carried forward to his long account.

ÆGISTHUS

    Bumpers! (*aside*) Dear me, I fear there's something wrong,
    This wine's so inconveniently strong;
    One stoup's enough to make one stupid, quite.   15

CLYTEMNESTRA

    (*aside*) There is a taste in this that don't seem right.
    (*Cheers from all the Guests— Orestes rises to respond.*)

80.3 SD 'Cheer up Sam or Sarah Bell: A Beautiful Ethiopian Melody' (1856) arranged by Charles G. Willis. African American Song. References to slavery and African American songs were constant in Victorian burlesque. See for example William Brough's *The Gipsy Maid* (1861).

94 SD Unclear SD. '*Repeat*' is in the third person plural form, yet it is not clear whether it should be Electra alone or Electra and Nemesis as the ones to repeat the lines. Furthermore, being at the beginning of the stanza, the lines that should be repeated are not clear either.

8 **Welcome Guest!** magazine founded by Henry Vizetelly in 1858. It was a weekly periodical aimed at a broad readership including women.

13 **Bumpers!** 'A cup or glass of wine, etc., filled to the brim, esp. when drunk as a toast' (*OED*, $n.^1$, 1).

ORESTES
>   My friends, I thank you, and attention claim
>   While, as I promised, I divulge my name;
>   Learn my parental tree can boast a stem none
>   Inferior to that of Agamemnon, (*sensation*)   20
>   Concerning whom I could a tale unfold,
>   Whose lightest word would make your blood run cold,
>   And while it might your very breath suspend,
>   Makes me his particular heir to stand on end.
>   Hence your guest's name, as you've already guessed, is   25
>   Orestes, and your king.

ALL
>   Long live Orestes!
>   (*The King and Queen are yielding to the narcotic influence
>   of the potions.*)

CLYTEMNESTRA
>   (*dreamily*) Of all this tumult what can be the reason?

ÆGISTHUS
>   It looks to me uncommonly like treason.

CLYTEMNESTRA   My son!

ORESTES
>   (*advancing*) Ah! that reminds me—now I'm warm,
>   I've an unpleasant duty to perform,   30
>   Imposed by fate. (*Draws.*)

ÆGISTHUS   Oh! spare yourself, my boy,
>   Ten minutes since—I mention it with joy,
>   My poisoned cup was drank from by your mother!

CLYTEMNESTRA
>   I've but one consolation—you're another!
>   For *of yours* let me tell you, every drop's   35
>   At least as deadly as cheap lollypops!

ÆGISTHUS
>   As many a victim, who, insanely willing
>   To have his likeness taken for a shilling,
>   Finds himself nothing like himself—so surely
>   I find, like him, I'm *taken very poorly*;   40

>   Both our cups drugg'd? It seems then I and you
>   Are both floored, and laid down with *drug-it* too!
>
> CHRYSOTHEMIS
>
>   Though I don't dote on aunty much, I vote
>   We do our best to get an *anti-dote!*
>   (*Nemesis rises, C.*)
>
> NEMESIS
>
>   Stir not! their time has come—leave them to me,   45
>   And let the Fates work out their own decree.
>   To you, Orestes, as of right belongs
>   (You the young martyr of a thousand wrongs,)
>   Mycenae's throne, and on it, by your side
>   Chrysothemis shall sit, your well-won bride.   50
>   (*to Electra*) For you, whom snow, nor rain, nor taunt, nor gibe
>   Could drive from duty's path, I'll now prescribe;
>   Henceforth you'll shun those dangerous nightdraughts please,
>   To take, if I may say it, your *pill-at-ease,*
>   Resting in pillowed ease with Pylades.   55
>
> ÆGISTHUS
>
>   (*raising his head*) I beg on this felicitous occasion,
>   To make the customary observation,
>   Bless you, my children! (*to Nemesis*) Thank you ma'am, good-day.
>   (*to Clytemnestra*) My dear, I think our carriage stops the way.
>   (*Ægisthus and Clytemnestra, with table, sink on C. trap.*)
>
> NEMESIS
>
>   Justice is done upon the guilty pair,   60
>   Yet, lest pollution hover in the air,
>   Tainting your future lives, these blood-stained halls,
>   Crime-clouded towers, and time-dishonored walls,

30–1 **I've ... fate** allusion to the oracle in Delphi, not a modern understanding of fate.

36 **lollypops!** juxtaposition of contemporary commodities with classical references. The earliest record of lollipop as a sweet in the OED dates from 1784.

50 **Chrysothemis** see List of Roles, 7n.

61 **pollution** in the summer of 1858 there was a pollution crisis known as the Great Stink. Human waste produced an overpowering stench that was widely recorded in the press and the literature of the period (see Halliday, *Great Stink*).

None here in their destruction to involve,
Must as a Polytechnic view, dissolve, 65

NEMESIS, CHRYSOTHEMIS, ORESTES, ELECTRA, PYLADES, LYCUS

And like the baseless fabric of a vision,
Leave not a track to mark their old position!
(*Nemesis waves her arm—the tables sink, and Scene breaks to pieces, or dissolves, revealing the last Scene.*)

FINALE.

AIR

Power of Love.

ORESTES

You've a power whose sway
   The author must adore,
Bidding him decay 70
   Or live a little more;
For in your verdict lies
   The hope he has reared above
All others—or—he dies,
   Such is your power—of glove! 75
Source of joy and woe,
   Sealers of his fate,
Don't let him vanquished go,
   Or quite repudiate
One who has known you well 80
   As vulture less than dove—
None can better tell
   Than he your power of glove!

Curtain

65 **Polytechnic** the Royal Polytechnic Institution opened to the public on 6 August 1838 and was equipped with various display rooms, among which the Great Hall was the most prominent, where exhibits were housed. The Polytechnic was also a site for cultural and scientific entertainment; for example, the exhibition of dissolving views were among its most famous shows (see Lightman, *Victorian*, 197–200). Only a week before the first performance of Talfourd's *Electra*, the Royal Polytechnic announced the display of 'Dissolving views of the Holy Land' after David Roberts's sketches (*Morning Chronicle*, Friday 15 April 1859, p. 1).

67 SD Common stage effects in the transformation scenes of Victorian burlesque.

67.5 SD Melody from William Balfe's opera *Satanella* (1858). Sung by an invisible choir closing the last scene of the opera.

72 **your verdict** addressing the audience.

75 A punning appeal to the audience to use their 'power of glove' and applause.

Textual notes

1.1

0–12] *not in LC*
0.2 SD *Mycenæ. ÆGISTHUS*] *this edn; 1859* Mycenæ ÆGISTHUS
0.4 SD *following*] *this edn; 1859 following*
17 touched] *LC* reached
39 SD] *LC* Enter-Lady
40 SD] *not in LC*
now?] *LC* now
49 SD] *not in LC*
50 SD] *not in LC*
51.2–3 SD] *LC* Exit Courtiers
<u>Chorus repeated</u>
52 SD] *not in LC*
56 nights] *LC; 1859 (*uights*)*
58 you] *LC* your
69 afraid] *LC* afraid of
75 head] *LC* hand
77 appear] *LC (*apear*)*
81 a parallel] *LC (*a pparallel*)*
85 beer] *LC* bier
94 SD] *not in LC*
97.1–2 SD *R ... dancing.*] *LC* & Nemesis
97.3–110 SD] *not in LC*
110.2 SD *tremulous*] *this edn; 1859* tremulo
114 fated] *LC* fatal
118 SD] *LC* (<u>Sinks</u>)
119 SD] *not in LC*
121 SD] *not in LC*
126 SD] *not in LC*
128 SD] *not in LC*
129 SD] *not in LC*
131 SD] *not in LC*
137 SD] *not in LC*
139 yet] *not in LC*
139 crime's] *LC (*crimes*)*
145 SD] *not in LC*

147 SD] *not in LC*
155] *not in LC*
156 see I] *LC* see
159 SD] <u>Enter Huntsmen</u>
160 SP] *not in LC*
167 *quartan*] *LC (quarten)*
177 SD] *LC* <u>Exit</u>
179 SD] *not in LC*
181 Proclaim] *LC; 1859 (Prolaim)*
188 hubby] *LC* honey
193 *as-well*] *LC (a sw<u>e</u>ll)*
194 that] *LC* my
195 fell] *LC* fell <u>Exit</u>
200–203] *LC* Oh cut &c &c

1.2
0 SD] *LC* A Chamber
<u>Enter Electra</u>
1 SP] *not in LC*
2 its] *LC; 1859* it's
7 gold] *LC* black
11–12 SD] *not in LC*
16.1 SD] *not in LC*
16.2 SD] *not in LC*
23 *blues*?] *LC (Blues)*
29 antipathy] *LC (Ant ipathy)*
35 SD *R.H.*] *not in LC*
36 SD *L*] *not in LC*
40 fables] *LC (fable)*
51 us.] *1859* us
64 may] *LC* pray
76 plagued] *LC (planged)*
81.1 SD] *not in LC*
81.2 SD *angrily, L*] *not in LC*
87 SD] Song—_∧^{air} nothing more
   Ive the matter farily pondered
   And its many pathways seen
   But I scarcerly know which road leads

  To the vengeance that I mean   Could I but see him face
  For what can a lonely maiden   to face
  With a task thats brimming o'er   With his worthleſs pa in law
  With difficulty, do but ask   That party would like nothing
    For her brother and —nothing   leſſ
    more   And I'd ask nothing more
     2
  Thus for weeks & months I'm brooding
  Over hopes too long deferred
  Orestes promised to return
  I know he'll keep his word

111 SD R] *not in LC*

1.3

0 SD] *LC* S*ᶜ* 3. The ~~sacred~~ Cypreſs Grove
   LC <u>Enter Orestes & Pylades</u>
4 one] *LC* (on)
5 Mycenæ] *LC* (Mycence)
SD] *not in LC*
9 the] *LC* aᵗʰᵉ
17 cinerary] *not in LC*
21 may] *LC* my
28 mere] *LC* (meer)
32 SD–50] *not in LC*
32.1 SD SONG. AIR] *this edn;* 1859 SONG, ORESTES. AIR
51 SD] *not in LC*
52 SD] *not in LC*
57 SD] *not in LC*
58 taper's] *LC* (tapers)
SD] *not in LC*
59 SD] *not in LC*
68 tail] *LC* tale
72 it] *LC* you
72.1 SD–96] *LC* <u>Enter Electra</u>
72.3 SD SYMPHONY—SONG.] *this edn;* 1859 SYMPHONY—SONG. ELECTRA
97 SP] *not in LC*
SD] *not in LC*
109 Lycean] *LC* (Lycaeum)

SD] *not in LC*
112 SD] *not in LC*
113 SD] *not in LC*
116 SD] *not in LC*
117 SD] *not in LC*
Mycenæ] *LC (Mycence)*
119] *not in LC*
125 Phocis] *LC (Phosis)*
126 news] *LC* of news
134 and here] *LC* there
134 SD *Sings*] Song
155 SD] *not in LC*
the] *LC* this
156 SD] *not in LC*
158 *um*] *LC* am
167 thought] *LC (though)*
168 Ppropriate] *LC (-appropriate)*
175 SD] *not in LC*
178 befell] *this edn; LC* befel; *1859 (befel)*
180 other] *LC (others)*
186 him] *LC; 1859 (him?)*
190 SD] *not in LC*
191 SD] *not in LC*
192 infer?] *LC (infer)*
197 SD] *not in LC*
Oh, rest easy] *LC* Orest-easy
205 invoice] *LC (in voice)*
212 SD] *not in LC*
213 *behoof*] *LC(* be hoof*)*
215 ill] *LC thin*
220 secrecy] *this edn; LC (secresy); 1859 (secrecy)*
223 It's] *LC (Tis); 1859 (Its)*
turning] *LC (turnings)*
225 SD] *not in LC*
229.1 SD] *LC* Exit
229.2–4 SD] *LC* Enter Agisthus
230 those] *LC* these
232 SD] *not in LC*
233 SD] *not in LC*

234 SD] *not in LC*
236 SD] *not in LC*
253] *not in LC*
253 SD] *not in LC*
262 us] *LC (as)*
265 show] *LC (shew)*
269 gladly] *LC* ~~greatly~~ *gladly*
269 SD–290 SD] *not in LC*
269 SD.1 TRIO] *this edn; 1859* TRIO— ÆGISTHUS, ORESTES, and PYLADES
270–286] *this edn; 1859 lines* fling,...ha! / Ha! / king, ha! ha! / thus / together...ha! / the / be / allowed...ha!/ nous / but...ha! / far...ha!/ condescension / mention /
290–1] *this edn; 1859 lines* your / chum...ha!/

1.4
0.1 SD] *not in LC*
0.2. SD *R.*] *not in LC*
1 SP] *not in LC*
6 you're] *LC (your)*
11 higher] *LC* the higher
15 Here] *LC* There
18 he'd] *LC* he
20 in] *LC* int
aunt] *LC* Ant-
20.1 SD *R.*] *not in LC*
20.2 SD *with...L.*] *LC* & Lycus
27 When] *LC* Where
29 SD] *not in LC*
32 &c.'] *LC* en
36 SD *R*] *not in LC*
38 SD] *not in LC*
42 I am] *LC (I'm)*
46 can't] *LC* wont
SD] *LC* <u>Re enter Chrysothemis</u>
51 SD] *not in LC*
63 I] *LC* a
68 down-strokes] *LC* down~~stairs~~strokes
SD] *not in LC*
72 SD] *not in LC*
73.1 SD] *not in LC*

73.2 SD] *not in LC*
75 it.] *1859* it
79.1 SD] *not in LC*
79.2 SD R] *not in LC*
80 SD] *not in LC*
84 SD] *not in LC*
92 SD] *not in LC*
94 SD] *not in LC*
97 SD] *not in LC*
99 SD] *not in LC*
100 SD] *not in LC*
106 SD] *not in LC*
108 SD] *not in LC*
109 fray!] *this edn*; *LC* (fray); *1859* (fray.!)
109.1 SD *R. 2 E*] *not in LC*
109.2 SD] Enter Ægisthus & Pylades
110 SD] *not in LC*
111 SD] *not in LC*
115.1 SD] *not in LC*
115.2 SD] *not in LC*
116.1 SD] *not in LC*
116.2 SD] *not in LC*
118 SD] *not in LC*
119 SD] *not in LC*
122 SD] *not in LC*
126 closely] *LC* close
131 SD] *not in LC*
132 SD] *not in LC*
133 this] *LC* ('tis)
134 SD] *not in LC*
136.1 SD] *not in LC*
136.2 SD] Enter Electra
137 SD] *not in LC*
144.1 SD] *not in LC*
144 are] *LC* ('re)
144.2 SD] *not in LC*
148.1 SD] *not in LC*
148.2 SD] *not in LC*
148.3 SD] *not in LC*

149 SD] *not in LC*
156–157] *not in LC*
157.1 SD QUINTETTE] *this edn; 1859* QUINTETTE | ÆGISTHUS, CLYTEMNESTRA, ELECTRA, PYLADES, CHRYSOTHEMIS; *LC* Quintette
157.2–3 SD] *not in LC*
170 SD *Exeunt [all]] this edn; 1859* | *Exeunt.*

1.5
0 SD] *LC* <u>The Great Square</u>
1 SD] *not in LC*
4 SD] *not in LC*
6 you'd] *LC* you
8 SD] *LC* (<u>groans</u>)
15 SD] *LC* Enter —Agisthus Clytemnestra Lycus—Chrysothemis
       Electra & Pylades
18 SD] *not in LC*
19.1 SD] *not in LC*
19.2 SD] *not in LC*
20 SD] *not in LC*
22 SD] *not in LC*
27 SD] *not in LC*
32 Gilliflower] *LC* (Gilli flower)
33 SD] *not in LC*
34 SD] *not in LC*
36 SD] *not in LC*
36 condition] *LC* ~~condition~~^position
37 position] *LC* condition
38.1 SD] *not in LC*
38.2 SD] *not in LC*
42 *too*] *LC* to
44 SD] *not in LC*
48 SD] *not in LC*
49 prythee] *not in LC*
52 pacified] *LC; 1859* (pacified?)
58 SD] *not in LC*
59 SD] *not in LC*
60 SD] *LC* <u>Enter Orestes</u>
61 sire] *LC* (Sir)
62.1 SD] *not in LC*

62.2 SD] *not in LC*
64 SP] *LC* C̶h̶r̶ Cly
SD] *not in LC*
66 SD] *not in LC*
70.1 SD] *not in LC*
70.2 SD] *not in LC*
77–101] *not in LC*
103.1 SD] *not in LC*
103.2 SD] *not in LC*
105 SD] *not in LC*
106.1 SD] *not in LC*
106.2 SD] *not in LC*
107 SD] *not in LC*
117 SD] *LC* Exit
117.1 SD *Exeunt*] *1859* | *Exeunt Aegisthus &c., &c*

1.6
0 SD] *not in LC*
9 works] *LC* rules
11–12] *not in LC*
13 in this] *not in LC*
16 poisoned] *not in LC*
18–20] *LC* The Queen has fixed her admiration
23 pangs endures] *LC* pangs of endures
27 *experienta*] *LC (experiential)*
it.] *this edn; LC (it); 1859 (it)*
30–33] *not in LC*
33.1 SD] *not in LC*
33.2 SD *Enter ÆGISTHUS, R.*] *LC* A̲i̲g̲i̲s̲t̲h̲u̲s̲ ̲E̲n̲t̲e̲r̲s̲
34 SP] *not in LC*
36 may] *LC* might
38–39] *not in LC*
42 SD] *not in LC*
43 Chrysothemis?] *not in LC*
48 SD] *not in LC*
Exit] *this edn; 1859* | *Exit* NEMESIS
51 lose] *LC (*loose*)*
53 SD] *LC* Song
61 crown the refection] *LC* g̶l̶o̶w̶ ̶i̶n̶ ̶t̶h̶e̶ ̶g̶l̶a̶ſs̶ ^crown the refection

66.1 SD *L*] *not in LC*
66.2 SD *R*] *not in LC*
67 SP] *not in LC*
71 SD] *not in LC*
72 SD] *not in LC*
79 work's] *LC (work)*
80 SD–95 SD] *not in LC*

1.7
1.7] *LC* S<u>cene 8</u>
0 SD] *not in LC*
0.4 SD *Music*] *this edn; 1859 | Musk*
1 SD] *not in LC*
5 SD] *not in LC*
8 copies] *LC* numbers
SD] *not in LC*
9 SD] *not in LC*
10.1 SD] *not in LC*
10.2 SD] *not in LC*
13 SD] *not in LC*
16.1 SD] *not in LC*
16 There is] *LC* Here's
20 SD] *not in LC*
26 SP] *not in LC*
26.1 SD] *not in LC*
27 SD] *not in LC*
29 SD] *not in LC*
31 SD] *not in LC*
32 since] *not in LC*
34 you're] *LC* your
35–36] *not in LC*
41 drugg'd? It] *LC (drugged it)*
44 SD *C*] *not in LC*
45 SP] *not in LC*
has] *LC* is
51 SD (*to Electra*)] *not in LC*
56–57] *not in LC*
58 SD] *not in LC*
59.1 SD] *not in LC*

59.2 SD] *LC* <u>Sinks</u>—
62 halls] *LC* walls
66 SP] *not in LC*
67 their] *LC* there
67 SD–83 (*Nemesis . . . glove*] *LC* Or like some Railway dividend division
                        Leave not a truck to mark the imposition
                        <u>End of Burlesque</u>

References

Adams, W. D., *A Book of Burlesque. Sketches of English Stage Travestie and Parody*, London: Whitefriars Library, 1891.

Anon., *The United States Songster. A Choice Selection of About One Hundred and Seventy of the Most Popular Songs*, Cincinnati: U. P. James, 1836.

Anon., *Great Exhibition of the Works of Industry of all Nations. Official Descriptive and Illustrated Catalogue by Authority of the Royal Commission*, London: Spicer Brothers, vol. II, 1851.

Anon., *London as It Is Today. Where to Go, and What to See During the Great Exhibition*, London: H. G. Clarke, 1851.

Anon., *Annual Report of the Registrar-General of Births, Deaths and Marriages in England*, London: George Eyre and William Spottiswoode, 1858.

Anon., *Apollo and the Flying Pegasus or the Defeat of the Amazons*, British Library Add. MS 52973, 1858.

Anson, W. S., *Shakespearean Quotations*, London: Routledge, 1907.

Atlantic Monthly

Auerbach, J., *The Great Exhibition of 1851: A Nation on Display*, New Haven: Yale University Press, 1999.

Austen, J., *Sense and Sensibility*, New York: Anchor, [1811] 2011.

Austen, J., *Northanger Abbey*, London: Penguin, 1817.

Balee, S., 'Wilkie Collins and surplus women: the case of Marian Halcombe', *Victorian Literature and Culture* 20 (1992), pp. 197–215.

Banks, S., *A Polite Exchange of Bullets: The Duel and the English Gentleman, 1750–1850*, Woodbridge: The Boydell Press, 2010.

Bath Chronicle and Weekly Gazette

Baugh, Ch., 'Stage design from Loutherbourg to Poel', in J. Donohue (ed.), *The Cambridge History of British Theatre Vol. 2 1660 to 1895*, Cambridge: CUP, 2004.

Bayley, P., *Orestes in Argos*, London: Thomas Dolby, 1825.

Berkshire Chronicle

Billings, J., Bundelman, F. and Macintosh, F. (eds), *Choruses Ancient & Modern*, Oxford: OUP, 2013.

Birmingham Journal

Blackstone, W., *The Commentaries of the Laws of England*, Dublin: John Colles, 1765–1769.

Blackwood's Lady's Magazine and Gazette

Blanchard, E. L., *Antigone Travestie*, British Library Add. MS 42982, ff. 166–173, 1845.

Blanchard, E. L., *The Life and Reminiscences of E. L. Blanchard*, London: Hutchinson, 1891.

Booth, M., *Theatre in the Victorian Age*, Cambridge: CUP, 1991.

Bowen, Z. R., *Musical Allusions in the Works of James Joyce: Early Poetry Through Ulysses*, Albany: State University of New York Press, 1974.

Braddon, M. E., *Lady Audley's Secret*, London: Penguin, [1862] 1998.

Bradford Observer

Bratton, J., *New Readings in Theatre History*, Cambridge: CUP, 2003.

Bratton, J., *The Making of the West End Stage: Marriage, Management and the Mapping of Gender in London 1830–1870*, Cambridge: CUP, 2012.

Brontë, Ch., *Jane Eyre*, London: Penguin, [1847] 2013.

Brough, R., *Medea; or, the Best of Mothers, with a Brute of a Husband. A Burlesque, in One Act*, London: Thomas Hailes Lacy, 1856.

Brough, R. and Brough, W., *The Sphinx*, London: National Acting Drama Series, 1849.

Brown, P. and Ograjenšek, S. (eds), *Ancient Drama in Music for the Modern Stage*, Oxford: OUP, 2010.

Burling, W. J., *A Checklist of New Plays and Entertainments on the London Stage 1700–1737*, London: Fairleigh Dickinson University Press; Associated University Presses, 1993.

Burnand, F. C., *Paris or Vive Lemprière. A New Classical Extravaganza*, British Library Add. MS 53049 N, 1866.

Butler, H. E., *War Songs of Britain*, London: Constable & Company Limited, 1909.

Byron, H. J., *Orpheus and Eurydice*, London: Thomas Hailes Lacy, 1864.

Byron, H. J., *Weak Woman*, London: Samuel French, 1875.

Caledonian Mercury

Carpenter, J. E. (ed.), *Songs for All Seasons*, London: George Routledge & Sons, 1867.

Cazden, N., Haufrecht H. and Studer, N., *Folk Songs from the Catskills*, Albany: State University of New York Press, 1982.

Chambers, R. (ed.), *The Book of Days: A Miscellany of Popular Antiquities in Connection with the Calendar Including Anecdote, Biography, & History Curiosities of Literature and Oddities of Human Life and Character*, London & Edinburgh: W. & R. Chambers, 1864.

Chantraine, P., *Dictionnaire étymologique de la langue grecque*, Paris: Klincksieck, 1968–1980.

Cibber, C., *Vernus and Adonis*, London: Bernard Lintott, 1715.

Clarke, M. L., *Greek Studies in England 1700–1830*, Cambridge: CUP, 1945.

Collins, T., Martin, J. and Vamplew, W., *Encyclopedia of Traditional British Rural Sports*, Abingdon: Routledge, 2005.

Collins, W., *The Woman in White*, London: Penguin, [1859] 2010.

Constantinidis, S. E. (ed.), *Text & Presentation 2005*, London: McFarland and Co., 2006.

Cork Examiner

Crombie, J. E., 'Shoe-throwing at weddings', *Folklore* 6 (6) (1895), pp. 258–281.

Curley, R., *The Britannica Guide to Inventions that Changed the Modern World*, New York: Britannica Educational Publishing, 2010.

Davis, J., '"They Shew Me Off in Every Form and Way": The Iconography of English Comic Acting in the Late Eighteenth and Early Nineteenth Centuries', *Theatre Research International* 26 (3) (2001), pp. 243–256.

Davis, J. and Emeljanow, V., *Reflecting the Audience: London Theatregoing, 1840–1880*, Hatfield: University of Hertfordshire Press, 2001.

Davis, T. C., *Actresses as Working Women: Their Social Identity in Victorian Culture*, London: Routledge, 1991.

Davis, T. C., *The Broadview Anthology of Nineteenth Century Performance*, Peterborough: Broadview Press, 2012.

Day Books indexing the Lord Chamberlain's Plays (1824–1903), 7 vols, Add. MSS 53,702–708.

Denvir, B., *The Early Nineteenth Century: Art, Design and Society 1789–1852*, London: Longman, 1984.

Derby Mercury

Devizes and Wiltshire Gazette

Dickens, Ch., *The Pickwick Papers*, London: Penguin, [1837] 2012.

Dickens, Ch., *Sketches by Boz. Illustrative of Every-Day Life and Every-Day People*, London: Chapman & Hall, [1836] 1895.

Dickens, Ch., *Martin Chuzzlewit*, Ware: Wordsworth, [1844] 1994.

Dickens, Ch., *Hard Times*, London: Penguin, [1854] 2012.

Dickens, Ch., *Dickens's Dictionary of London*, London: Macmillan & co., 1879.

Disraeli, B., *Sybil: or the Two Nations*, London: Penguin, [1845] 1980.

Dowling, L., *Hellenism and Homosexuality in Victorian Oxford*, Ithaca, London: Cornell University Press, 1994.

Dublin Gazette

Eagle, M. K. O., *The Congress of Women Held in the Woman's Building*, World's Columbian Exposition (Chicago), 1895, in *The Gerritsen Collection of Aletta H. Jacobs*, College University Library. http://gerritsen.chadwyck.com [accessed 15 October 2013].

Edinburgh Evening News

Egan, P., *The Pilgrims of the Thames in Search of the National*, London: W. Strange, 1838.
Elmes, J., *A Topographical Dictionary of London and its Environs*, London: Whittaker, Treacher and Arnot, 1831.
Eltis, S., *Acts of Desire: Women and Sex on Stage 1800–1930*. Oxford: OUP, 2013.
Engels, F., *Die Lage der arbeitended Klasse in England*, Leipzig: O. Wigand, 1845.
Era
Erbsen, W., *Cowboy Songs, Jokes, Lingo and Lore*, Asheville, NC: Native Ground Books & Music, 1995.
Erickson, A. L. B. and McCarthy, Fr. J. R., 'The Yelverton Case: civil legislation and marriage', *Victorian Studies* 14 (3) (1971), pp. 275–291.
Examiner
Exeter and Plymouth Gazette
Fahnestock, J., 'The rise and fall of a convention', *Nineteenth-Century Fiction* 36 (1) (1981), pp. 47–71.
Field, J. F., 'Domestic service, gender, and wages in rural England, c.1700–1860', *The Economic History Review* 66 (2013), pp. 249–272. http://xv9lx6cm3j.search.serialssolutions.com/?url_ver=Z39.88-2004&rft_val_fmt=info%3Aofi%2Ffmt%3Akev%3Amtx%3Ajournal&rft.genre=article&rft.jtitle=The%20Economic%20History%20Review&rft.atitle=Domestic%20service%2C%20gender%2C%20and%20wages%20in%20rural%20England%2C%20c.1700%E2%80%9318601&rft.volume=66&rft.issue=1&rft.spage=249&rft.epage=272&rft.date=2013-02-01&rft.issn=0013-0117&rft.eissn=1468-0289&rfr_id=info%3Asid%2Fwiley.com%3AOnlineLibrary [accessed 20 April 2013].
Finson, J. W., *The Voices That Are Gone: Themes in 19th-Century American Popular Song*, Oxford: OUP, 1994.
Fiske, S., *Heretical Hellenism: Women Writers, Ancient Greece, and the Victorian Popular Imagination*, Athens: Ohio University Press, 2008.
Foley, H. P., *Reimagining Greek Tragedy on the American Stage*, Berkeley: University of California Press, 2012.
Foster, T., *The Perennial Calendar, and Companion to the Almanack*, London: Harding, Mavor, and Lepard, 1824.
Foulkes, R., *Lewis Carrol and the Victorian Stage: Theatricals in a Quiet Life*, Aldershot: Ashgate Publishing, 2005.
Francis, J., *Chronicles and Characters of the Stock Exchange*, London: Longman, Brown, Green and Longmans, 1855.
Gay, J., *The What D'Ye Call It*, London, 1716.
Genest, J., *Some Account of the English Stage from the Restoration in 1660 to 1830. In ten volumes. Vol. VI*, Bath: E. H. Carrington, 1832.

Gilbert, W. S., *Ruddigore; or, the Witches Curse*, London: Chapell, 1887.

Glasgow Herald

Goc, N., *Women, Infanticide and the Press, 1822–1922: News Narratives in England and Australia*, Aldershot: Ashgate Publishing, 2013.

Goldhill, S., *Victorian Culture and Classical Antiquity: Art, Opera, Fiction, and the Proclamation of Modernity*, Princeton and Oxford: Princeton University Press, 2011.

Grafton, A., Most G. M. and Settis, S. (eds), *The Classical Tradition*, Cambridge, Massachusetts, and London, England: The Belknap Press of Harvard University Press, 2010.

Gray, Th., *Elegy Written in a Country Churchyard and Other Poems*, London: Penguin, 2009.

Griswold, R. W., *The Poets and Poetry of England in the Nineteenth Century*, Philadelphia: Carey & Hart, 1846.

Hager, K., *Dickens and the Rise of Divorce: The Failed-Marriage Plot and the Novel Tradition*, Aldershot: Ashgate Publishing, 2010.

Hall, E., 'Classical Mythology in the Victorian Popular Theatre', *International Journal of the Classical Tradition* 5 (1999), pp. 336–366.

Hall, E., 'Sophocles' Electra in Britain', in J. Griffin (ed.), *Sophocles Revisited. Essays Presented to Sir Hugh Lloyd-Jones*, Oxford: OUP, 1999.

Hall, E. and Wrigley, A., *Aristophanes in Performance 421 BC–AD 2007. Peace, Birds, and Frogs*, Oxford: Legenda, 2007.

Hall, E. and Macintosh, F., *Greek Tragedy and the British Theatre 1660–1914*, Oxford: OUP, 2005.

Halliday, S., *The Great Stink of London: Sir Joseph Bazalgette and the Cleansing of the Victorian Capital*, Stroud: Sutton, 1999.

Hamilton, C., *Marriage as Trade*, London: Chapman and Hall, 1909.

Hampshire Telegraph

Harper's New Monthly Magazine

Harper, M., 'British Migration and the Peopling of the Empire', in A. Porter (ed.), *The Oxford History of the British Empire. Vol. III, The Nineteenth Century*, Oxford: OUP, 1999.

Hartman, M. S., *Victorian Murderesses: A True History of Thirteen Respectable French and English Women Accused of Unspeakable Crimes*, New York: Schocken Books, 1977.

Hereford Journal

Hereford Times

Higginbotham, A. R., ' "Sin of the Age": Infanticide and Illegitimacy in Victorian London', *Victorian Studies* 32 (3) (1989), pp. 319–337.

Howard, D., *London Theatres and Music Halls 1850–1950*, London: The Library Association, 1970.

Hughes, J., *Apollo and Daphne*, London: Jacon Tonson, 1716.

Hume, R. D., *The Development of English Drama in the Late Seventeenth Century*, Oxford: Clarendon Press, 1976.

Humphreys, A., 'Breaking apart: the early Victorian divorce novel', in N. D. Thompson (ed.), *Victorian Women Writers and the Woman Question*, Cambridge: CUP, 1999.

Hurst, I., *Victorian Women Writers and the Classics: the Feminine of Homer*, Oxford: Oxford University Press, 2006.

Hurst, I., 'Ancient and Modern Women in the Woman's World', *Victorian Studies* 52 (2009), pp. 42–51.

Ibsen, H., *A Doll's House and Other Plays*, London: Penguin, 1965.

Illustrated London News

Jackson, R., *Victorian Theatre*, London: A&C Black, 1989.E

Jenkins, R., *Dignity and Decadence: Victorian Art and the Classical Inheritance*, Cambridge, Mass.: Harvard University Press, 1992.

Jordan, E., *The Women's Movement and Women's Employment in Nineteenth-Century Britain*, London: Routledge, 1999.

Kendrew, J., *Penny Books*, York, 1826.

Kentish Gazette

Ketterer, R., *Ancient Rome in Early Opera*, Urbana: University of Illinois Press, 2009.

Kilday, A., *A History of Infanticide in Britain c. 1600 to the Present*, Basingstoke: Palgrave, 2013.

King, A., 'George Godwin and the Art Union of London 1837–1911', *Victorian Studies* 8 (2) (1964), pp. 101–130.

Labern, J., *Labern's Comic Minstrel; A Collection of Popular Comic Songs*, London: Thomas Allman and Son, 1857.

Leeds Times

Légouve, E., *Medea: a Tragedy. Translated from the Italian Version of Joseph Montanelli by Thomas Williams*, London: R. S. Francis, 1856.

Lemon, M., *Medea; or A Libel on the Lady of Colchis*, British Library Add MS 52,960L, 1856.

Lemprière, J., *Lemprière's Classical Dictionary of Proper Names mentioned in Ancient Authors*, F. A. Wright (ed.), London: Routledge, [1788] 1948.

Levitan, K., 'Redundancy, the "surplus woman" problem, and the British census, 1851–1861', *Women's History Review* 17 (2008), pp. 359–376.

Leveridge, R., *The Comick Masque of Pyramus and Thisbe*, London: Mears, 1716.

Lewes, G. H., *On Actors and the Art of Acting*, London: Smith, Elder & Co., 1875.

Lhamon, W. T., *Jump Jim Crow: Lost Plays, Lyrics and Street Prose of the First Atlantic Popular Culture*, Cambridge: Harvard University Press, 2003.
Lightman, B., *Victorian Popularizers of Science: Designing Nature for New Audiences*, Chicago: University of Chicago Press, 2007.
Lloyd's Weekly Newspaper
London Daily News
London Gazette
London Standard
Lord Chamberlain's Plays Supplementary Papers
Lumley, B., *Reminiscences of the Opera*, London: Hurst and Blackett, 1864.
Macdonald, M., *Sing Sorrow: Classics, History and Heroines in Opera*, Westport: Greenwood Press, 2001.
Macintosh, F., 'Medea transposed: burlesque and gender on the mid-Victorian stage', in E. Hall, F. Macintosh and O. Taplin (eds), *Medea in Performance: 1500–2000*, Oxford: Legenda, 2000.
MacKay, Ch., *Songs of England. The Book of English Songs*, London: Houlston & Wright, 1857.
MacKay, Ch., *The Collected Songs of Charles Mackay. With Illustrations by John Gilbert*, London: G. Routledge & Co., 1859.
Mackie, C., 'Frederick Robson and the evolution of realistic acting', *Educational Theatre Journal* 23 (2) (1971), pp. 160–170.
Manchester Courier and Lancashire General Advertiser
Mann, H., 'The blue coat school, Liverpool', in *The Common School Journal for the Year 1844*. Vol. VI, Boston: William B. Fowle and N. Capen, 1844.
Marsh, Ch., *The Clubs of London: With Anecdotes of Their Members, Sketches of Character and Conversations*, London: Henry Colburn, 2 vols, 1828.
Marshall, G. 'Introduction: Thinking Through Reception', in Ch. Martindale and R. T. Thomas (eds), *Classics and the Uses of Reception*, Oxford: Blackwell, 2006.
Marshall, G. (ed.), *Shakespeare in the Nineteenth Century*, Cambridge: CUP, 2012.
Marshall, G. and Thomas, R. F. (eds), *Classics and the Uses of Reception*, Oxford: Blackwell, 2006.
Martineau, H., *Autobiography*, Vol. II, Cambridge: CUP, 3 vols, [1877] 2010.
Mayhew, H., *London Labour and the London Poor*, London: Griffin, Bohn and Company, 1861.
Mayhew, H. and Binny, J., *The Criminal Prisons of London and Scenes of Prison Life*, Cambridge: CUP, [1862] 2011.
Mill, J. S., *The Spirit of the Age*, Chicago, Ill.: University of Chicago Press, [1831] 1942.

Milligam, H. V., *Stephen Collin Foster: A Biography of America's Folk-Song Composer*, New York; G. Schirmer, 1920.

Millington, E. J., *Characteristics of the Gods of Greece: A Manual for School-Girls*, Bristol: I. E. Chilcott, 1867.

Monholland, C. S., *Infanticide in Victorian England, 1856–1878: Thirty Legal Cases (England)*. Masters Thesis (Rice University, 1989), http://hdl.handle.net/1911/13382 [accessed 15 December 2013].

Monrós-Gaspar, L., *Cassandra the Fortune Teller: Prophets, Gipsies and Victorian Burlesque*, Bari: Levante Editori, 2011.

Moody, J., 'The Drama of Capital: Risk, Belief, and Liability on the Victorian Stage', in F. O'Gorman (ed.), *Victorian Literature and Finance*, Oxford: OUP, 2007.

Moore, R.J., Jr. and Haynes, M., *Lewis & Clark. Tailor Made, Trail Worn. Army Life, Clothing & Weapons of the Corps of Discovery*, Helena: Farcountry Press, 2003.

Morley, H., *The Journal of a London Playgoer. From 1851 to 1866*, London: George Routledge & Sons, 1866.

Morning Chronicle

Morning Post

Murray, J., *Strong-Minded Women and Other Lost Voices from Nineteenth Century England*, New York: Pantheon, 1982.

The Musical World

Nelson, C. C., *A New Woman Reader: Fiction, Articles, and Drama of the 1890s*, Peterborough: Broadview Press, 2000.

Newey, K., 'Women and theatre', in J. Shattock (ed.), *Women and Literature in Britain 1800–1900*, Cambridge: CUP, 2001.

Newcastle Journal

New Observer

The New York Times

Nicoll, A., *A History of English Drama. 1660–1900* Vol. IV, Cambridge: CUP, 1955.

Nightingale, F., *Cassandra*, London: Pickering & Chatto, [1852] 1991.

Norfolk Chronicle and the Norwich Gazette

North American Review

Northampton Mercury

Northern Star

Norton, C., *English Laws for Women in the Nineteenth Century*, London, printed for private circulation, 1854.

Norwood, J., 'A reference guide to performances of Shakespeare's plays in nineteenth-century London', in G. Marshall (ed.), *Shakespeare in the Nineteenth Century*. Cambridge: CUP, 2012.

O'Gorman, F. (ed.), *Victorian Literature and Finance*, Oxford: OUP, 2007.

O'Hara, K., *Two Burlettas of Kane O'Hara: Midas and The Golden Pippin* (edited by Ph. T. Dircks), New York: Garland, 1987.
O'Malley, A., *Children's Literature, Popular Culture, and Robinson Crusoe*, Basingstoke: Palgrave Macmillan, 2012.
Oxford Dictionary of National Biography
Oxford English Dictionary
Pache, C. O., *Baby and Child Heroes in Ancient Greece*, Champaign, Ill.: University of Illinois Press, 2004.
Paisley Herald and Renfrewshire Advertiser
Partridge, E., *Routledge Dictionary of Historical Slang*, London: Routledge, 1973.
Pascoe, Ch. E., *The Dramatic List. Living Actors & Actresses on the British Stage*, London: Hardwicke & Co., 1879.
Pearsall, R., *Victorian Popular Music*, Newton Abbot: David & Charles, 1973.
Penny Magazine
Perry's Bankrupt and Insolvent Gazette
Pilbeam, P., *Madame Tussaud: and the History of Waxworks*, London, New York: Hambledon and London, 2003.
Planché, J. R., *The Paphian Bower; or, Venus and Adonis*, British Library Add. MS 42919, ff. 21, 753–775, 1832.
Planché, J. R., *The Golden Fleece; or, Jason in Colchis and Medea in Corinth*, British Library Add. MS 42983, ff. 10, 316–328, 1845.
Planché, J. R., *The Birds of Aristophanes*, London: Thomas Hailes Lacy, 1846.
Planché, J. R., *Theseus and Ariadne*, London: Thomas Hailes Lacy, 1848.
Planché, J. R., *The Yellow Dwarf*, London: Thomas Hailes Lacy, 1854.
Planché, J. R., *The Vampire*, London: John Dicks, 1888(?).
Poovey, M., 'Covered but Not Bound: Caroline Norton and the 1857 Matrimonial Causes Act', *Feminist Studies* 14(3) (1988), pp. 467–485.
Pope, A., *The Works of Alexander Pope. Containing his Satires, Essays on Man, Moral Essays and Miscellaneous Pieces in Verse*, Edinburgh: James Donaldson, 1789.
Prettejohn, E., 'Reception and Ancient Art: The Case of the Venus de Milo', in Ch. Martindale and R. T. Thomas (eds), *Classics and the Uses of Reception*, Oxford: Blackwell Publishing, 2006.
Prins, Y., *Victorian Sappho*, Princeton, NJ., Chichester: Princeton University Press, 1999.
Punch
Reading Mercury
Reece, R., *Agamemnon and Cassandra; or, the Prophet and Loss of Troy*, Liverpool: Daily Post Steam Printing Works, 1868.
Reformers Gazette
Reynolds's Newspaper

Richards, J. H., *The Ancient World on the Victorian and Edwardian Stage*. Basingstoke, Hampshire: Palgrave Macmillan, 2009.

Richards, J. H., *The Golden Age of Pantomime: Slapstick, Spectacle and Subversion in Victorian England*, London: I. B. Tauris & Co., 2015.

Richardson, A. E., *Monumental Classical Architecture in Great Britain and Ireland*, New York: W.W. Norton & Company, 1982.

Richardson. E., 'A Conjugal Lesson: Robert Brough's Medea and the discourses of Mid-Victorian Britain', *Ramus Critical Studies* 32(1) (2003), pp. 57–83.

Richardson. E., *Classical Victorians: Scholars, Scoundrels and Generals in Pursuit of Antiquity*. Cambridge: CUP, 2013.

Ritchi, J. E., *The Night Side of London*, London: Tinseley Bros., 1861.

Roberts, J. (ed.), *The Oxford Dictionary of the Classical World*, Oxford: OUP, 2007.

Rose, L., *The Massacre of the Innocents: Infanticide in Britain, 1800–1939*, London: Routledge, 1986.

Rossetti, Ch., *Goblin Market*, London: Macmillan & Co., 1862.

Rousseau, G. S., *Oliver Goldsmith: the Critical Heritage*, London: Routledge, 1974.

Rowell, G., *Nineteenth Century Plays*, Oxford: OUP, 1972.

Rowell, G, *Theatre in the Age of Irving*, Oxford: Blackwell, 1981.

Roy, D., *Plays by James Robinson Planché*, Cambridge: CUP, 1986.

Ryan, W. B., *Infanticide – Its Law, Prevalence, Prevention and History*, London: J. Churchill, 1862.

Sala, G. A., *Robson: A Sketch*, London: John Camden Hotten, 1864.

Sands, M., *Robson of the Olympic*, London: The Society for Theatre Research, 1979.

Saumarez Smith, C., *The National Gallery: A Short History*, London: Frances Lincoln, 2009.

Schoch, R. W., '"Chopkins, late Shakespeare": the bard and his burlesques, 1810–66', *English Literary History* 67 (4) (2000), pp. 973–991.

Schoch, R. W., *Not Shakespeare: Bardolatry and Burlesque in the Nineteenth Century*, Cambridge: CUP, 2002.

Schoch, R. W., *Victorian Theatrical Burlesques*, Aldershot: Ashgate, 2003.

Scott, W., *The Poetical Works of Sir Walter Scott*, Edinburgh: Robet Cadell, 1851.

Selby, Ch., *The Judgement of Paris; or, the Pas de Pippins*, British Library, Add. MS 42995, ff. 31, 891–898, 1846.

Shakespeare, W., *The Oxford Shakespeare. The Complete Works edited by Stanley Wells and Gary Taylor*, Oxford: OUP, 1998.

Shanley, M. L., *Feminism, Marriage and the Law in Victorian England 1850–1895*, Princeton, NJ.: Princeton University Press, 1989.

Showalter, E., *A Literature of their Own. From Charlotte Brontë to Doris Lessing*, London: Virago, [1977] 2009.

Shrimpton, N., ' "Even these metallic problems have their melodramatic side": Money in Victorian Literature', in F. O'Gorman (ed.), *Victorian Literature and Finance*, Oxford: OUP, 2007.

Southampton Herald

Speaight, G., *The History of English Puppet Theatre*, London: Hale, 1990.

Stern, B. H., *The Rise of Romantic Hellenism in English Literature 1732-1786*, New York: Octagon, 1969.

Stewart, J., *The Acrobat: Arthur Barnes and the Victorian Circus*, Jefferson: McFarland, 2012.

Storey, G., House, M. and Tillotson, K., *The Letters of Charles Dickens: the Pilgrim Edition*, Oxford: OUP, 1995.

Stowell, S. (ed.), *A Stage of Their Own. Feminist Plays of the Suffrage Era*, Manchester: Manchester University Press, 1992.

Strachey, R., *The Cause. A Short History of the Women's Movement in Great Britain*, London: Virago, [1928] 1989.

Stray, Ch., *Classics Transformed: Schools, Universities, and Society in England, 1830-1960*, Oxford: Clarendon Press, 1998.

Sullivan, J. A., *The Politics of the Pantomime. Regional Identity in the Theatre 1860-1900*, Hatfield: STR, University of Hertforshire Press, 2011.

The Sunday Times

Symmons, J., *The Agamemnon of Aeschylus*, London: Taylor and Hessey, 1824.

Talfourd, F., *Macbeth Travestie*, Oxford: E. T. Spiers, 1847.

Talfourd, F., *Alcestis, the Original Strong-Minded Woman: a Classical Burlesque in One Act*, London: Thomas Hailes Lacy, 1850.

Talfourd, F., *Shylock; or, the Merchant of Venice Preserved*, London: Thomas Hailes Lacy, 1853.

Talfourd, F., *Atalanta, or the Three Golden Apples*, British Library Add. MS 52965 S, 1857.

Talfourd, F., *Electra in a New Electric Light*, British Library Add. MS 52982, C, 1859.

Talfourd, T. N., *Ion*, London: John Dicks, 1836.

Taunton Courier and Western Advertiser

Taylor, G., *Players and Performances in the Victorian Theatre*, Manchester: Manchester University Press, 1989.

Taylor, H. and Mill, J. S., 'The Enfranchisement of Women', *Westminster Review* 55 (1851), pp. 189-311.

Taylor, T., *Payable on Demand*, London: Thomas Hailes Lacy, 1859.

Taylor, T., *Settling Day*, London: Thomas Hailes Lacy, 1865.

Tennyson, A., *In Memoriam, Maud, and Other Poems*, J. D. Jump (ed.), London: J. M. Dent, [1855] 1995.

Thackeray, W., *The Newcomes*, London: Bradbury and Evans, 1855.

Thiselton-Dyer, T. F., *Folk-lore of Women*, Los Angeles: Indo-European Publishing, 2010.

Thompson, N. D. (ed.), *Victorian Women Writers and the Woman Question*, Cambridge: CUP, 1999.

Thorn, J. (ed.), *Writing British Infanticide: Child-Murder, Gender, and Print, 1722–1859*, Newark: Delaware University Press, 2003.

Timbs, J., *Club Life of London with Anecdotes of the Clubs, Coffee-Houses and Taverns of The Metropolis During the 17th, 18th and 19th Centuries*, London: Richard Bentley, 1866.

Upton, G. P., *The Standard Operas*, Teddington: The Echo Library, 2009.

Vance, N., *The Victorians and Ancient Rome*, Oxford: Blackwell Publishers, 1997.

Wakefield, P., *The Juvenile Travellers: Containing the Remarks of a Family During a Tour Through the Principal States and Kingdoms of Europe*, London: Darton & Harvey, 1801.

Walton, J. M., 'Aristophanes and the Theatre of Burlesque', in Stratos E. Constantinidis (ed.), *Text & Presentation 2005*, London: McFarland and Co., 2006.

Weiss, B., *The Hell of the English: Bankruptcy and the Victorian Novel*, Lewisburg: Bucknell University Press, 1986.

Wells Journal

Westmeath, E., *A Narrative of the Case of the Marchioness of Westmeath*, London: James Rideway, 1857.

Westmorland Gazette

West Middlesex Advertiser and Family Journal

Whale, P. B., 'A Retrospective View of the Bank Charter Act of 1844', *Economica*, New Series 11 (43 A) (1944), pp. 109–111.

White, E. W., *A Register of First Performances of English Operas*, London: The Society for Theatre Research, 1993.

Whitehead, Ch., *The Public Art Museum in Nineteenth Century Britain: The Development of the National Gallery*, Aldershot: Ashgate Publishing, 2005.

Willier, S. A., *Vicenzo Bellini: A Guide to Research*, London: Routledge, 2002.

Wilson, P., *Murderess: A Study of the Women Executed in Britain since 1843*, London: Joseph, 1971.

Woman's Herald

Woman's Signal

Women's Penny Paper

Wood, E., *East Lynne*, London: Richard Bentley, 1861.

Wooler, J., *Jason and Medea*, British Library Add. Ms 43036, ff. 267–307, 1851.

Worcestershire Chronicle

Woolmer's Exeter and Plymouth Gazette

Worsnop, J., 'A re-evaluation of "the problem of surplus women" in 19th-century England: the case of the 1851 Census', *Women's Studies International Forum* 13 (1) (1990), pp. 21–31.

Wyndham, H. S., *The Annals of Covent Garden Theatre From 1732 to 1897*, London: Chatto & Windus, 2 vols, vol. II, 1906.

Young, A. R., *Punch and Shakespeare in the Victorian Era*, Bern: Peter Lang, 2007.

York Herald

Zeitlin, F. I., 'A Study in Form: Three Recognition Scenes in the Three Electra Plays', *Lexis* 30 (2012), pp. 361–378.

Index

Adelphi Theatre
   and Brough's *Frankenstein* 135
   and Lemon's *Medea* 55
   Robert Taylor's designs for 50
   and Selby's extravaganzas 5
   and Williams' *Medea* 16, 57, 60
   Miss Woolgar in 35
Aeschylus
   Agamemnon as a source of burlesque 10
   in the portico at Covent Garden 6
   in the Victorian press 52 n. 50
Apollo
   in *Apollo and the Flying Pegasus* 14
   in Hughes' *Apollo and Daphne* 7, 51 n.36
   in O'Hara's *Midas* 50 n.30
   Madame Vestris as 7
Apollonius, *Argonautica* as a source of burlesque 10
Ariadne
   in the 1851 Exhibition 3
   in Planché 14
   in Titian 3
Aristophanes
   and Julia Ward Howe's lecture at The Congress of Women 18
   and Planché 10
   in the portico at Covent Garden 6
   as a source of burlesque 10
audience 1, 7, 8, 10, 11, 12, 17, 18, 19, 24, 26, 28, 31, 32, 33, 35, 36, 38, 56 n.112–3
Austen, J. *Sense and Sensibility* 37

Bacchantes in the 1851 Exhibition 3
Bacchus
   in the portico at Covent Garden 6
   in sculpture 4
   in Titian 3
Balfe, W. *Satanella* 19, 16

Bellini, V. *Norma* 5
   in Brough's *Medea* 159 n.274
Blanchard, E. L.
   Antigone Travestie 2, 8, 10, 15, 16, 17, 18–23
   debtor's plot in 21–3
   in Dublin 19
   George Wild in 19, 23
   Harry Hall in 19, 54 n.80, 64 n.4
   and Sir Peter Laurie 21, 68 n.66
   and 'West Middlesex' swindle 21
   The Road of Life 19
   debtor's plot in 21
Bodichon, B. as strong-minded woman 34
Braddon, M. E.
   and bigamy plots 29
   Lady Audley's Secret 29, 34
   on 'strong-minded women' 34
breeches roles 9, 12
Brontë, Ch. *Jane Eyre* 13
Brough, R.
   Medea; or the Best of Mothers 2, 9, 14, 17, 23, 24–31, 33, 38, 39, 40, 41, 45
   and Brough, W. 10
   The Sphinx 14
   Ristori in 9
   Robson as 9, 16, 23, 24–8, 29
Brough, W. 136
Burnand, F. C. 8, 10, 53 n.57, 54 n.80
   Paris, or Vive Lemprière 11
Byron, G. G., Lord, anticipating Victorian burlesque 7
Byron, H. J. 10, 52 n.53
   Orpheus and Eurydice 15

Cerrito, F. 5
classical burlesque
   general characteristics of 1–2, 5–17, 23, 31, 39
   politics of 12

collections
   Angerstein and Beaumont 3
   of Greek sculpture 7
   at the National Gallery 3
   Sir Robert Walpole's 2
Compton, H. 12, 24, 90, 91 n.25, 211
Correggio, A. A. da *Venus with Mercury and Cupid* 3
Covent Garden 5
   Antigone in 18, 19
   Kane O'Hara in 7
   restoration of 6
Cupid
   in Correggio 3
   and the 1851 Exhibition 3
   Marie Wilton as 12

Davies, E. as a 'strong-minded woman' 34
De Quincey, Th. 18
Dibdin, Ch. 7
Dickens, Ch. 26
   on Frederick Robson 26
   Hard Times 28
   Pickwick Papers 13
   on Richardson's show in *Sketches by Boz* 19, 65 n.0.SD
   on 'strong-minded' women in *Martin Chuzzlewit* 34
Dido
   Queen Caroline as 8
   in Turner 3
divorce 12, 14, 31, 261 n.36–7, 263 n.38–9
   divorce laws and burlesque 14, 15, 23, 28–9, 32, 163 n.55
   and the Forrest case 29
   press coverage of 14, 28, 29
Drury Lane 5
   and Hughes' *Apollo and Daphne* 51 n.36
   pantomimes at 23, 62
   rebuilding of 6

education 10, 14, 18, 34, 151 n.145–54, 227 n.6
   Blue Coat School 9, 164, 165 n.71
   and the classics 2, 11, 15
Eliot, G. and Antigone 18
entertainment 1, 4, 6, 10, 16, 18, 23, 36, 77 n.210, 117 n.480, 139 n.37, 141 n.49, 213 n.102, 219 n.68, 269 n.65
fairground entertainments 6, 16, 19
marionette and puppet shows 7, 8
popular theatre 10, 15, 31
Richardson's shows 16, 19, 54 n.74, 65 n.0SD
Euripides
   Alcestis 9, 10, 33
   in burlesque 10
   Medea 10
   parodied by Lord Byron 7

Farren, W. 91 n.16, 91 n.21, 91 n.23
   and family 16
   as manager 24, 40
Fornasari L. as Belisario 5
Frost, W. E. and *Diana surprised by Actaeon* 4

Galatea 3, 5, 10
Gay, J. *The What D'Ye Call It* 7
Gibson J. and Antigone 18
Gilbert, W. S. 10
Gilbert à Beckett, G. A. 10
Glück, Ch. W. 5
Grahn, L. 5
Great Exhibition 3, 13
Greece
   eighteenth-century rebirth of interest on 7
   at the Great Exhibition 3
   indoctrination of the press on 4
   referents from 2
   and travel literature 8
Greek Revival architecture 6

Hamilton, C. *Marriage as Trade* (1909) 31
Hecate at the portico of the Covent Garden 6
Her Majesty's Theatre 5
   and Taglioni's Electra 36
Homer
   Iliad 10
   in Lemprière 11
   Odyssey 10
Howe, J. W. at The Congress of Women 18

intertheatricality 17, 18, 21, 23, 31, 38–9

Juno, in ballet 5

Leclerq family 9
Leech, J. and caricatures 13
Legouvé, E. 145
   Medea 24–6
      burlesques of 55 n.105
Lemprière's dictionary 10–11, 52 n.51, 52 n.52
Leveridge, R. 7
Lorrain, C. at the National Gallery 3

Medusa at the 1851 Exhibition 3
Menander in the portico of the Covent Garden 6
Mendelssohn, F. *Antigone* 5, 18–20
Mill, J. S. 22
   and Harriet Taylor Mill 14, 28, 30, 34
Millington, E. J. *Characteristics of the Gods of Greece* 10
Milton, J. *Comus* 5
Minerva
   in ballet 5
   in the portico at Covent Garden 6
Montanelli's translation of Légouvé 24–6

National Gallery and the Eastlake controversy 16
Neo-Palladian architecture 6
New Strand Theatre
   and Blanchard's *Antigone* 10, 19, 22
   and Talfourd's *Alcestis* 31, 91 n.21
Norton, C. 13–14, 30
   English Laws for Women in the Nineteenth Century 28
   Infants Custody Act, 13
   Stuart of Dunleath 28

O'Hara, K. *Midas* 7
Olympic Theatre 10, 19, 23, 24–6
   and Planché 9–10
   and Robson 24–6, 56 n.112
Ovid
   in Lemprière 11
   Metamorphoses 4, 10
   as a source of burlesque 10

Phelps, E. S. and Antigone 18
Pinero, A. W., Sir, *The Second Mrs. Tanqueray*, 31
Planché, J. R. 7, 8, 10, 14
   The Birds of Aristophanes 10
   The Golden Fleece 14, 25
   Olympic Revels 8–9
   praising Robson 24
   Theseus and Ariadne 14
   The Vampire 31–2
   'the vampire trap' 32
   The Yellow Dwarf 24
Poussin, N. *Nymph with Satyrs*, 3
Psyche 3, 49 n.12
   in Duffet 8

Rachel, Mlle in *Les Horaces* 5
Reece, R. 8, 10, 33, 35
repertoire 17, 31
Ristori, A.
   burlesque of 55 n.105
   and Robson 16, 24–7
   statue of 9
Robson, F.
   as Medea
      in the Olympic 24–6, 56 n.112
      and Ristori 16, 24–7
Rossetti, Ch. *Goblin Market* 37
Royal Strand Theatre 11

Sadler's Wells 23
Selby, Ch. 51 n.43, *The Judgment of Paris; or, the Pas de Pippins* 5
Simpson, J. P. *The World and the Stage* 36
Smirke, R. 6
Society of Dilettanti 7
Sophocles 36
   Antigone 18
   Electra 10, 37, 38
   as a source of burlesque 10

tableaux vivant 4, 9
Taglioni, M. 5
Talfourd, F. 10
   Alcestis; or the Original Strong-minded Woman 2, 8, 28, 31–6
   and the Infantry Brigade 12, 16, 17, 32
   and police 9, 32

and strong-minded women 33–6
and the 'vampire trap' 32
Atalanta, or the Golden Apples 12, 14
Electra in a New Electric Light 2, 9, 10, 11
   and electric lighting 36
   and strong-minded women 35
   and Taglioni's ballet *Electra* 36, 37
   Miss Ternan in 9
   in the Haymarket Theatre 87
Macbeth Travestie 26
Shylock; or, the Merchant of Venice Preserved 25
Talfourd, T. N. *Ion* 5
Taylor, T. 51 n.43
   Settling Day 23
Titian *Bacchus and Ariadne* 3
transvestite and cross-dressed roles 9, 23
Turner, J. M. W. *Dido Building Carthage* 3

Venus
   in ballet 5
   in Colley Cibber's *Venus and Adonis* 7
   Correggio's 3
   at the 1851 Exhibition 3
   in modern refigurations after Romanticism 12, 53 n.57
   in puppet theatre 7
   at Reimer's Anatomical Museum 4
Vestris, Madame 7, 9
Virgil *Aeneid* 10

Wagner, R. 5
Wilde, O. *A Woman of No Importance* 31
Wilkins, W. 6
Williams' translation into English of Legouvé's *Medea* 26, 41
Wilson, R. *The Destruction of the Children of Niobe* 3
women
   abandoned 14, 29, 30, 36
   and adultery 28, 29
   as an 'angel in the house' 29, 35, 38
   and bigamy 26, 28, 29, 56 n.115
   and divorce 12, 14, 15, 23, 28–31, 32
   in *Apollo and the Flying Pegasus* 14
   as financial agents 23
   and infanticide 28, 29, 30
   Burke Ryan, W. *Infanticide* 30
   married women 14, 26, 28
   'condition of marriage plays' 31
   New Women 12, 57 n.163
   in sensation novels 28–9
   and sisterhood 36–7
   strong-minded women 22, 32, 33–6, 38
   and suffrage/suffragette drama 31
   Surplus Women Question 37
   unmarried women 37–8
   Woman Question 14, 18, 28, 31
Wood, E. *East Lynne* 29, 37
Wooler, J. *Jason and Medea* 31
Wyatt, B. D. rebuilding of Drury Lane 6